The Good Reader's Guide

(read for real)

Program Author
David W. Moore

NATIONAL GEOGRAPHIC   Hampton-Brown

Acknowledgments

The author wishes to thank two individuals for their significant efforts on *The Good Reader's Guide*.

Sharon Arthur Moore's professional knowledge and experience helped shape the advice in many of these chapters.

Jacalyn Mahler, the Executive Editor and project head, deserves enormous credit for her insightful editorial contributions, which are evident on every page.

Cover Photo: Mark Thiessen, National Geographic Magazine.

Acknowledgments continue on page 473.

National Geographic School Publishing
Hampton-Brown
P.O. Box 223220
Carmel, California 93922
800-333-3510
www.NGSP.com

Printed in the United States of America

ISBN 10: 0-7362-3411-X
ISBN 13: 978-0-7362-3411-5

ISBN 10: 0-7362-3410-1
ISBN 13: 978-0-7362-3410-8

07 08 09 10 11 12 13 14 15 9 8 7 6 5 4 3 2 1

Contents

Reading for Real

Can You Read Me?

Connect to Reading

Unlocking Words

Your Job as a Reader

Be an Active Reader
Theme: Nature's Mysteries

Plan and Monitor 218
Theme: Mavericks, Heroes, and Pioneers

Skills in Action

Reading for Real

"Life happened because I turned the pages."

—ALBERTO MANGUEL

Why Read?

Get inspired

Experience the past

Discover where you're going

Stay connected

Make informed decisions

Become an expert

Get the power

Sharpen your viewpoint

Discover where you come from

Get Inspired

Reading can motivate you to become more than you are. Poet Benjamin Zephaniah found inspiration in the works of a "dead white poet" with an unlikely name: Percy Bysshe Shelley.

Benjamin Zephaniah

I Love Shelley

—Benjamin Zephaniah

Shelley's my man. If he were alive now he wouldn't be sitting in an ivory tower only leaving to attend the odd literature festival; he would be demonstrating against the exploitation of the third world and performing at the Glastonbury festival.

I used to think of Shelley as just another one of those dead white poets who wrote difficult poetry for difficult people, but then I learnt how dedicated he was to justice. He gave up his riches and hung out with beggars on the streets; he was angry about the treatment of the poor by the rich, and although he probably saw very few black people he was passionately against the slave trade. It was this that turned me on to Shelley, his humanity, passion, and his rock and roll attitude.

He did not write for children, but he certainly wrote about children. In his day his poetry was easily understood by everyday people; he wrote for the masses. Imagine this, there was no TV, no radio, no Internet, but

**Benjamin Zephaniah
(b. 1958)**

his poetry was being quoted on the streets and chanted at demonstrations. Think of him as the rock star of his time, women loved him, the authorities hated him, and everyone knew when he was in town.

Shelley once said. 'My soul is bursting, ideas, millions of ideas are crowding into it.' Hey, I feel like that sometimes. I feel worried that I won't live long enough to say all the things that I want to say, but if my life is long I feel like I could never run out of things to say when on one hand there is so much trouble in the world, and on the other hand, there is so much loveliness to be had.

Bob Marley wrote. 'If you are a big tree/we are the small axe/ready to cut you down/well sharp, to cut you down.' Shelley wrote. 'Let the axe strike the tree/the poison tree will fall.' Zephaniah wrote. 'When the small hear the call/how the high and mighty fall.' We are all saying that the bully in the playground will get his/her comeuppance; they that mock the poor and needy will one day be brought down by the power of love and justice.

Shelley was the intelligent rapper of his age, compassionate and good looking, but we all still wonder what his wife Mary was thinking of when she wrote Frankenstein!

Percy Shelley

Become an Expert

Reading is a way to learn about something that interests you. What do you want to know more about? When author Patrick Jones was growing up, he read everything about his favorite sport—professional wrestling.

Wrestling with Reading
—Patrick Jones

You have to understand that the world was different then. I was growing up in Flint, Michigan, and was a huge fan of professional wrestling. But it wasn't like now, with just Vince and the WWE. Then, every major city had its own wrestlers: my guys were The Sheik and Bobo Brazil. Every other city had its wrestlers who would often visit Flint to fight, and lose to, The Sheik. The only way you could know about those other wrestlers was through magazines. There was no Internet, no cable, no e-mail, no way of sharing information. The only way I could find out about these other wrestlers was through the newsstand wrestling magazines.

So, I'm twelve and I go to my local public library to get something for school. I wasn't a big reader or library user; it just wasn't something I did. I'm at the library and I see a whole shelf of different magazines. As I go to check out my books, I summon up all my twelve-year-old

Patrick Jones
(b. 1961)

courage and ask the librarian if the library has any wrestling magazines. That is what I thought I asked; instead I think I asked her to show me what her face would look like if she sucked on a lemon for a hundred years. She looked like she was about to stroke out at the mere mention of wrestling magazines in her library. She made me feel stupid, and I never went back.

Flash forward now to the summer of 2000. Former professional wrestler and then best-selling author Mick "Cactus Jack Mankind Dude Love Hardcore Legend" Foley is the guest of honor at the American Library Association convention. I'm the one getting to ask him questions as some five hundred plus librarians sit in the audience, then later stand in line to have Foley autograph his book. Sometimes there is justice in the universe.

So it was newsstand wrestling magazines that started me reading, and, for that matter, writing. By the time I was eight, I had already published some articles in a wrestling fan newsletter (*In This Corner*, edited by Danny Shelburg).

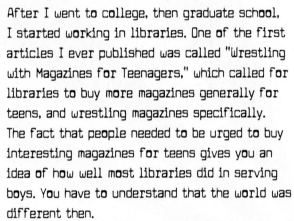

After I went to college, then graduate school, I started working in libraries. One of the first articles I ever published was called "Wrestling with Magazines for Teenagers," which called for libraries to buy more magazines generally for teens, and wrestling magazines specifically. The fact that people needed to be urged to buy interesting magazines for teens gives you an idea of how well most libraries did in serving boys. You have to understand that the world was different then.

Imagine my delight as the past couple of years have seen an explosion of books written by (and sometimes for) professional wrestlers: some about the new breed (The Rock), some about the old legends (Freddie Blassie), and some about the best of both worlds (Mick Foley). I don't read much fiction anymore, even though I try to write it now. I don't read the newsstand wrestling magazines anymore, either. Instead the highlight of every Saturday is when the *Wrestling Observer* newsletter arrives in my mailbox.

But maybe you don't like wrestling. That's OK, but that's not the point. The point is how

something I saw on TV captured me and how reading everything that I could about it made me enjoy it even more. In doing so, it made me enjoy reading, as I learned the lesson about the value of reading for fun and for facts. Reading can be, for many folks, good in and of itself. But for me—for lots of men and boys—reading is the means to reach an end. The end being a fuller understanding, appreciation, and even expertise in an area: wrestling, baseball, fly fishing, computer graphics, model rockets, science fiction films, rap music, or martial arts. Boys want to read about something. We'll see a movie or something on TV, and want to know more. A lot more, and that is what reading books and magazines—and Web pages—can do for us.

I'm not sure what happened to that librarian in Flint, and I never got my wrestling magazines from the library. My hope is that boys going into libraries now can find wrestling magazines or something similar. Everyone has to understand that the world is different now.

Stay Connected

In this poem, Naomi Shihab Nye writes about an Iraqi American friend whose two "home" countries are at war. When everything else around her changes, reading remains a constant.

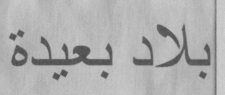

Ducks

—Naomi Shihab Nye

In her first home each book
had a light around it.
The voices of distant countries
floated in through open windows,
entering her soup and her mirror.
They slept with her in the same thick bed.

Someday she would go there.
Her voice, among all those voices.
In Iraq a book never had one owner—it had ten.
Lucky books, to be held often
and gently, by so many hands.

Later in American libraries she felt sad
for books no one ever checked out.

Naomi Shihab Nye
(b. 1952)

أصوات

She lived in a country house beside a pond
and kept ducks, two male, one female.
She worried over the difficult relations
of triangles. One of the ducks
often seemed depressed.
But not the same one.

During the war between her two countries
she watched the ducks more than usual.
She stayed quiet with the ducks.
Some days they huddled among reeds
or floated together.

She could not call her family in Basra
which had grown farther away than ever
nor could they call her. For nearly a year
she would not know who was alive,
who was dead.

The ducks were building a nest.

Experience the Past

In school, Maurice Duhon, Jr., was asked to read some of Langston Hughes' work. This is Maurice's response. It shows how an era in history came alive for Maurice.

THERE'S A Harlem Renaissance IN MY HEAD

—*Maurice E. Duhon, Jr., age 17*

This first appeared in a collection of writings by teenage boys called You Hear Me?

The trombones slap me in the face with their high-life beats, and the piano's glamorous tunes tap me on my shoulder and whisper in my ear. As I look down into the Juke-Joint from my bedroom floor, rotted house, rotted life, plain rotten seems forgotten as the music plays and the beats go down to the rhythm of my heart's pound. There's a Harlem Renaissance in my head, there's a Harlem Renaissance in my head.

Through the floor a light, where the music roared, overtakes the darkness that surrounds me as I look through this floorboard. I can see the hoppin' and a dancin' and the suave men a prancin' around the young ladies who stand stunning on the floor. . .

The music stops, the poet stands up, and with each turn of the page, his mind's thoughts he will emancipate and everybody in the room he will captivate. His pen his only weapon with which injustice he must eradicate. As I look down into the Juke-Joint from my bedroom floor, rotted house, rotted life, plain rotten seems forgotten as the music plays and the beats go down to the rhythm of my thoughts' pound. There's a Harlem Renaissance in my head.

Let your ink run rampant, Langston Hughes. Let your fingers tickle the ivories forever, Duke. At every moment history being made in my own personal Juke-Joint. I lean my ears to hear even closer and find my mind in a past tense, opening my eyes to see beauty, but surrounded by pure silence. There's a Harlem Renaissance in my head, a Harlem Renaissance in my head.

Discover Where You Come From

In 2002 Ilyasah Shabazz wrote *Growing Up X*, a memoir about what it was like growing up as Malcolm X's middle daughter. In this excerpt, she talks about why she decided to read her father's autobiography when she went to college.

from Growing Up X

—Ilyasah Shabazz

Crisspell was a single-sex dorm and the girls in it were, for the most part, white. My roommate, whose name I can no longer remember, had a curly blonde Afro; she looked a bit like Little Orphan Annie. She was nice, from what I remember; all the girls in my suite were nice. But I barely got to know them because no sooner had my mother kissed me good-bye and departed than a group of older African American students decided I should be in the "black" dorm, named after W.E.B. Du Bois.

These students knew who I was because a girl from Mount Vernon named Darlene, who used to hustle with us at my friend Tony's house, was now a student at New Paltz and had already spread the word. The group presented its decision to me as a *fait accompli*; they arrived, packed up my things, moved me down the hill to Du Bois. It never occurred to me that I had anything to say about this move. I was a tumbleweed blowing in the wind and that wind, usually provided by my mother, was now blowing from a different direction. My people wanted me. I smiled and tumbled along.

For the first time in my life I became MALCOLM X's DAUGHTER! Everywhere I went on campus, people

Ilyasah Shabazz
(b. 1963)

already knew who I was or, at least, who they thought I should be. I'd be walking along the path, thinking about my next class, and suddenly someone I didn't know was right up in my face. "Are you Malcolm X's daughter?" It was demanded with such undisguised skepticism I felt like pulling out my ID to prove it to all concerned. "What are you doing here?" Other people would just point and whisper as I passed, their voices traveling on the wind. *There she goes! Are you certain that's Malcolm X's daughter? She sure doesn't look it!* It was startling and bewildering and a little disturbing. I was sixteen-years-old. What did they want from me?

What I knew about my father at this point in my life came not from what I'd read but from what was shared by Mommy and family friends. I knew about Malcolm the husband, Malcolm the father, Malcolm the friend, not Malcolm X the spokesman, the revolutionary, the icon. I knew he was a great man who had made significant contributions to people of the African diaspora and the world, but I didn't know precisely what those contributions were.

I didn't know why some people were surprised to learn I was his daughter. I decided I needed to find out.

I had brought a copy of my father's autobiography with me from home. I sat down to read it, trying to distance myself from the man in its pages, trying not to think of him as my father but as simply a man.

Even so, it was a very emotional experience. Although I'd lived with and played with the *Autobiography of Malcolm X* all my life, this was the first time I read it with anything approaching adult comprehension. The story of Malcolm Little's transformation into Malcolm X and then El-Hajj Malik El-Shabazz is one of the most powerful stories of the twentieth century. In some ways it is *the* story of the twentieth century, of the brutal oppression and degradation of one group of people by another and of that first group's fight to reliberate themselves physically, emotionally, and psychologically.

Night after night during those first summer months I sat in my dorm room reading and crying. My roommates must have thought I was losing my mind! But reading the story of Malcolm X filled me with awe for the man, for the human being he was. He was different from any man I had ever met or read about or saw on television, so honest and loyal and committed and genuine and deeply, deeply spiritual. Reading the *Autobiography* made me prouder than I already was to be the daughter of Malcolm X. But it also worried me. How in the world could I possibly ever live up to a man like that?

Much later in my life Attallah told me that all of us sisters called her during our freshman or sophomore years with questions about our identities. She always seemed to have the answers, to have the gift of knocking out our insecurities and uncertainties. "You don't owe an explanation to anyone," she said. "You are Malcolm X's daughter—you don't have to pass a test. You are his daughter and all he would want for you is to be whole as you explore yourself in this new space."

Make Informed Decisions

Reading lets you gather the facts so you can make informed decisions. Here Opus takes such action, but is his decision a good one?

19

Discover Where You're Going

Reading can open doors to careers you may never have thought about. When Wyland was a teenager, he read a book that changed the course of his life.

Something Very Rare and Beautiful

—*Wyland*

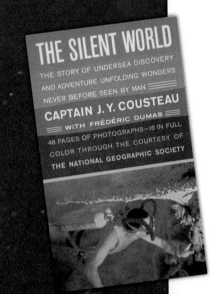

I was born and raised just outside Motor City—Detroit, Michigan. Considering that my life is dedicated to making the art of the ocean visible for the whole planet, my birthplace seems a mistake. I've always felt I should have been born on the West Coast, closer to the whales and other marine life I've come to love so well. But in truth, it hardly matters where I was born, since my love affair with the ocean actually started with a book—*The Silent World*, by Jacques Cousteau.

I was around 13 years old when I read it. Even then, I knew that I wanted to be an artist. At the age of 3, I had painted my first murals—on the back of the headboard on my parents' bed. I would slide underneath the bed with the paint and brushes and paint these detailed landscapes of the world of dinosaurs. Later, my mom let me set up a studio in our basement, and I spent hours there painting. It was a way for me to relax after sports and schoolwork.

Wyland
(b. 1956)

I didn't go out looking for *The Silent World*; a friend of mine just handed it to me. I had no idea that I would find it so compelling. The book was first published in 1953 and has sold more than five million copies in 22 languages. Cousteau is mainly known for his films, but his writing is tremendous. Using words, he paints an incredibly vivid picture of the undersea world. I believe Cousteau was able to do this because he knew that world so well. He had an emotional bond with the sea; people often say it was like his mistress. His descriptions of his encounters with marine animals are powerful, too. He writes about swimming with sharks and manta rays. At the time his book was published, most people feared the undersea world, but he made it very clear that the most dangerous animals in the sea were not the sharks or whales, but us.

Cousteau transported people into the marine world in a way that nobody else had. I immediately fell under the book's spell and couldn't put it down—I was up until two, three o'clock in the morning reading it. When I finished, I knew I wanted to be just like Jacques Cousteau. *Someday, I vowed to myself, I too will be an ocean explorer and diver.*

Jacques Cousteau

After I read *The Silent World*, I began to lobby my mother to take our family on a vacation to California to visit her sister, my Aunt Linda. It took a year of pushing, but when I was 14, we finally went. When I saw the ocean for the first time at Laguna Beach, my budding interest in it, inspired by Cousteau's book, blossomed into a full-fledged passion. As we stood on the beach, the waves crashing onto the rocks and the sand, I looked out to the horizon. A few hundred yards out from shore, I saw two black backs covered with clusters of yellow barnacles, accompanied by magnificent sprays of water blowing up into the air. I was looking at living whales for the first time. I couldn't see the entire body of each whale—only their backs as they surfaced to blow. But that was enough for me. I was ecstatic. I had never seen an animal that large in the wild. I felt as if I were seeing something very rare and beautiful—as if it were a miracle to be there when they swam by. Words alone can't describe how this first sighting affected me; I can only say I'll never forget what I saw that day. I was changed by each and every detail of it.

I told myself that one day I'd live here. Sure enough, 10 years later, I moved to Laguna Beach

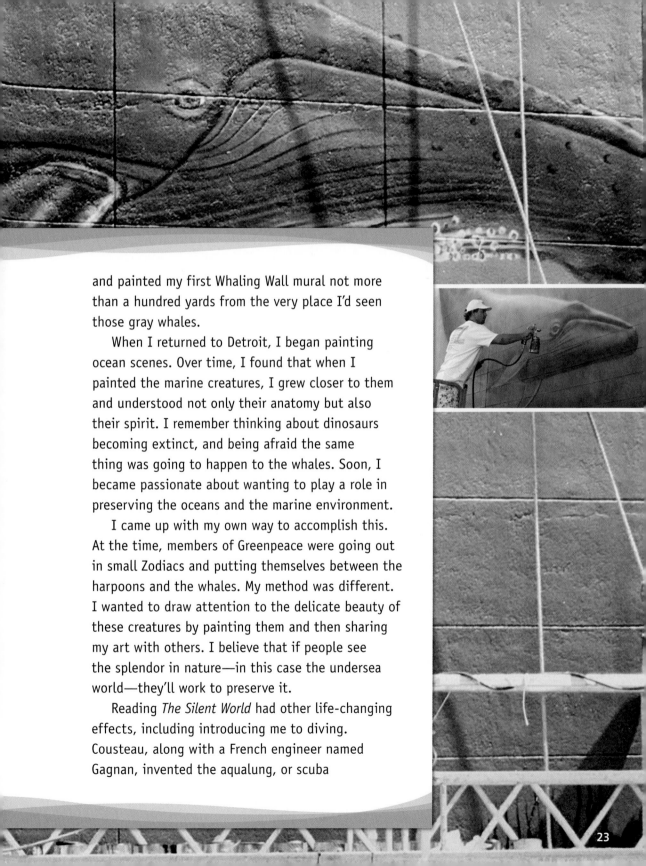

and painted my first Whaling Wall mural not more than a hundred yards from the very place I'd seen those gray whales.

When I returned to Detroit, I began painting ocean scenes. Over time, I found that when I painted the marine creatures, I grew closer to them and understood not only their anatomy but also their spirit. I remember thinking about dinosaurs becoming extinct, and being afraid the same thing was going to happen to the whales. Soon, I became passionate about wanting to play a role in preserving the oceans and the marine environment.

I came up with my own way to accomplish this. At the time, members of Greenpeace were going out in small Zodiacs and putting themselves between the harpoons and the whales. My method was different. I wanted to draw attention to the delicate beauty of these creatures by painting them and then sharing my art with others. I believe that if people see the splendor in nature—in this case the undersea world—they'll work to preserve it.

Reading *The Silent World* had other life-changing effects, including introducing me to diving. Cousteau, along with a French engineer named Gagnan, invented the aqualung, or scuba

(self-contained underwater breathing apparatus), and he was one of the first people to swim unrestricted: without an air tube connected to a remote oxygen source. In the book, he shares his experience of that remarkable underwater freedom in this beautiful description of his first scuba dive, taken in the Mediterranean Sea in June of 1943:

> "At night I had often had visions of flying by extending my arms as wings. Now I flew without wings. . . . From this day forward we would swim across miles of country no man had known, free and level, with our flesh feeling what the fish scales know."

Although *The Silent World* is mostly text, it has one great photo of Jacques Cousteau diving. That photo, combined with Cousteau's description, intensified my desire to learn to dive. When I started a few years later, it was everything Cousteau said it was—and more. Diving has become a spiritual experience for me. Like Cousteau, I feel that I am actually flying underwater. Each dive has its own magical moments.

I think diving has an even greater power for me because of the physical limitations I had as a small boy. Born with a severe clubfoot, I underwent 11 major surgeries before the age of five and was continuously hobbled by a corrective cast that prevented my swimming. I wasn't able to go into the water like everybody else; I could only dream about and imagine it. When all the casts were finally off and we took our first vacation to Cass Lake, I couldn't wait to get in the water. The very first time I jumped in, I was swimming well; it felt so natural. In fact, I'm more comfortable in the water than out. I'm more of a sea mammal, I guess.

It's amazing how important a book can be. Before I read Cousteau, I mostly read books about all kinds of art; I was inspired by artists such as Salvador Dali and Robert Bateman. And although I loved the water, I hadn't made a connection to the ocean. Reading *The Silent World*, art and nature came together for me. It was "the barnacle that broke the whale's back" and changed the course of my life. Cousteau inspired people to respect, love, and protect the ocean and its inhabitants with his artful use of words. Today, I do the same thing with a paintbrush.

Sharpen Your Viewpoint

Reading can show you other people's viewpoints and help
you clarify your own point of view. Liz Bahe attended high
school at the Institute of American Indian Arts. In this poem,
she remembers how she felt when she read textbooks about
European pioneers.

Man Poling a Canoe into Camp,
Noah Billie, 1992, Seminole Tribe
of Florida Ah-Tah-Thi-Ki Museum.

PRINTED WORDS

—Liz Sohappy Bahe

I stared at the printed words
hazed, blurred, they became grey.
I trailed down the page
to a picture shouting what I read.

I thought about my people
up North—
far from here.
My land, the hot dry basin,
the pine on the mountain ranges
and the snowcapped peaks.

I thought of the killing word;
Civilization.
The steel buildings stabbing the earth,
stabbing old religions now buried on the hilltop,
to have their tears drip black
from Industry's ash clouds.

I thought of the unseen tears
in eyes watching our valley
gashed by plows,
proud trees uprooted, dragged aside,
giving way to smothering tar roads.
And river veins pumped away
never knowing the path to the Columbia River.

I glanced at the blurring printed words
and felt an ancient anger swell,
bubble like a volcano in birth,
anger blackening the printed words
about your land being only a swamp
useless to Civilization.

I saw in a flash
the unknowing eyes of the Everglades—
alligators, egrets, water turkeys, ibises.
Animals I've never seen, never known
except from sadness that their fate lies
in printed words.

The words about the Everglades—
moist, mysterious, very much a land—
useless.
Words forgetting the animal people,
the Seminole, the Miccosukie,
who are standing in the way of the thing called
Civilization.

Everglades and Seminole Camp Scene,
Noah Billie, 1987, Seminole Tribe
of Florida Ah-Tah-Thi-Ki Museum.

Get the Power

What does reading have to do with power? Natalie Merchant and Robert Buck wrote this song about someone who can't read. It describes what it's like to depend on other people to make sense of all the "lines and circles."

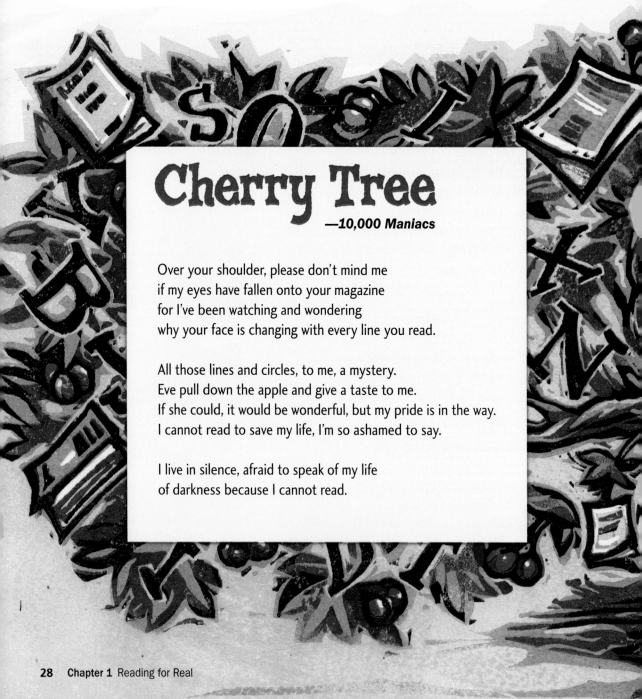

Cherry Tree

—10,000 Maniacs

Over your shoulder, please don't mind me
if my eyes have fallen onto your magazine
for I've been watching and wondering
why your face is changing with every line you read.

All those lines and circles, to me, a mystery.
Eve pull down the apple and give a taste to me.
If she could, it would be wonderful, but my pride is in the way.
I cannot read to save my life, I'm so ashamed to say.

I live in silence, afraid to speak of my life
of darkness because I cannot read.

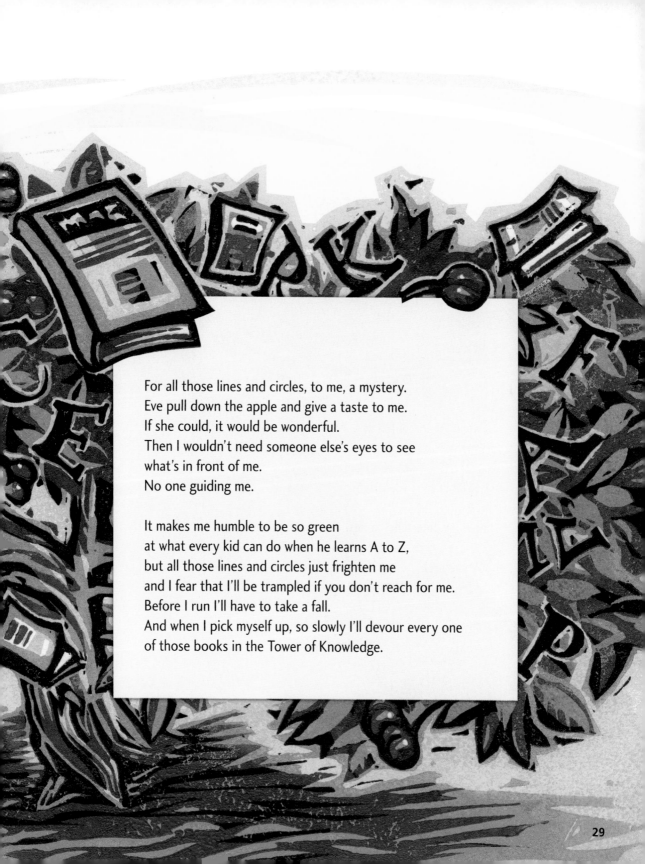

For all those lines and circles, to me, a mystery.
Eve pull down the apple and give a taste to me.
If she could, it would be wonderful.
Then I wouldn't need someone else's eyes to see
what's in front of me.
No one guiding me.

It makes me humble to be so green
at what every kid can do when he learns A to Z,
but all those lines and circles just frighten me
and I fear that I'll be trampled if you don't reach for me.
Before I run I'll have to take a fall.
And when I pick myself up, so slowly I'll devour every one
of those books in the Tower of Knowledge.

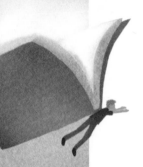

Can You Read Me?

*"***R**eading is a discount ticket to everywhere.*"*

—MARY SCHMICH

IN THIS CHAPTER

Connect to Reading

How Do You Connect?

Read much? Believe it or not, you probably do. Just look at all the reading materials featured in this chapter. From maps to web pages, food labels to brochures, there's always a reason to read. You can learn everything from how to microwave a pizza to the migratory habits of *Blasturus cupidus*.

Try this. Make a log like the one shown here. Every time you read something, whether it's a label or a novel, write it down. Keep the log for one week. Then see how much you read.

READING LOG — DAY 1: SEPTEMBER 8

1. Shampoo label
2. Headlines on sports page
3. Movie schedule
4. Lab notes
5. Cafeteria menu
6. Science textbook
7. Teacher comments on English essay
8. Street signs: Detour, No Crossing, Yield
9. Sign on front of subway car
10. Ads in subway and subway car
11. FlashFury CD cover
12. Camp brochure
13. E-mails from friends
14. Act 1, "A Raisin in the Sun"
15. Cooking directions on pizza box
16. Manual for driving test
17. Tag with washing instructions
18. Directions on laundry detergent box
19. Text message
20. Jamilla's diary (!)

Who Else Is Connected?

According to a recent study, although most teens believe that reading is the key to getting into college and finding a good job, only 16% of 15 to 17-year-olds read every day for fun. For most, the problem is finding books they like.

So how can you discover some great reads? Find out how other people connect to reading. Make a copy of the four-square shown here. Fill in each box. Then survey your classmates. Find people who responded the way you did. Write their initials in the box. Talk about your common interests.

1. What are some things you like to do outside of school?	2. What things do you read that come from having these interests?
play basketball drive listen to music take photos	Sports page of newspaper Maps CD inserts How-To Manual
3. What are some other things you read? Graphic novels E-mails	4. Why do you read? • To learn more about the sports I like • To forget about my life for a while • To learn how to use my digital camera

Advertisement

Think of fashion ads as fairy tales that always tell the same story: *Buy (insert product name), and you'll live happily ever after.* Of course, the ad doesn't actually say that. The message is much more subtle, but still very powerful.

Advertisements use lots of tricks to get you to buy the product. The photo shows models with an attitude you admire—confident, energetic, popular, whatever. This suggests that the attitude comes with the product.

Ad writers also choose words very carefully. They use the word *you* to try to put you in the picture: *You set the style. You wear (insert brand name).* This advertising technique is called "transfer," and it's very persuasive. Phrases like *break away* make you think that you can stand out from the crowd and lead the pack—if only you had those jeans!

Watch out for words like *unforgettable* that amplify, or exaggerate, the appeal of the product. And of course, when all else fails, there's always sex appeal: *The fit is unforgivable.* Can one brand of jeans really offer all that? Well, hurry to a store near you to find out, and don't forget your wallet.

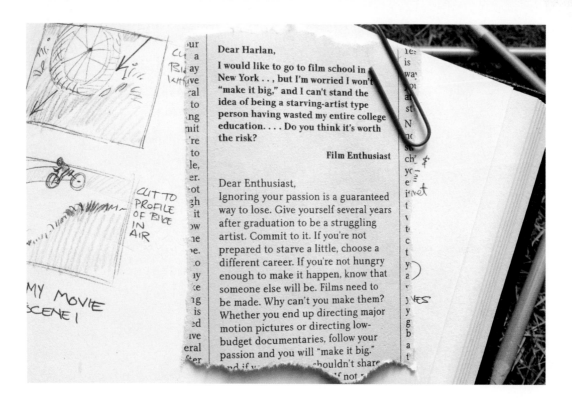

Dear Harlan,

I would like to go to film school in New York . . , but I'm worried I won't "make it big," and I can't stand the idea of being a starving-artist type person having wasted my entire college education. . . . Do you think it's worth the risk?

Film Enthusiast

Dear Enthusiast,
Ignoring your passion is a guaranteed way to lose. Give yourself several years after graduation to be a struggling artist. Commit to it. If you're not prepared to starve a little, choose a different career. If you're not hungry enough to make it happen, know that someone else will be. Films need to be made. Why can't you make them? Whether you end up directing major motion pictures or directing low-budget documentaries, follow your passion and you will "make it big."

Advice Column

Have you ever read an advice column? What the columnist says usually confirms your own judgment about the best way to solve a problem, and that can really boost your confidence.

Not all advice columns are equal though. In fact, some sources of teen advice like chat rooms can be very dangerous. That's because the people giving the "advice" aren't experienced and may be personally involved with the reader.

Advice columns in newspapers and magazines, on the other hand, give advice from experienced adults who have no personal stake in the problem. When you read an advice column, ask yourself, "How does this person's problem apply to my life now, in the past, or maybe in the future?" Most of the letters teens send to advice columnists ask questions about family issues or "first time" situations: first girlfriends or boyfriends, first break-ups, first concerns about sex.

For a columnist, these are the same issues that come up year after year. But for the teens who are reading the column, these issues are headline news. Whether the letter is signed **Waiting in West Virginia** or **Confused in Cleveland**, the best advice is always, "Be comfortable with yourself, and find people you can trust to advise you."

Application for a Job

A job application is a foot in the door to employment. When a manager reads your application, you have his or her undivided attention. It's your chance to stand out—so make sure you fill it out completely and accurately.

If you're able to complete the application at home, great! Then you can gather all the information you need—social security number, dates, addresses, phone numbers, etc. If you have to fill it out at the workplace, arrive prepared with all the information in hand.

Job applications always ask for *employment experience.* What previous jobs have you had? If you have no employment experience, just say so and don't worry. Job applications also ask for *references.* These are people who know you and can speak well of you, like teachers, coaches, or former bosses.

When you get to the section called *Job Related Skills,* don't be shy. Tell why you are the best person for the job and get more than your foot in the door.

Employment Experience

Please provide the following information of your past and current employers.

Employer	Phone ( )
City, State	Date of Hire
Title	Salary
Supervisor	Reason for Leaving
Employer	Phone ( )
City, State	Date of Hire

Application for College

It's important to read a college application VERY carefully. Take your time reading through it so that you understand exactly what information the college is asking for. Read through the entire form once. Then gather together all the dates and personal documents you will need like school and financial records, ID cards, and essays. Having this information at hand will make your task a lot easier.

What's the best way to make a good impression? Make sure the application is filled out completely. For example, did you list the names of all the schools you attended and the graduation dates? Your previous school experiences are important. And make sure that the information you provide is correct. One small mistake and the form will be sent back to you.

If you don't understand a term like *citizenship status,* don't guess the meaning. Ask an adult at home or school to explain it to you. Take your time, read and answer the items carefully, and best of luck!

▼ *A CLOSER LOOK*

5	CITIZENSHIP STATUS
	U.S. CITIZEN ☐ Yes ☒ No

If not a U.S. citizen, indicate status below:
- ☒ (2) Permanent Resident / Date Issued: 1/13/97
- ☐ (3) Temporary Resident / Date Issued: _____
- ☐ (4) Amnesty
- ☐ (5) Refugee
- ☐ (6) Student Visa (F-1 or M-1)
- ☐ (7) Other Status (Specify): _____

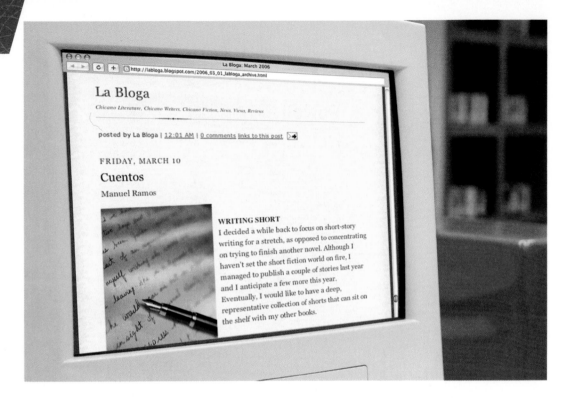

Blog

A blog is a good way to stay connected with your friends. But what exactly is it? A blog is a website with entries organized in chronological order, from the most recent date to the oldest. This means it's always being updated. (At first, people called sites like this a *web log*, but then clipped the two words into one word: *blog*.)

Think of a blog as a container. It can hold anything the editor—the person who created the blog—wants to put into it: poetry, journal entries, photographs, song lyrics, political commentary, or quotations. Often there are links that connect you to interesting websites you might never find on your own. Click one and see where it takes you.

Read what the editor says about that link and add your comments. A blog is like an ongoing conversation. But before your comments are posted, the editor has to approve them to make sure they're appropriate for the Internet.

A blog is not a place to find factual news. It is where you go to read opinions, to connect with people who share your interests. You can read 1,000 blogs before you find one that really speaks to you. Then you're hooked. You read that blog day after day. You follow the links to news articles, other websites of interest, and even more blogs!

Book Review

What is the book about? Is it the kind of book that you'd like? Is the writing dull or really gripping? A good book review answers these questions, but doesn't give away too much.

When your favorite author writes a new book, look for reviews in magazines, newspapers, and on the Net. Then you can decide if you want to spend your time—and maybe some money—to read it. Some reviewers use a rating system like the one movie critics use. The more stars, the more the reviewer liked the book.

Even after you read a book, check out the book reviews. Often different people react differently to the same book. You may discover something you completely missed.

Of course, some books may not be worth a second thought, but some may be worth a second and a third. The stars will tell you.

▼ *A CLOSER LOOK*

★★★★☆ *STAFF PICKS*
Monster by Walter Dean Myers
Reviewer: Eddie V.

Do you ever feel like your life is a movie? Imagine being only sixteen and on trial for murder. In this book, Steve Harmon uses journal entries and a movie screenplay to tell us the story of his murder trial. Is he guilty or innocent? Follow the facts, and you decide! This is one of Walter Dean Myers's best novels. It stayed with me for days.

Inside the brochure image:

RAMP IT UP

SKATEBOARDING CAMP

...n up now for the summer session.
All levels welcome.
Guaranteed FUN.

CAMP SCHEDULE
Session 1   June 6–June 10
Session 2   June 13–June 17
Session 3   June 20–June 24
Session 4   June 27–July 1

Challenging indoor
and outdoor ramps.
Street or vert skater!
Try our new concrete bowl with
6 ft. extensions! Or our vert
ramp 12 ft. tall x 36 ft. wide.
Learn to
your friends.
...es, handrails, gat...

Fee: $650 per person
per session (includes
meals and transportation
to and from Port Lowell
train station).

Brochure

Brochures are printed handouts, folded over, slim and slick, filled with inviting photographs and bite-sized bits of information. They have titles like *5 Steps to Quitting Smoking, Getting a Job with a Radio Station,* or *Upgrade Your Internet Service.* You've seen them in doctors' offices, guidance counselors' offices, electronics stores, and other high traffic areas.

You'll never read most brochures because they're written for special audiences or consumers. But suppose you're seriously into skateboarding and you see a brochure about *RAMP IT UP Skateboarding Camp*? You'll read it. You may even take it home and start dreaming about spending a week popping ollies over the gap. But then, of course, there's the issue of money.

Brochures are informational, but many are also made to promote something that costs money. That "something" can be a product, a service, a camp, or even a school. That's when brochures start to cross the line into advertising.

You may not even know you want something until you see the glossy pictures and the glowing description. A brochure will tell you about the good things, but it won't tell you everything. That comes later, when you call the toll free number on the back.

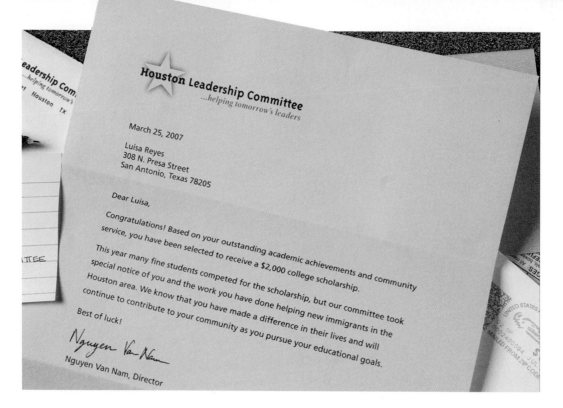

Houston Leadership Committee
...helping tomorrow's leaders

March 25, 2007

Luisa Reyes
308 N. Presa Street
San Antonio, Texas 78205

Dear Luisa,

Congratulations! Based on your outstanding academic achievements and community service, you have been selected to receive a $2,000 college scholarship.

This year many fine students competed for the scholarship, but our committee took special notice of you and the work you have done helping new immigrants in the Houston area. We know that you have made a difference in their lives and will continue to contribute to your community as you pursue your educational goals.

Best of luck!

Nguyen Van Nam
Nguyen Van Nam, Director

Business Letter

Look at the envelope—it's long enough to hold a document folded in thirds. Whatever is inside must be important. That's what a lot of young people think. And at least sometimes, they're right.

A business letter is just an efficient way to do business. Look at the letterhead at the top. It tells you the name of the company or organization. Next, read the greeting. Does the sender know you? Probably not if it says, *Dear Student* or *Dear Sir or Madam*.

What's the purpose of the letter? The first few sentences will tell you. *We are happy to inform you . . .*

means "Keep smiling. We have good news for you."

Many business letters ask you to do something by a certain date. So slow down, and read carefully. Reread parts if you need to, and check the meanings of any formal language used. Are you ready to do business?

Houston Leadership Committee
...helping tomorrow's leaders
35 South Main Street
Houston, TX 77057

Luisa Reyes
308 N. Presa Street
San Antonio, TX 78205

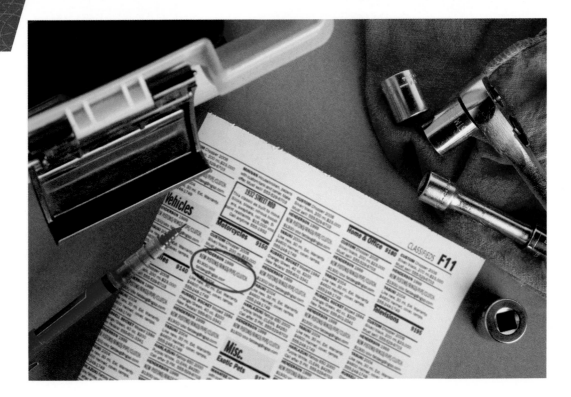

Classified Ad

A classified ad is a description of a product that's listed for sale in the newspaper. How do you read a classified ad? *Between the lines.* After all, what does *like new* really mean?

The first step is to know some facts about the product you want to buy. What features are important to you? What are you willing to pay?

Let's say you're looking for a motorcycle. Check the brand name and the year it was made. That tells you a lot. Consider the real age of the product. A three-year-old motorcycle with 30 miles could be a better buy than this year's model with 500 miles.

Look for what the ad does and doesn't say. Is the warranty still in effect? If so, the manufacturer will cover some repair work. Of course, the real test will come when you ride it. If you can't live without it, pay the seller's price, *obo* (or make your best offer.)

▼ *A CLOSER LOOK*

Motorcycles   9150

CUSTOM Chopper 2006
Silver/black, 200 mi.$23,000
Must sell! 555-529-6703

HENDERSON 1999
NEW PISTONS/RINGS/PIPE/CLUTCH
$1300/obo
fatdawg@HBgoodreaders.com

YASUKI 2004
Like new, 30mi. Ext. Warranty.
$4600 Helmet, cover, ramps.

Comic Strip

Comic means "funny." But not all comic strips are funny, so scratch that. They are strips, though— strips of sequential pictures, read from left to right, with words that tell a story or joke.

The pictures show the characters' actions and feelings. Words of dialogue are shown inside speech balloons with "tails" that point to the character who's speaking.

Cartoonists have to make their point in a small space. Unlike graphic novels that go on for many pages, comic strips convey a message about life and human nature in just a few panels. You may have to make some inferences to figure out the message. What do the characters represent? Look for clues in the setting and in the character's clothes.

Those are the basics. From this point on, the rules vary from one comic strip to another. Animals may talk. Heroes may fly, and kids may never grow up. It can get pretty weird.

In the comic strip *Calvin and Hobbes,* a boy thinks his toy tiger is alive. The tiger talks and acts like a best friend, but all the adults think he's just a toy tiger. It's a clever device that is sometimes funny, but always fun. The point is, when you read a comic strip, let go of your disbelief, buy into the fantasy, and just enjoy the ride.

Electronic Communication

E-mail. Text messages. E-cards. Instant messages. Blogs. Are you plugged in? Many people are, especially teens because electronic communication is fast and it's fun.

E-mail is electronic mail that's sent online from one computer to another. Anyone with a computer and an e-mail address can send and receive messages. Different e-mail programs have different mailbox designs. But there are some basic things you'll always see like the name of the person who sent the e-mail and a *Cc* list if other people received the same message.

When you get an e-mail, look for the subject line. That will tell you what the e-mail is about. Also look for attachments like text files or photographs. You can reply to an e-mail as soon as it arrives in your mailbox, or you can wait and reply at a later time.

Want to communicate really fast? Some cell phones can send text and picture messages. But watch out! The costs can really add up. You save time with text messaging, but not money.

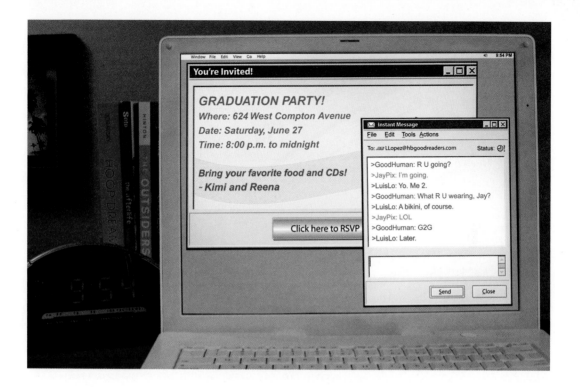

If speed is what you're after, try instant messaging. Unlike e-mail, there's no delay when you "IM." You communicate in real time.

All you have to do is create a list of friends, or *buddy list*. Then whenever someone in your list is online, a small window opens up and you can start a conversation. You and your friends type in messages that immediately appear in the window. One WORD OF CAUTION: When you IM, keep in mind that it's not considered a secure way to communicate. Never send any private or confidential information.

Instant messaging is much faster than sending e-mail because you don't have to go through a lot of steps. It's also less formal. Since people like the speed of IM, they often combine words or use alternate spellings. They also use abbreviations and acronyms. It's like reading a private language, but you soon catch on to it. Here are some examples:

Y = why   **R** = are   **U** = you

One of the most popular acronyms is **LOL**, which means "I'm **L**aughing **O**ut **L**oud." That's what you might do when you get an E-card like an electronic party invitation. It's a great way to spread the word about a party, and your friends can click on a link to tell if they plan to go. Uh oh. It's time for the party. **G2G**.

Nutrition Facts
Serving Size 1 oz. (28g/About 20 chips)
Servings Per Container About 12

Amount Per Serving

Calories 150   Calories from Fat 90

% Daily Value*

Total Fat 10g

Saturated Fat 3g

Trans Fat 0g

Cholesterol 0mg   15%

Sodium 180mg   15%

Total Carbohydrate 15g

Dietary Fiber 1g   0%

Sugars 0g   8%

Protein 2g   5%

4%

Vitamin A 0%   •   Vitamin C 10%

Calcium 0%   •   Iron 0%

Vitamin E 6%   •   Thiamin 4%

Niacin 6%   •   Vitamin B6 4%

Phosphorus 4%   •   Zinc 2%

*Percent Daily Values are based on a 2,000 calorie diet.
Your Daily Values may be higher or lower depending on
your calorie needs.

Food Label

Why are my clothes getting tighter? Why is my nose one big, ugly zit? The simple answer is, "You are what you eat." But wait! You don't have to give up all the foods you love in order to be healthy. By reading the Nutrition Facts on food labels you can make choices that let you eat—but not overeat— foods you like.

For example, look at the food label on a bag of potato chips. Read the serving size, the number of servings in the package, and the number of calories in each serving. Now do the math: If there are 20 chips in one serving and 150 calories per serving, how many calories are in one chip? What if you were to eat just a half serving instead of a full serving?

Calories only tell part of the story. You also need to consider Daily Values, or the amount of nutrients that public health experts recommend you eat each day. The % Daily Value that's shown on the label is for a single serving of the food. It's based on a daily diet of 2,000 calories.

Read the % Daily Value for fats, cholesterol, and sodium (salt). If the percentage is high, eat less of the food. Eat more foods that are high in fiber, protein, vitamins, and minerals. In other words, if you eat a small serving of potato chips, balance out your meal with more nutritious foods—and save yourself a trip to the clothing store.

Graphic Novel

Reading a graphic novel takes some practice. Do you read the words first, or do you look at the pictures? How do you move through the page? And what's with the slanted panels and jagged text balloons? Do they mean something? Uh huh. Everything means something in a graphic novel.

The pictures are a good place to start since they set the scene and show the action. Move through the page the way you usually read: start at the top and move from left to right across the panels. Then go down the page to the next panel on the left.

Look at the shape of the text balloons. Often they're a clue to what the characters are saying. If the outline is sharp and jagged, the person may be angry or shouting.

Does the novel have slanted panels? This indicates speed or dramatic intensity. When a panel is divided into several parts it means that the story events are happening very quickly or that the events are happening at the same time but in different places.

Even the font, or typeface, can carry information. The penciller may use a *flowery font* to show magical powers or romance. Robotic or mechanical speech may look like **THIS**. Sound effects **BAM!** also play a big part. Reading a graphic novel is meant to be a full-body experience— more like viewing a movie than reading a book.

▼ From the graphic novel
Shock Rockets

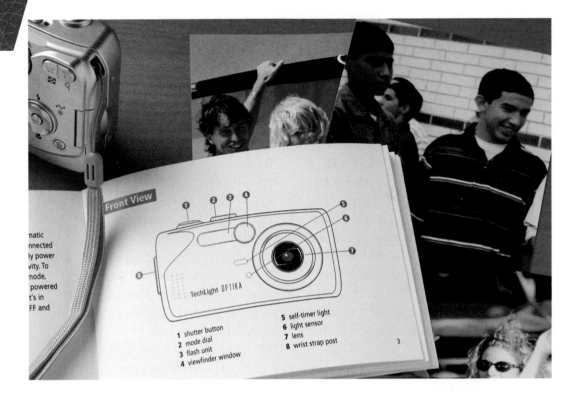

Front View

TechLight OPTIKA

1 shutter button
2 mode dial
3 flash unit
4 viewfinder window

5 self-timer light
6 light sensor
7 lens
8 wrist strap post

3

natic
nnected
ly power
vity. To
node,
powered
t's in
FF and

How-To Manual

Okay, you have a new digital camera that takes photos, makes videos, downloads movies, and sings you to sleep. You're eager to try it out, but where do you begin? First, get to know the product.

Find the diagram in the manual that shows the parts. Each part will be numbered and labeled with its name. If there are parts to assemble, use the Table of Contents to find the instructions for putting the parts together.

Now you're ready to learn how to use the product. The Table of Contents will help you with that, too. Start with the basics like *Operating Your Camera* or *Taking Pictures*.

Inside, you will find how-to directions. These are commands given in order: 1. *Remove this.* 2. *Turn that,* etc. Follow the commands. But before you remove or turn anything, read through all the directions once, paying special attention to information that's marked **CAUTION!** or <u>**WARNING**</u>. You'll be glad you did.

Inserting the Memory Card

To insert the card:

1. Turn off camera.
2. Open card door.
3. Orient card so arrows point toward camera.
4. Insert card into slot. Make sure connector is sealed.
5. Close card door.

CAUTION! *Forcing the memory card may cause damage.*

Interview

An interview is a tool for collecting information. It consists of an interviewer asking questions (**Q**) and of an interviewee giving the answers (**A**). A good interviewer keeps the interviewee on track by saying, "Getting back to. . ." and "Can you tell me more about . . . ?"

When you read an interview, you're usually reading a written record of questions and answers that were spoken aloud. It's not as spontaneous as a live interview, but it's more concise. All the "ums, ers" and "you knows" have been edited out.

Writers also reorganize interviews to get a better flow of ideas. It's easy to get information from a written interview because the writer has done all the work for you.

▼ *A CLOSER LOOK*

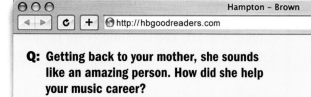

Q: Getting back to your mother, she sounds like an amazing person. How did she help your music career?

A: She called the Spanish radio station in our hometown of San Antonio, Texas. She spoke to the director and got me a job singing jingles. This led to my first recording experiences and appearances on local TV talk shows.

Magazine

A magazine is like a box of candy for the brain. It offers a variety of reading experiences—ranging from chewy to soft, from nutty to hard. It invites you to pick what you like and leave the rest in the box. But how do you choose?

Start with the delicious cover. It's designed to tempt your eye and capture your interest. The title and cover usually show the focus of the magazine so you can choose one on a topic you like— maybe science, sports, or music.

But is this issue of the magazine for you? To decide, read the "teaser copy" on the cover. Teasers announce high-interest articles inside the issue so you can tell if you want to look inside and find out more.

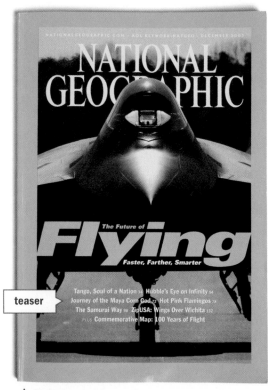

teaser

▲ Magazine cover

The table of contents is a great way to find out more. The pictures and bite-size descriptions give you a taste of each article. Use the page numbers to quickly locate an article.

When you get to the article, scan the title and section headings. Flip through the other pages. Do the photos and captions make you want to read the article?

Once you're hooked, settle in and really read. Look for the "who, what, when, where, and how" information. Be sure to read with a critical eye. Is the writing clear and interesting? If so, you may want to read other issues of the magazine.

▼ Magazine article

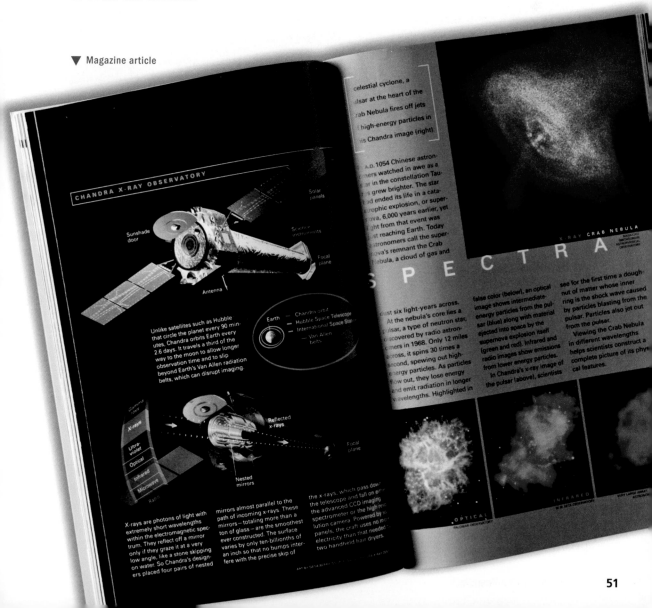

CHANDRA X-RAY OBSERVATORY

Sunshade door

Solar panels

Scientific instruments

Focal plane

Antenna

Unlike satellites such as Hubble that circle the planet every 90 minutes, Chandra orbits Earth every 2.6 days. It travels a third of the way to the moon to allow longer observation time and to slip beyond Earth's Van Allen radiation belts, which can disrupt imaging.

Earth — Chandra orbit
— Hubble Space Telescope
— International Space Station
— Van Allen belts

X-rays
Ultraviolet
Optical
Infrared
Microwave

Reflected x-rays

Focal plane

Nested mirrors

X-rays are photons of light with extremely short wavelengths within the electromagnetic spectrum. They reflect off a mirror only if they graze it at a very low angle, like a stone skipping on water. So Chandra's designers placed four pairs of nested

mirrors almost parallel to the path of incoming x-rays. These mirrors—totaling more than a ton of glass—are the smoothest ever constructed. The surface varies by only ten-billionths of an inch so that no bumps interfere with the precise skip of

the x-rays, which pass down the telescope and fall on either the advanced CCD imaging spectrometer or the high resolution camera. Powered by solar panels, the craft uses no more electricity than that needed for two handheld hair dryers.

celestial cyclone, a pulsar at the heart of the Crab Nebula fires off jets of high-energy particles in this Chandra image (right).

A.D. 1054 Chinese astronomers watched in awe as a star in the constellation Taurus grew brighter. The star had ended its life in a catastrophic explosion, or supernova, 6,000 years earlier, yet light from that event was just reaching Earth. Today astronomers call the supernova's remnant the Crab Nebula, a cloud of gas and

dust six light-years across. At the nebula's core lies a pulsar, a type of neutron star, discovered by radio astronomers in 1968. Only 12 miles across, it spins 30 times a second, spewing out high-energy particles. As particles flow out, they lose energy and emit radiation in longer wavelengths. Highlighted in

false color (below), an optical image shows intermediate-energy particles from the pulsar (blue) along with material ejected into space by the supernova explosion itself (green and red). Infrared and radio images show emissions from lower energy particles.

In Chandra's x-ray image of the pulsar (above), scientists

see for the first time a doughnut of matter whose inner ring is the shock wave caused by particles blasting from the pulsar. Particles also jet out from the pulsar.

Viewing the Crab Nebula in different wavelengths helps scientists construct a complete picture of its physical features.

X RAY   CRAB NEBULA

S P E C T R A

OPTICAL

INFRARED

Map

Some maps are works of art. There are maps from Greece dating back to the 1400s that have fantastic sea serpents and wind spirits painted in the margins. In 1680 a Dutch map maker included a man riding an elephant in his map of Central Asia. Today, cartographers use computers and satellite imagery to produce beautiful maps.

Cartography has changed, but every map ever made has one thing in common: it is a physical representation of a specific place. It could be the floor of the ocean, the surface of Mars, your school, or the entire world. But keep in mind that not all maps of a geographic location provide the same information.

When you pick up a map, check the title to make sure it has the type of information you want. A map like the one on the next page may help you understand Afghanistan's physical features and its political borders with other countries. But the map can't show you how to get around in an Afghani city or show you shifts in the country's population. For that information, you would need different, specialized maps.

After you check a map's title, read the map legend. The legend explains the symbols that are used to represent boundary lines, cities, airports, roads, and other features. The legend is the most important tool for reading and understanding a map.

A map legend also includes a scale for calculating distance. Maps covering large areas might use a scale of 100 miles for every inch on the map. It's good to know the true scale of a map, because all flat representations of the earth are somewhat distorted.

Cartographers have to stretch and shrink the natural configurations of the earth to show it on a flat, two-dimensional map. The further you get from the center, the more distortion you get. Luckily, this doesn't affect how useful maps are. People can still navigate from one place to another, measure distance, and locate sites based on map information.

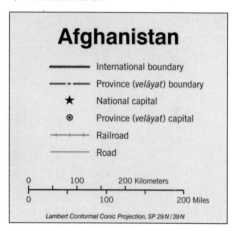

Afghanistan

——— International boundary
—·—·— Province (velāyat) boundary
★ National capital
◉ Province (velāyat) capital
+—+—+ Railroad
——— Road

0   100   200 Kilometers
0   100   200 Miles

Lambert Conformal Conic Projection, SP 29 N / 39 N

▼ Topographical map
of Afghanistan

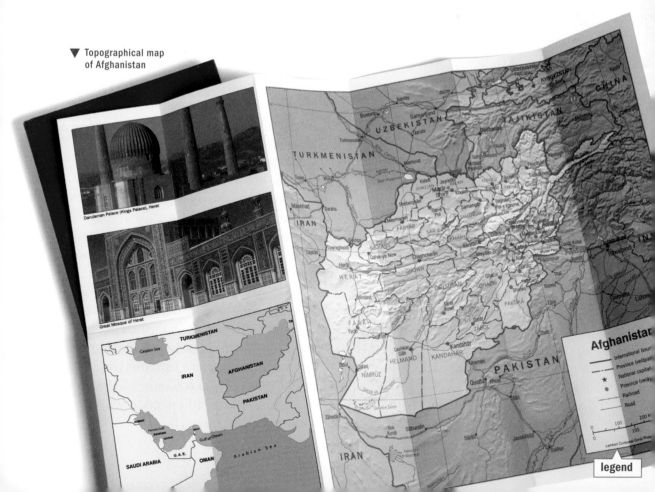

legend

Menu from Teresa's Cafe:

Teresa's Cafe

Appetizers

CHILE CON QUESO
Large Bowl......$6.25   Medium Bowl.......$3.50

DELUXE NACHOS
Tortilla Chips, topped with refried beans,
cheese dip, picadillo meat and jalapeños.
Full Order.......$7.95   Half Order.......$4.25

TERESA'S NACHOS
Beef or chicken fajita, over tortilla chips, refried beans, cheese dip and jalapeños.
............$7.95   Half Order.......$4.25

Chalupas

TERESA'S CHALUPAS
Two chalupas, covered with refried beans,
taco meat, shredded lettuce, diced tomatoes,
guacamole and cheddar cheese $5.95

CHALUPAS SABROSAS
Two chalupas, covered with refried beans,
shredded lettuce, diced tomatoes, guacamole
and cheddar cheese $4.95

BEANS CHALUPAS
Two chalupas, covered with refried beans,
shredded lettuce and diced tomatoes.....$4.50

THE TOSTADA
A large deep-fried flour tortilla, covered with
.... beef or chicken fajita, shredded
.... cheese.............$5.25

RANCHERITO
Cheese enchila
guacamole sa
refried beans

CHIMICHAN
Large rolled
topped witl
refried bea

POE
Stu
or
sp
g

Menu

Whether you're eating at The Fast Eats Diner or Teresa's Cafe, the meal begins with the menu. What will you order? Read the menu to help you decide. All of the items are arranged into categories like *Appetizers, Soups, Salads, Dinners, Beverages,* and *Desserts.* Some menus have more categories, some have fewer, but each one is clearly marked to help you find what you want.

Let's say you and a friend go to Teresa's Cafe for dinner. The first items on the menu are the appetizers. An appetizer is a small serving of food that begins a meal. Read the descriptions of each food. The Deluxe Nachos sound good. You could share a full order with your friend for $7.95 or get a half order just for yourself for $4.25. Hmmm. What's your budget? And how hungry are you? Before you decide, glance through the dinners. (On some menus you'll see a section called *Entrées,* which is French for "dinners.")

Compare the amount of food and the price for each dinner. At Teresa's, all the dinners come with rice, refried beans, and salad. That seems generous and the prices are good. Now it's time to get serious. Look for foods you like, and narrow down the choices to two or three. Compare the choices, then select one to order. Be sure to factor in money for a tip. And you better make that a *half order* of Deluxe Nacho's to share. You need to leave some room for dessert!

Movie Review

How do you read a movie review? *Any way you want to.* Why read a movie review? Ah! That's a better question. Read a movie review to find out what a movie *is*: a comedy, an action thriller, a mystery, a documentary, a musical, or a chick flick romance.

Many movies are *adaptations,* or film versions of a novel or a play. Others are *based on a true story,* which means they're about a real person's life or a real event, but don't always stick to all the facts.

Does the review make you want to rush out and see the movie? You can get a fast read by checking the icons, or little pictures. If the reviewer gives the movie thumbs down, one star out of five, or a rotten tomato, it's time to start rethinking your plan. Even after you've seen a movie it's fun to read the reviews. They're like a bonus feature for before and after your movie-going experience.

▼ *A CLOSER LOOK*

Newspaper

Newspapers are pretty amazing. Each and every day, they give millions of readers the latest news, along with editorial opinions, special features, sport stories, financial advice, classified ads, comics, book reviews, obituaries, TV schedules, and weather forecasts—all fresh off the press.

Whether it's a local paper covering news close to home or a national paper focusing on national and international events, a newspaper can inform and entertain you every day of the week. Think of all those pages covered in all that ink! How do you get through it?

Luckily, newspapers are divided into sections. Different kinds of articles appear in different sections. Sections A and B cover the top news stories of the day. Other sections might focus on *Business*, *Sports*, *Travel*, or *Entertainment*.

What interests you? Use the Index on the first page of the newspaper to find the sections you want to read. The letter stands for the section and the number is the page number.

▼ A CLOSER LOOK

Index

Advice	D10	Local News	B1
Book Reviews	D15	National News	A1
Business	E1	Movies	D2
Classifieds	F1	Obituaries	B6
Comics	D4	Sports	C1
Crossword	D6	Travel	G1
Editorials	A14	TV	D8
Entertainment	D1	Weather	B13

Still, the amount of information in a newspaper can be overwhelming. Where do you begin? Start by scanning the headlines that appear above each article. The bigger and bolder the headline, the more important the story.

If you're an athlete, the headline **TAX CUTS THREATEN HIGH SCHOOL SPORTS** may be important to you. Scan the article for the basic facts. *What* tax is being cut, and *why* does it threaten school sports? *When* and *where* is this happening? *Who* supports the tax cuts and *who* is against them?

News reporters try to answer the questions *Who? What? Where?* *When? Why?* and *How?* by presenting the facts that are known about the subject. In the tax cuts story, the facts involve issues that stir up debate and may even personally affect you.

Should the proposed tax cut be allowed? If so, how will the schools support their sports programs? Read and form your own opinion.

When you read a news article, it's important to read with a critical eye. Examine the facts and decide. Are you convinced? Is the information believable and is it complete? Are both sides of the issue fairly reported? Sometimes important information is left out of the story.

▼ Front page of a local newspaper

PRESIDENT TO ADDRESS NATION
Page A2

Possible Water Shortages
Page B1

Local Teen Wins Scholarship
Page D4

Today's forecast/813

73 Low 56
High

Lake County Daily

Monday, May 15

58 CENTS

Since 1871

STATE

TAX CUTS THREATEN HIGH SCHOOL SPORTS

RECREATION

CRIME

Suspects arrested in hacking case

Local men held for questioning

By SCOTT RUSSELL
Lake County Daily

LAKE COUNTY — The proposed cut in business taxes will reduce the already tight 2007 budget of the Lake County School District. Revenue from the current business tax provides 33% of an already inadequate school budget and rising costs have forced the School Board to eliminate all art and music programs, Grades K-12. "If this tax ....roved, we will need to ...programs,"

Abner Hackman

▲ Sports page

THE DAY IN THE NATIONAL LEA[GUE]

CENTRAL	W	L	PCT	GB	L10	STR.	HOME
St. Louis	21	16	.568	—	6-4	W-1	9-8
Cincinnati	21	16	.568	—	9-1	W-4	10-12
Houston	19	17	.528	1½	6-4	L-2	10-7
Milwaukee	18	19	.486	3	6-4	L-1	10-10
Chicago	18	19	.486	3	4-6	W-1	11-9
Pittsburgh	11	26	.297	13	4-6	L-1	8-9

CT	GB	L10	STR.	HOME	AWAY
68	—	6-4	W-1	9-8	12-8
.568	—	9-1	W-4	10-12	11-4
.568	1½	6-4	L-2	10-7	9-10
.528		6-4	L-1	10-10	8-9
.486	3	6-4	W-1	11-9	7-10
.486	3	4-6	W-1		

	L	PCT	GB	L10	STR.	HOME	AWAY
	16	.568	—	6-4	W-1	9-8	12-8
	16	.568	—	9-1	W-4	10-12	11-4
	17	.528	1½	6-4	L-2	10-7	9-10
	19	.486	3	6-4	L-1	10-10	8-9
	19	.486	3	4-6	W-1	11-9	7-10

N	L	PCT	GB	L10	STR.	HOME	AWAY
			—	6-4	W-1	9-8	13-7
		568	—	6-4	W-1	9-8	12-8
					W-4	10-12	11-9

Yellow Jackets overpower Eagles

DETROIT — Adolfo Ruiz hit a three-run homer off Jake Nolan in the ninth inning, and the surging Yellow Jackets rallied for their 6th victory in 6 games, beating the slumping Eagles 5-2 on Friday. "Proud. Very proud," Ruiz said to his fans. This was ... of the season.

Newspaper, continued

And speaking of sports, what's yours? Well, check out the *Sports* section. Read about the triumphs and defeats of your favorite athletes. Sports articles are like instant replays played back in fast forward. Be prepared for colorful adjectives, strong verbs, and enough scores and statistics to fill a fan's happy brain.

Read the description of an exciting baseball game between the Yellow Jackets and the Eagles. Cheer the *surging* Yellow Jackets as they *rally,* or come back, for a big win. Sigh as you read how the *slumping* Eagles have now lost five games in a row. Read how Adolfo Ruiz brought in three runs off one pitch, giving the Yellow Jackets a winning score of 5–2 and Adolfo his 14th home run of the season. How did he feel about it? "Proud. Very proud," he said.

▼ *A CLOSER LOOK*

Yellow Jackets overpower Eagles

DETROIT — Adolfo Ruiz hit a three-run homer off Jake Nolan in the ninth inning, and the surging Yellow Jackets rallied for their 6th victory in 6 games, beating the slumping Eagles 5-2 on Friday. "Proud. Very proud," Ruiz said to his fans. This was his 14th home run of the season.

Pssst! Over here, on the Editorial page, there's something you have to see. It's the First Amendment of the Bill of Rights in action. Yup. This is the page where people exercise their freedom of speech.

Of course, the entire newspaper is an example of free speech, but the Editorial page features persuasive articles that express personal opinions. This is where famous and not-so-famous writers complain, protest, whine, and rant—all hoping to bring attention to an issue. The issue could be the price of gas, teen curfews, or even video games and their use in schools.

As you read an editorial you need to make judgments. Does the writer build a strong argument based on fact? For example, *Video games have changed a lot during 30 years* is a fact. However, *educators still think of them as animated comic books* is not. Some educators may feel that way, but not *all* of them.

In the end, though, the most important question is *Does the editorial make a point worth thinking about?* Remember, you always have the right to disagree. Then it's your turn to send a letter to the editor of the newspaper. Spread the word!

▼ Editorial page

Monday, May 15

EDITORIAL

A14

RANTS

OTHER VIEWS

Video Games in the Classroom

By MALVA JACKSON

We may not think video games belong in the classroom, but perhaps they do. I'm not talking about the blast and bash games. No. I'm referring to the ones that are intellectually challenging, the ones that encourage our kids to *reason and strategize.*

Although the content of current games doesn't match the school curriculum, I think game companies would be eager to design games for the panies would be eager to design games for the

Anti-smoking law good for business

Re off th

By A. Gi

Qui sequa augia lobo am dur ero adi ve ill fe l

Author's Book Signing
Saturday, May 16
10:00 a.m. to 1:00 p.m.

Meet Jacqueline Woodson
Author of *Miracle's Boys*

Novel

Who says you can't judge a book by its cover? That's where you should start every novel. Look at the book title, author's name, and cover art. What's your first impression? Then check out the back cover and any book summaries or reviews. They'll give you an idea of what the novel is about and introduce you to some of the characters.

Wonder what the author's writing style is like? Read the excerpts. Hopefully they'll get you interested enough to turn to chapter 1, page 1. That's where the journey begins.

Enter a novel as if you are entering a new neighborhood. You are the visitor who is just starting to get to know the neighbors and their stories.

Who's showing you around the neighborhood? The narrator. As the reader, it's up to you to interpret what the narrator tells you. In the novel *Miracle's Boys,* the narrator is a thirteen-year-old boy. He tells you that his older brother Charlie has changed and is now *cold.* You have to read between the lines to know that the brothers were once close, but events drove them apart.

▼ Novel excerpt

Right after he came home from Rahway, I got up in the middle of the night to look at him. He'd been away for more than two years, and the guy sleeping across from me was a stranger. Some days he'd just sit on that bed with his hands hanging down between his knees. Just staring out the window and looking evil. But when he was asleep, his face **spread out**—all the frowns and scowls just kind of faded and he looked like Charlie again, ready to care about something, to be happy, or to cry about stray animals.

When you read a novel, think about the setting, or the time period and place in which the events happen. In *Miracle's Boys*, the brothers live in a modern-day city. This setting causes some of the problems in the boys' lives. In another environment or another time, the characters might face different problems.

Novels are often about conflict. As the story moves along, the characters' needs and desires run smack into obstacles, causing tension and frustration. As you read, ask yourself, "What does this character want and what is standing in the way?" The obstacle could be another person. It could be a flaw within the character's own personality.

Or it could be a force of nature. The ultimate question is, "How will the character overcome the obstacle? What choices will she or he make?"

Get involved when you read a novel. Make predictions about what will happen next. Then read on to see if you were right. Go ahead and judge the characters. Do they act cowardly or bravely, smart or stupid? Often the results of their actions are not known until the end of the story.

Before you exit a novel, think about the characters' choices and the consequences. You might even see ways the story applies to the choices you make in your own life. You can learn a lot from a novel. Even if you don't like all the neighbors.

▼ Front and back cover
of *Miracle's Boys*

Ty'ree, Charlie, and Lafayette are Miracle's sons. When Miracle dies, the boys have to keep their family together.

Staying together isn't easy. Charlie goes to jail. Ty'ree cannot go to college because he has to work full-time to support them. And Lafayette's head is full of unanswered questions.

How can Miracle's boys survive when so much is set against them?

JACQUELINE
WOODSON

Miracle's Boys

Play

To act out a play is an art. To watch it is entertainment. To read it is a bit of both. Reading a play, whether it's *Hamlet* or *A Raisin in the Sun*, gives you time to capture all the characters' words and think about their meaning. And it lets you use your own imagination to *visualize* the action.

Reading a play can be very satisfying, but it helps if you know a few things first. Read the introduction so you'll have an idea of what to expect. It's especially helpful to have background information for a play based on historical events. For instance, knowing that *A Raisin in the Sun* is about an African American family's struggles in the 1950s puts you in the right time frame and gives the story weight.

Look for information about the genre of the play. If it's a tragedy, expect it to end bravely but sadly. If it's a satire, expect it to poke fun at everything. And you already know what to expect from a comedy or a romance: ha-ha, kiss-kiss.

Once you have some background information, read the cast of characters. You can start to figure out their relationships and you may even find some clues to the plot. What events will bring these characters together? How will their interests intersect or conflict?

With these questions in mind, you're ready for the play to begin. The curtain goes up and the stage lights dim. Where is the playwright taking you? Most plays start with a description of the setting.

The first scene in *A Raisin in the Sun* takes place in a small, cramped apartment in Chicago's Southside. The only sunlight comes from one small window. Ruth is waking her son Travis for school. Although she's only thirty, "disappoinment has already begun to *hang in her face.*" You know the mood is already weary and tense.

Be sure to read the character descriptions and the stage directions that are scattered throughout the play between the lines of dialogue.

This information will help you visualize the characters and their actions. Are you still there? Good, because now comes the story.

Plays, like novels, are about conflict. First the scene is set. Then the main character's problem is introduced. The problem develops with tension building toward a final conflict. Finally, there's the resolution—it might be a happy ending, or not so happy. All of this can happen in one, three, or five acts, which are divided into shorter scenes.

As you read the scenes, keep your focus on the characters. Do they learn something about life? Do they change as the play unfolds? Whether the playwright's message is depressing or uplifting, read to enjoy!

Plays by three playwrights ▶

Poem

Even when the subject is sleep, some poems are just fun to read.

from DREAM-LAND

Where sunless rivers weep
Their waves into the deep,
She sleeps a charmed sleep:
Awake her not.
Led by a single star,
She came from very far
To seek where shadows are
Her pleasant lot.

—CHRISTINA ROSSETTI

The language in this poem is so musical that the words sweep you along to the end. In only a few lines, the poet paints a scene that you can see, hear, taste, and smell.

Not all poems are easy to read. But the first time you read any poem, don't worry about the hard parts. Read the poem once straight through just for enjoyment. Read it out loud to get an idea of how it sounds and what it's about. Does it follow a rhyme pattern and have a steady rhythm?

After your initial taste, read the poem a second time. Slowly. This is so that you can focus on the meaning. What is the poet describing? Does she repeat certain words or lines?

Start to make sense of the poem by explaining the lines in your own words. Write down your thoughts. Is the woman dreaming about *sunless rivers,* or do the rivers represent something else? Check a dictionary for word meanings and if there are footnotes with the poem, read them, too. They often give useful background information.

The third time you read a poem is when things get really interesting. That's when you start to examine the poet's word choice and the descriptions that appeal to your senses. It's also when you focus on how the poem makes you feel.

A poem doesn't have to rhyme. It doesn't have to be grammatical or even pretty. It only has to reveal a true insight about life.

Pablo Neruda thought the first poems he wrote were "pure nonsense, pure wisdom." Recognizing the truth in a poem may take effort, but don't give up. Draw from your own experience and connect the poet's message to your own life. Each poem means different things to different people. Only you know what's true for you.

▼ From the poem "La Poesía"
by Pablo Neruda

LA POESÍA

Y fue a esa edad . . . Llegó la poesía
a buscarme. No sé, no sé de dónde
salió, de invierno o río.
No sé cómo ni cuándo,
no, no eran voces, no eran
palabras, ni silencio,
pero desde una calle me llamaba,
desde las ramas de la noche,
de pronto entre los otros,
entre fuegos violentos
o regresando solo,
allí estaba sin rostro
y me tocaba.

Yo no sabía qué decir, mi boca
no sabía
nombrar,
mis ojos eran ciegos,
y algo golpeaba en mi alma,
fiebre o alas perdidas,
y me fui haciendo solo,
descifrando
aquella quemadura
y escribí la primera línea vaga,
vaga, sin cuerpo, pura
tontería,
pura sabiduría
del que no sabe nada,
y vi de pronto
el cielo
desgranado

POETRY

And it was at that age . . . poetry arrived
in search of me. I don't know, I don't know where
it came from, from winter or a river
I don't know how or when,
no, they were not voices, they were not
words, nor silence,
but from a street it called me,
from the branches of the night,
abruptly from the others,
among raging fires
or returning alone,
there it was, without a face,
and it touched me.

I didn't know what to say, my mouth
had no way
with names,
my eyes were blind,
Something knocked in my soul,
fever or forgotten wings,
and I made my own way,
deciphering
that fire,
and I wrote the first, faint line,
faint, without substance, pure
nonsense,
pure wisdom
of one who knows nothing,
and suddenly I saw
the heavens
unfastened

Public Service Poster

Some information is so important it needs to be printed on a poster and publicly displayed. Government agencies use posters to spread the word about important issues like workers' rights and harmful chemicals at the workplace.

Does Lady Liberty catch your eye? The U.S. Department of Agriculture created the poster to announce that it's illegal to discriminate against anyone who takes part in Special Nutrition programs. All offices, schools, clinics and other places that offer the programs are required to display this poster in a highly visible area. That's how important it is.

When you see a public service poster, think, "This information may affect my life." Take time to read it, even the small print. Pay attention to legal terms such as *ordinance* ("rule or law") and *prohibit* ("does not allow"). The message on a public service poster isn't for some other guy: it's for you.

▼ A CLOSER LOOK

In accordance with Federal law . . . this institution is prohibited from discriminating on the basis of race, color, national origin, sex, age or disability.

De acuerdo a lo establecido por las leyes Federales . . . se prohíbe a este organismo la discriminación por raza, color, origen nacional, sexo, edad, o impedimentos de las personas.

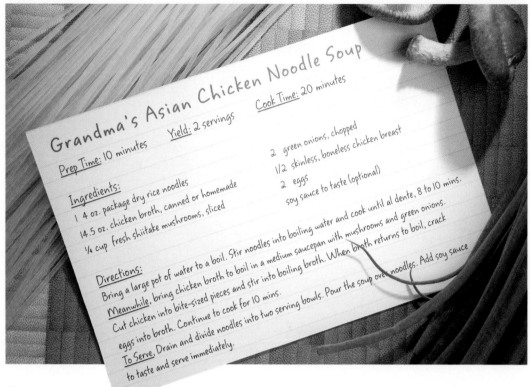

Grandma's Asian Chicken Noodle Soup

Prep Time: 10 minutes   Yield: 2 servings   Cook Time: 20 minutes

2 green onions, chopped
1/2 skinless, boneless chicken breast
2 eggs
   soy sauce to taste (optional)

Ingredients:
1 4 oz. package dry rice noodles
14.5 oz. chicken broth, canned or homemade
1/4 cup fresh shiitake mushrooms, sliced

Directions:
Bring a large pot of water to a boil. Stir noodles into boiling water and cook until al dente, 8 to 10 mins. Meanwhile, bring chicken broth to boil in a medium saucepan with mushrooms and green onions. Cut chicken into bite-sized pieces and stir into boiling broth. When broth returns to boil, crack eggs into broth. Continue to cook for 10 mins.
To Serve, Drain and divide noodles into two serving bowls. Pour the soup over noodles. Add soy sauce to taste and serve immediately.

Recipe

A recipe is a chemical formula. You have to measure, combine, and usually heat the ingredients. To make sure your lab experiment will be successful, read the recipe before you actually do anything with it.

First, read it once straight through. Then read it again, *carefully,* beginning with the list of *measured* ingredients. Keep in mind that *cup* means a measuring cup, not a coffee cup and *tbs.* (tablespoon) or *tsp.* (teaspoon), means "measuring spoons," not the spoons you eat with.

Notice the size of packaged ingredients. If you're using a can of chicken broth, is it an 8 oz. or a 14 oz. can? Once you check the list of ingredients, reread the directions for preparing the food. Look up the meaning of unfamiliar words, such as *al dente.* Some cookbooks have glossaries of cooking terms at the back of the book.

As you've learned in science class, timing is crucial. So, check to see how long it will take to prepare all the ingredients and to cook the food. Finally, do a mental check. Do you have all the ingredients, the tools, and enough time? Great! You're good to go.

Video Arts Summer Institute
June 26–July 28
Daily Schedule

Class	Days	Time	Room
Digital Filmmaking	M–W–F	8:00–11:45	Rm
Digital Storytelling: Video Production	T–Th	1:00–3:45	Stu
Extreme Sports Video I Beginner	T–Th	9:00–5:45	Stu & A
Extreme Sports Video II Advanced	W–Th	9:00–5:45	Stu & A
Video Editing	M–T–F	4:00–5:45	La
Game Design	W–Th	8:00–12:45	Rm
Hollywood Visual Effects	T–Th	1:00–3:45	La
3D Modeling & Animation	M–W–F	1:00–3:45	La
Music Video Production	M–T–F	1:00–2:45	Stu
Skateboarding & Videography	M–W–F	4:00–5:45	Stu &

	8:00 – 11:45	9:00 – 11:45	1:00 – 3:45	4:0
Mon.	Digital Filmmaking Room 603		3D Modeling/ Animation Lab 5	Skat Stu + A
Tue.		X Sports Video I Studio 3 + Arena	Digital Storytelling Studio 4	
Wed.	Digital Filmmaking Room 603		3D Modeling/ Animation Lab 5	Skat Stu +
Thur.		X Sports Video I Studio 3 + Arena	Digital Storytelling Studio 4	
Fri.	Digital Filmmaking Room 603		3D Modeling/ Animation Lab 5	Ska Stu +

Schedule

Whether it's showing class times, train arrivals and departures, or the bands in a music festival, a schedule is a tool to help you plan your time. Not all schedules are alike. But all schedules have one thing in common. They are organized around time, usually starting with the earliest hour.

Let's say you want to take summer classes to learn video arts. You're reading the schedule to decide which classes to attend. Run your eye down the list of classes offered. When you see one you like, follow the grid from left to right to find the days it meets, the times, and the room number.

The class on Digital Filmmaking you'll take for sure. You see that it meets on Monday, Wednesday, and Friday, from 8:00 to 11:45. You write that down, including the room number. Next you see Digital Storytelling. It's scheduled on Tuesday and Thursday, 1:00 to 3:45. That works. . . but wait! What about the beginning Extreme Sports Video class? That's what you're really interested in.

That class also meets on Tuesday and Thursday, and it goes all day from 9:00 to 5:45, which means it overlaps with Digital Storytelling and all other classes on those two days. One thing schedules can't solve is how to be in two places at the same time. You'll have to choose. No contest. Extreme Sports Video it is!

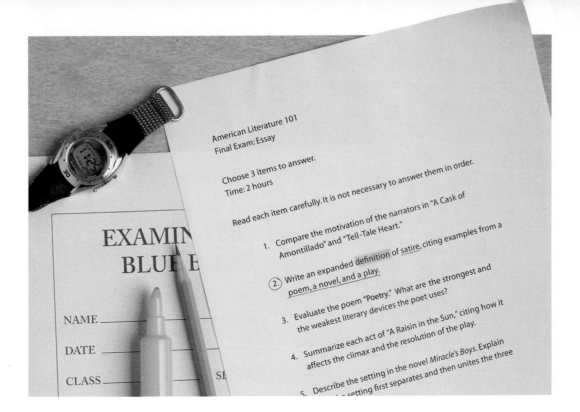

American Literature 101
Final Exam: Essay

Choose 3 items to answer.
Time: 2 hours

Read each item carefully. It is not necessary to answer them in order.

1. Compare the motivation of the narrators in "A Cask of Amontillado" and "Tell-Tale Heart."

2. Write an expanded definition of satire, citing examples from a poem, a novel, and a play.

3. Evaluate the poem "Poetry." What are the strongest and the weakest literary devices the poet uses?

4. Summarize each act of "A Raisin in the Sun," citing how it affects the climax and the resolution of the play.

5. Describe the setting in the novel Miracle's Boys. Explain how setting first separates and then unites the three...

EXAMIN
BLUE E

NAME

DATE

CLASS   S

Test

You have studied hard and you know a lot, but you're afraid you don't know "everything." Now you have to take an essay test and you're in Stress City. Relax. You don' t have to know everything to do well. At this point, it's more important to think clearly and present what you do know in the best way.

First, take time to read through the directions and all the questions. Look for commands like *compare, evaluate, summarize,* and *define.* What you write depends on these commands. For example, when an item says *evaluate,* you're being asked to judge or assess the quality of something, not just describe it.

As you read each question, underline key words or phrases. It's always a good idea to give examples in your essay, but if the item asks for *several examples,* you better count on giving at least three.

Once you understand the questions, the next step is to get organized. Before you start writing, map out your ideas in a brief outline, or list of key points. In a timed test you probably won't have much time to go back and refine your first draft.

Use your writing plan to draft a response. And check your work by reading your answers. If you finish early, (yeah!) add details and descriptive language. And yes, neatness does count.

Textbook

A textbook is a tool for learning that works best when you know how to use it. A textbook, like the latest cell phone or digital camera, has many features. Each feature has its own purpose.

Start by checking out the Table of Contents at the beginning of the book. It lists all the chapters and main parts and their page numbers. This gives you an overview of the topics you'll be reading about.

At the very back of the book, you'll find the Index. That's an alphabetical listing of every important idea and term mentioned in the text. When you want to find specific information, use the index to locate the right pages.

Ready to dive in and start reading? To make textbooks user-friendly, the information is organized under headings. The largest heading, or title, introduces the broad topic. Subheads organize the information into narrower, more specific subtopics.

For example, a chapter entitled *Space Exploration* might have these subheads: **Dreams of Space, Early Space Travelers,** and **Astronauts at Work.** Can you guess what each section is about? Before you begin to read, skim the heads and subheads to get a preview of the contents.

Suppose you've been asked to read 64 pages *by tomorrow*. Need a plan for getting through it? Start with the list of key terms and questions.

You may find Focus Questions at the beginning of a chapter. These are your road map for reading.

While you're reading, try to answer these questions and the review questions at the end of the chapter. If there are some you can't answer, just reread the text. Rereading is another secret tool that good readers use.

Here's another tip: When you're hung up on the meaning of a word, see if it's in the Glossary, usually located at the end of a textbook before the Index. A glossary is like a mini-dictionary that explains how the word is used in your textbook.

Footnotes also provide information about difficult words. If you see a raised number beside a word or phrase, look for a footnote at the bottom or side of the page.

Are pictures really worth one thousand words? Well, maybe one hundred. Textbooks are filled with photographs, illustrations, and other graphic elements like maps, diagrams, charts, and graphs. These visual features let you *see* what you are reading, making new or complex concepts easier to understand and remember.

Your brain loves all this visual input because it instantly upgrades comprehension. *Thinking.* That's what you do to make a textbook work for you. Without the thinking you bring to it, a textbook is like a cell phone without batteries.

▼ Science article in a textbook

Chapter 1

A Polish Astronomer Dares to Wonder

In the spring of 1493, Nicolaus Copernicus found himself amazed. Christopher Columbus's discovery of distant lands proved that the world was much bigger than the maps of the day said it was. Nicolaus knew that Ptolemy had made those maps centuries before. If Ptolemy made mistakes in his maps, Copernicus wondered, could he have been wrong about other things, too?

Nicolaus Copernicus

15th-century map of Europe, based on Ptolemy's teachings

Stargazing

Nicolaus had liked astronomy since he was a little boy. He loved learning the ancient Greek stories of the constellations. He knew they were just stories, but they were fun. He learned them by heart.

As Nicolaus grew older, he had many questions about the stars. He wondered why some stars were brighter than others. Why were some planets next to certain stars on some nights and next to other stars on other nights? What was a shooting star, and where did it go?

The professors and church leaders depended on the writings of Aristotle, Ptolemy, and other ancient thinkers for the answers. But Nicolaus always wondered. . . .

Nicolaus studied astronomy at a university in Cracow, Poland. One night, an astronomy professor invited a few students to use instruments to measure

Painting of astronomer and explorer Amerigo Vespucci using an astrolabe to make a star map

where stars and planets were. Nicolaus was thrilled. He would learn how to make star maps, like Ptolemy's. The main instrument he would use was an astrolabe. He would line up a part of the astrolabe with a star to measure where it was in the sky. By using mathematics, he could then place the star on paper and make a star map.

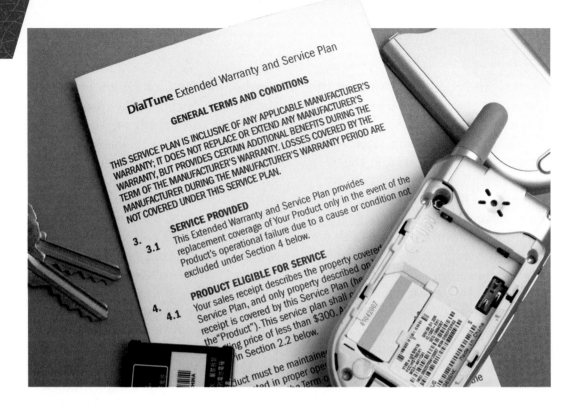

DialTune Extended Warranty and Service Plan

GENERAL TERMS AND CONDITIONS

THIS SERVICE PLAN IS INCLUSIVE OF ANY APPLICABLE MANUFACTURER'S WARRANTY; IT DOES NOT REPLACE OR EXTEND ANY MANUFACTURER'S WARRANTY, BUT PROVIDES CERTAIN ADDTIONAL BENEFITS DURING THE TERM OF THE MANUFACTURER'S WARRANTY. LOSSES COVERED BY THE MANUFACTURER DURING THE MANUFACTURER'S WARRANTY PERIOD ARE NOT COVERED UNDER THIS SERVICE PLAN.

SERVICE PROVIDED

3.

3.1   This Extended Warranty and Service Plan provides replacement coverage of Your Product only in the event of the Product's operational failure due to a cause or condition not excluded under Section 4 below.

PRODUCT ELIGIBLE FOR SERVICE

4.

4.1   Your sales receipt describes the property covered Service Plan, and only property described on receipt is covered by this Service Plan (he the "Product"). This service plan shall c ling price of less than $300. A in Section 2.2 below.

uct must be maintaine ted in proper oper Term o

Warranty

It is said there are no guarantees in this world, but there *is* a limited guarantee for most products you buy. It's called a *warranty.* Many products come with a *standard warranty,* or a company's promise to "cover" (replace or repair) a faulty product within a limited amount of time.

Warranties are written using a bunch of legal terms and phrases. The standard type of warranty usually covers *only manufacturing defects: all other causes and conditions are excluded.* Meaning, "if you misuse the product, crush it, flush it, or throw it around and break it, too bad for you."

Many warranties *expire,* or end, after ninety days. Some last for one,

two, or three years, depending on the cost of the product. Of course, as a product gets older, the risk of it breaking down *after the warranty expires* increases.

To cover this risk, you can buy an *extended warranty* when you purchase the product. Read the fine print before you buy it. Does the coverage overlap the standard warranty? That's not good.

But if you have a habit of putting your cell phone in the washing machine, a warranty that covers *accidental damages* may be good. Okay, reading a warranty *is* pretty boring, but you'll be glad you did. That's guaranteed.

Washing Instructions

According to a survey, eight out of ten people in Sweden read the washing instructions before they wash new clothes. Where would you fall in the survey? Do you read the little labels that are attached to your clothing? Ignore them at your own risk. If you've ever had a red shirt turn all your white clothes pink, you know why.

Washing instructions get right to the point. Some say *Dry clean only,* which means, "Take to a professional cleaner." Some say *Machine wash.* But be sure to read on. Check for a recommended water temperature. If it says *wash cold,* it means cold wash *and* cold rinse. Some labels don't say much at all and use symbols instead.

☐ means "machine wash on a gentle setting"; ☒ means "do not put in the dryer"; and ⊿ means "iron on a low temperature setting."

Finally, be sure to follow these instructions: *Wash with like colors.* Otherwise, you may be wearing pink.

▼ *A CLOSER LOOK*

COLOR MAY
TRANSFER
WHEN NEW

WASH BEFORE
WEARING

MACHINE WASH COLD

GENTLE CYCLE
WITH LIKE COLORS

TUMBLE DRY

Weather Map

Let's get scientific. The study of weather is, after all, a science. Look at the map. See the giant **H** over Montana and Wyoming? That **H** represents a high-pressure system where cool, dry air sinks and rotates in a direction *opposite* from the Earth's rotation.

What does the **H** mean weatherwise? Well, if you live in Billings, it means, "put on your shorts." High pressure usually brings sunshine.

Guess what a big **L** means. Right! It's a low-pressure area, caused by a low amount of winds rotating in the same direction as the Earth. Low pressure often means a chance of stormy weather, or "better take your umbrella." Just in case.

Now look at the line of blue triangles that runs from Kansas City to Canada. It represents the leading edge of a mass of cold air, or a *cold front*. Rain usually travels with or just behind a cold front, and as you can see, it's raining in Chicago.

However, south of Kansas City there are alternating blue and red lines. This means that the cold front has stopped moving, so it is called a *stationary front*. There is usually a noticeable difference in the temperature and wind direction on either side of a stationary front. So where does that leave Lubbock?

Hey, no one ever said predicting the weather was an *exact* science.

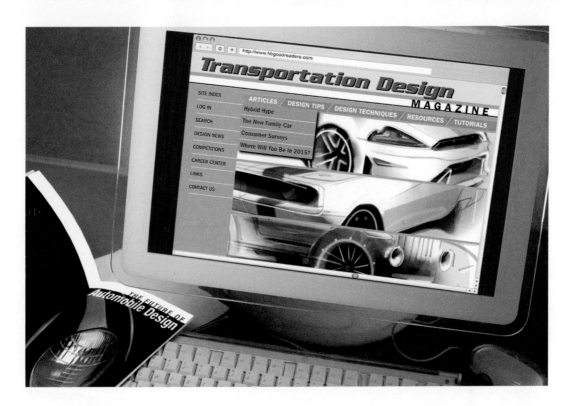

Web Page

There are over 80,000,000 Web sites on the World Wide Web and the number is growing. With the help of your Internet browser, you can find a site that answers your questions and suits your needs, and that's pretty amazing.

Web sites provide access to products, services, and information. Most sites are made up of Web pages which are like layers of information. Your starting point is always the Home Page. It's the first page you see when you type in a Web address and enter a site.

Let's say you've found the home page for a magazine about car design. The first thing to do is skim the menu of choices to see if the site has what you're looking for. If you're not sure, check the Site Index.

If you've come to this site, you're probably looking for more information about an article you read. Under *Articles*, you'll see a list of titles. If you click on *Hybrid Hype*, a page pops up with a menu in the sidebar. Choose **Learn More** and you'll go to a page with links to other Web sites about hybrid car design and a bibliography of recommended books.

The site may also have information about careers and tips for finding jobs. If that's what you're interested in, click *Career Center*. You may be on your way to designing the cars of the future!

Unlocking Words

"The words you use tell *what* you think and *who* you are."

—JACALYN MAHLER

Access Words

What can you do when you come across a tough word and you have no idea what it means? The first step is to decide if you really need to know what it means in order to understand the selection. If not, just keep reading. But if you do need to know, try these tips:

- Ask yourself what looks familiar about the word: *Have I seen it before? Do I know other words in English or another language that look like it?*

- Reread the words and sentences that come before and after the hard word. Sometimes they are clues to what the word means.

- Look for parts of the word you might recognize. Is there a prefix like *dis-* at the beginning? Or, a suffix like *-less* at the end?

- Check a dictionary, or ask someone to explain the word. Take this route once you've tried all the others.

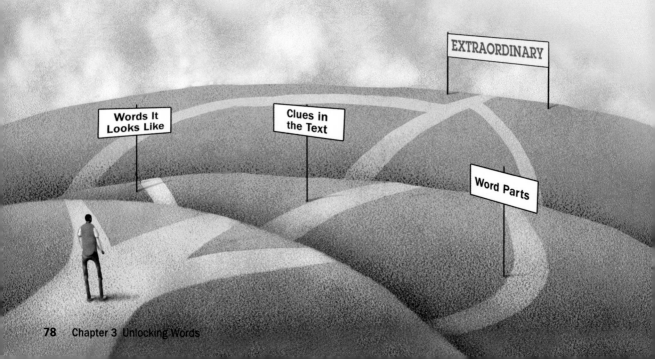

EXTRAORDINARY

Words It Looks Like

Clues in the Text

Word Parts

How Do You Figure Out New Words as You Read?

" When I see a new English word, I think about words I know in my home language. Then I check to see if the meaning I know for the Spanish word makes sense for the English word. "

—Magda

" I usually skip over the hard word and read the entire sentence. When I know what the sentence is all about, I can often get an idea of what the word means. "

—Oscar

" Sometimes I know other words that look like the hard word, but shorter. I use the meaning of *ordinary* to figure out the longer word *extraordinary*. I read ahead a little, too. If those things don't work, I check a dictionary. "

—Greg

" I think about the meaning of each word part. Then I put the pieces together. If I come across a word like *improbable*, I think about the meaning of *im-* and the word *probable*. Then I can tell what it means. "

—Stella

You can download more Readers Talk tips.  hbgoodreaders.com

Use What You Know

What's It Like?

When you travel around your town, you probably navigate by familiar sights. If someone needs directions to the music store, you can say, "Go up one block. The music store is next door to the library." Like traveling, learning new words is easier when you look for something familiar.

Does It Look Familiar?

If you're not sure what a word means, ask yourself if it looks like any other words you do know. Then use what you know about those words to figure out the meaning of the new word.

- Suppose you know that the word *class* can mean "a group or category." You can use that information to figure out what the longer words *classify* and *classification* mean. *Class*, *classify*, and *classification* are a **word family** because the words look similar and have related meanings.

- Word pairs like the English word *category* and the Spanish word *categoría* are called **cognates**. If you speak another language, you may know words that look like English words and have similar meanings.

FOCUS POINT Read "Three Gorges Dam" on the next page. How did the readers use what they know to figure out a new word? Do any words look like another word you already know?

THREE GORGES DAM

IMAGINE LIVING IN A PLACE where yearly floods destroy the land. Imagine having to reconstruct your home all the time. For many people living along the Yangtze River in China, this was a way of life. Government leaders decided to do something about the flooding by building an enormous dam.

Construction began on Three Gorges Dam in 1994. The dam is designed to control the waters of the Yangtze River. It will also provide power to many people whose homes are located near the river. The dam will be so big that it may force millions of people to relocate.

Even though they had to move, some people were happy about the dam. But many other people, including those outside of China, were worried. They feared that the creation of the dam might cause more ecological harm than good. Some thought that it might not even solve the flooding problem. Despite these worries, the dam is scheduled to be finished in 2009. When completed, it will be the largest dam in the world.

What Matters?

Construction has to do with building. So, reconstruct might mean "to build something again." And relocate probably means "to locate again."

Ecological and problem look like ecológico and problema in Spanish. The meanings I know make sense in the article.

Word Families

A **word family** is a group of words that look alike and are related in meaning. For example, the words *popular, popularity,* and *unpopular* belong to one family. They all come from the Latin word *populus,* which means "people."

When you know one word in a word family, you can often figure out the meanings of other words in the family. How are the words in this family related?

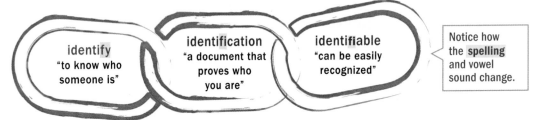

identify
"to know who someone is"

identification
"a document that proves who you are"

identifiable
"can be easily recognized"

Notice how the **spelling** and vowel sound change.

Nonfiction Article

THE ROOF OF THE WORLD

Mt. Everest

A few adventurous people know what it's like to stand on the roof of the world. They are the brave men and women who have the expertise to climb Mount Everest in Nepal. It's the highest mountain in the world. Climbers have to adjust to dangerous conditions. Many people have been hurt or even killed while climbing the giant. Yet the thought of injury or death does not keep climbers from trying to reach the peak.

How to Use Word Families

To figure out the meaning of *adventurous,* use what you know about the meaning of *adventure.*

What words look like *expertise, climbers,* and *dangerous?*

Your Home Language

Turn on the radio in Detroit and you might hear an announcer saying: *Important, marvelous, stupendous!* Turn on the radio in Mexico City and you might hear an announcer saying: *¡Importante, maravilloso, estupendo!*

Although the words are in different languages, they look and sound a lot alike. You can probably guess that they mean the same thing, too. That is because they are **cognates**, or pairs of words from two different languages that are similar in spelling, pronunciation, and meaning.

Nonfiction Article

RAINFOREST

Rainforests are thick, tropical forests found near the equator. They cover only a small part of the total area of the Earth. In one year, most rain forests get more than 80 inches of rain! This large amount of rainfall allows trees and other plants to flourish. The ecology of rainforests is perfect for diverse species. That is why rainforests are home to more than half of the world's plants and animals. Some are so rare they only can be found in the rainforests.

How to Use Cognates
1. Think of a word in your home language that looks like the highlighted word.

2. Check that the meaning you know makes sense.

What other cognates can you find?

Word Families

Use What You Know

When you come across a tough word, think of words that are in its **word family**. For example, you may be stumped by the word *computational*, but you can use what you know about *computer* to help you figure it out.

analyze

to study something by examining its parts

analyzer

analysis

analytic

analytical

> The suffix *-er* changes a verb to a noun. A person who *analyzes* is an *analyzer*.

conclude

to form an opinion or make a judgment

conclusion

conclusive

inconclusive

inconclusively

> Try using this word with your friends. It means "not in a way that convinces me."

category

a group of things that have something in common

categories

categorize

categorization

categorizing

> The suffix *-tion* is very common. It signals a noun.

create

to make something

creation

creative

creativity

creator

compute

to determine an answer or result using math

computation

computational

computer

computerized

define

to state or describe something clearly

defining

definition

redefine

undefined

concept

an idea

conceptual

conceptually

conceptualization

conceptualize

estimate

to use your judgment to guess an amount

estimated

estimation

overestimate

underestimate

> These are compound words, or words made up of two separate words.

interpret

to figure out or explain the meaning of something

interpretive

interpretation

misinterpret

reinterpret

legal

allowed by law

legalize

legality

legislation

illegal

occur

to happen or come about

occurred

occurrence

occurring

reoccur

> When the ending was added to the base word *occur*, the final *r* was doubled.

participate

to do an activity with other people

participant

participating

participation

participatory

perceive

to understand something by using the senses

perceiving

perception

perceptive

imperceptible

proceed

to move forward or carry out an action

proceeded

procedure

proceedings

process

respond

to answer

response

responsive

responsiveness

unresponsive

strategy

a plan to achieve a goal

strategic

strategically

strategies

strategist

English/Spanish Cognates

Use What You Know

¿Hablas español? Great! You have a huge advantage when it comes to figuring out the meanings of words in technical materials and textbooks.

That's because many English words used in the fields of science, social studies, and math come from Greek and Latin, and these words look and sound a lot like Spanish words you may know.

Study the word charts. When you are reading and see the English word, think of its Spanish cognate. Check to make sure that the meaning of the Spanish word makes sense because word pairs that sound the same can fool you.

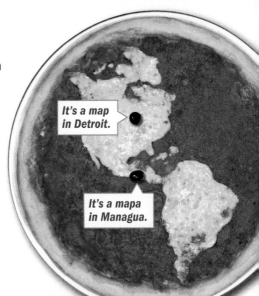

It's a map in Detroit.

It's a mapa in Managua.

Science

When you see...	think of	When you see...	think of
analysis	análisis	formula	fórmula
astronomer	astrónomo	galaxy	galaxia
atmosphere	atmósfera	gas	gas
biology	biología	human	humano
camouflage	camuflaje	hypothesis	hipótesis
chemical (*adj.*)	químico(a)	identification	identificación
classification	clasificación	insect	insecto
constellation	constelación	investigate	investigar
current	corriente	microscope	microscopio
deciduous	deciduo	nucleus	núcleo
diagram (*noun*)	diagrama	ocean	océano
ecology	ecología	organism	organismo
electricity	electricidad	planet	planeta
energy	energía	resources	recursos
examine	examinar	species	especie
experiment (*noun*)	experimento	telescope	telescopio
explosion	explosión	theory	teoría

READER'S FILE

Social Studies

When you see...	think of
agriculture	agricultura
biography	biografía
ceremony	ceremonia
coast	costa
colony	colonia
continent	continente
democratic	democrático(a)
dictator	dictador(a)
economy	economía
exploration	exploración
govern	gobernar
guide (*noun*)	guía
history	historia
immigrants	inmigrantes

When you see...	think of
independence	independencia
invent	inventar
island	isla
leader	líder
liberty	libertad
map	mapa
monument	monumento
navigate	navegar
pioneer	pionero(a)
population	población
poverty	pobreza
route	ruta
society	sociedad
vote (*verb*)	votar

Math

When you see...	think of
algebra	álgebra
angle	ángulo
area	área
base	base
calculation	cálculo
circle	círculo
determine	determinar
distance	distancia
division	división
equation	ecuación

When you see...	think of
geometry	geometría
line	línea
million	millón
number	número
object	objeto
point (*noun*)	punto
problem	problema
solution	solución
triangle	triángulo
value	valor

Use Context Clues

Sometimes when you come across a new or strange-looking object, you're not sure what it's used for. It's not until you see it in context that you understand its purpose. The same is true when you're reading new words. Sometimes you can figure out a word's meaning by seeing how it's used in a sentence.

What Are Context Clues?

Often you can find words and phrases right on the same page that can help you figure out a new word. These on-page clues to a word's meaning are called **context clues**.

Here are different types of context clues to look for:

- a direct definition signaled by *is* and *means*
- a restatement set off by commas, often beginning with the word *or*
- a synonym or an antonym
- examples signaled by *such as* and *including*

Sometimes the clues don't provide enough information; other times the clues can mislead you. So always try out your predicted meaning to see if it makes sense in the original sentence.

FOCUS POINT Read "Teen Inventors" on the next page. Which kind of clue did each reader use to predict the meaning?

TEEN INVENTORS

Have you ever had a great idea for a product? Some teens have put their ideas into action. Louis Braille invented a writing system for the blind when he was just 12 years old. At first, many people thought this invention was useless, but later they found it to be very beneficial.

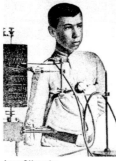

Igor Sikorsky

Blaise Pascal was another young inventor. At the age of 18, he conceived, or thought, of a great idea: a machine that could add and subtract. He built the first digital calculator in 1645. Teens have also come up with designs for aviation equipment such as helicopters and airplanes. Igor Sikorsky built his first helicopter when he was 19. These teens and their inventions prove that success comes from putting thoughts into action.

Context Clues

The word *but* gives me a hint that *beneficial* might mean the opposite of *useless*. Maybe it means "helpful."

I think the word *or* is a clue. Maybe "thought" is another way to say "conceived."

Definition Clues

A **definition clue** is just what it sounds like. The definition, or meaning of a word is given right in the text. To find these clues, look for signal words like *is, are, called, refers to,* and *means.* A definition may follow.

Magazine Article

A Bike with *Wings*

Have you ever heard of the flying bike? Probably not. The flying bike is exactly what it sounds like—a bike that can fly. The person who dreamed up this idea wanted a fast way to get around. So he made a bike powered by fans and a gas-inflated wing. The fans provide enough thrust to lift a rider off the ground. *Thrust* refers to the forward motion produced by an engine.

Imagine people taking to the skies on their daily commute! What is even more interesting is that in 2003 the U.S. government gave the inventor the right to be the only person who can make and sell the flying bike. This type of agreement is called a *patent.* Just think, one day, you too might be pedaling through the clouds!

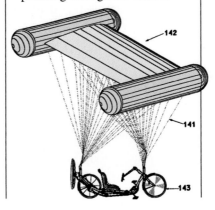

Signal words to a definition

What words are defined in the passage?

Restatement Clues

Are you an inquisitive, or curious, reader? The sentence you just read includes a **restatement clue**—words that are another way to say the same thing. The words are set off in a sentence by commas and often begin with the word *or*. Another name for a restatement clue is **appositive clue**.

Synonym and Antonym Clues

A **synonym clue** is a word or phrase that is similar in meaning to an unfamiliar word. The words *also* and *like* can signal synonyms.

An **antonym clue** is a word or phrase that means the opposite of an unfamiliar word. The words *but* and *unlike* often signal antonyms.

Magazine Article

SMART SHADES

Today, computers come in all shapes and sizes. Some are enormous. They are so large that they fill a room. Others are portable, or easy to carry from place to place. But have you ever heard of a computer that you can wear? Well, soon you will. One conglomerate, a large company made up of several small companies, has teamed up with a fashion designer to create sunglasses that house a minuscule computer screen. A tiny screen inside the left lens lets you read e-mails and surf the Internet. Unlike the simple sunglasses you wear now, the new ones have an intricate design.

Synonym clue for *enormous*

Restatement clue for *portable*

Antonym clue for *intricate*

Example Clues

"Electronics, including video games, go on sale today!" This sentence includes an **example clue**: video games are a type of electronics. Clues that name examples of unfamiliar words help you understand their meaning. The phrases *for example, including,* and *such as* are signal words for example clues.

Essay

Way Back When

I don't rely too much on technology. Really, I don't. OK, so when I lost my cell phone last week, I sat down and cried. That means nothing, but to be truthful, I did throw a few things across the room. Well, maybe I am too dependent on modern conveniences like DVD players and the Internet. I mean, what did we do before these things existed? If I had to use antiquated technologies, such as VCRs or landline phones, I would go crazy!

Example clue for *modern conveniences*

Example clue for *antiquated technologies*

All Kinds of Clues

When you're reading, you'll often come across an unfamiliar word. Here's what to do next:

1. Look for clues to its meaning.

2. Use the clues to predict the word's meaning.

3. Test the predicted meaning to see if it makes sense.

4. If not, check the definition in a dictionary.

What type of clue can you find for each hard word in this essay?

Essay

A TECHIE SPEAKS OUT

I don't know what I'd do if I couldn't communicate with my friends by e-mail. If I had to find writing paper and an envelope, no one would ever hear from me! Besides, think of all the trees I save by not using stationery. That's a great rationale, don't you think? Do I really need a good reason to use my computer?

Speaking of which—I wasn't too upset when I couldn't access my e-mail account for fifteen whole minutes. By the way, yesterday I had to tell someone that an account is a business record. Anyway, I thought I remained quite serene. Unlike the day I shouted and cried because I didn't have Internet service. Well, perhaps I shouldn't be so hard on old-fashioned media like radio. After all, you can listen to tunes on that anytime . . . can't you?

Multiple-Meaning Words

What does the word *track* mean? You might say that it's a footprint left on the ground. Or the path you run on at school. Or a song on a CD. It all depends because *track*, like many other words in English, has more than one definition.

Which Meaning Is Correct?

When you come across a word that has many possible meanings, you can use context clues to help you figure out the correct one. You may know the meaning of the word *strike* in a baseball game, but that definition doesn't fit in the example below.

Monday, May 15

EDITORIAL

RANTS & RAVES

Lessons from recent bus strike

By Will Jackson

Now is the time for the city to decide if it wants to support mass transportation, or if every commuter is going to have to fend for himself or herself. Where do you stand? During the recent bus driver's **strike** many people had to use the trains or taxis to get to work. Of course, the bus drivers were protesting low pay and loss of health insurance. You may not have been directly affected, but thousands of people were. And for them, taking trains or taxis or driving their own cars was an enormous expense and inconvenience.

How to Figure Out a Multiple-Meaning Word

1. First, look in the same sentence for words and phrases that may be **clues to the word's meaning.**

2. Next, look for clues in the sentences that come before or after.

3. Use the clues to figure out the correct meaning of the word.

   Here a *strike* means "when people stop working to protest something."

Each highlighted word is used twice in this article. Compare the word's meanings and parts of speech.

WHAT A CRIME

Crime scene investigation shows are very popular these days. One show features actors who are able to solve crimes in the course of just a few days. Crimes take much longer to solve in real life. But the process is becoming easier. New tools are helping the city's police force solve many cases.

When criminals force their way into a building, they often leave behind fingerprints and shoeprints. Today, the police can figure out a person's physical features from a shoeprint left at a crime scene. Officers take a course to learn how to make a cast from a shoe-print. The cast gives key information about a person's age, weight, and height.

DNA testing has also helped solve crimes. The police can use a strand of hair to identify who was at a crime scene! New ways of solving crimes are being discovered all the time. These days criminals have to outrun not just the police but the pace of technology, too!

▶ Police use fingerprints to solve crimes.

Multiple-Meaning Words

Compare the Meanings

Many English words have more than one meaning. Some common multiple-meaning words are shown below.

When you see these words, look in the text for clues to their meaning. It helps to think about how the word is being used. For example, is it a noun that names something, or a verb? It's also good to check a dictionary, but be sure to read through all the meanings to find the one that makes the most sense.

Word	Sample Sentences	Part of Speech	Possible Meanings
approach	Andrew had a creative **approach** to the problem.	noun	a way to do something
	It's wise to **approach** dogs with caution.	verb	to go near
	I will **approach** Joe about helping with the party.	verb	to go to with a request
	How should we **approach** this assignment?	verb	to begin to work on
area	I have never been to that **area** of town.	noun	a place or region
	The doctor's **area** of expertise is pediatrics.	noun	a field of study
	The **area** of the room is 200 square feet.	noun	measurement of a space
brief	This meeting will be very **brief**.	adjective	taking a short time
	He kept his speech very **brief**.	adjective	using few words
	I will **brief** you on what happened in today's meeting.	verb	to give a short explanation
challenge	It's a real **challenge** to train for the ten-mile race.	noun	something difficult that tests your skills
	Yolanda likes to **challenge** me to chess.	verb	to invite into a contest or fight
	I **challenge** their authority to ban those books.	verb	to question the right of
	That movie will **challenge** your thinking.	verb	to make active

Word	Sample Sentences	Part of Speech	Possible Meanings
code	Our school has a strict dress **code**.	noun	a set of rules
	During the war, messages were written in a secret **code**.	noun	a system of signs and symbols
	She used a different **code** for the new software.	noun	instructions for a computer program
conduct	At work it's important to **conduct** yourself professionally.	verb	to behave
	Who will **conduct** the tour of the museum?	verb	to lead or guide
	The wires **conduct** electricity in the house.	verb	to carry or allow passage through
	Miguel will **conduct** the orchestra.	verb	to direct in a performance
document	A birth certificate is a legal **document**.	noun	a written paper that gives information
	I will carefully **document** all of my research.	verb	to give evidence for
draft	The final **draft** of the story was exciting to read.	noun	a version of a piece of writing
	At age 18, men used to register for the military **draft**.	noun	selection of a person for a specific duty
	The **draft** from the window feels cold.	noun	a current of air in a room
	My lawyer will **draft** the contract.	verb	to write something that will probably change
file	He keeps all the stories he writes in a special **file**.	noun	a box or folder for storing papers
	I named the **file** "historyreport.doc."	noun	electronic information stored on a computer
	The school has a **file** on every student.	noun	a collection of information about a person or topic
	He used a **file** to shape his nails.	noun	a tool used to smooth and shape something that is rough

Compare the Meanings, continued

Word	Sample Sentences	Part of Speech	Possible Meanings
issue	The first **issue** of the magazine goes out today.	noun	edition of a newspaper or magazine
	Stem cell research is a big **issue**.	noun	a point or subject that people are discussing
	The team will **issue** new uniforms tomorrow.	verb	to give out or distribute
link	There is a definite **link** between smoking and cancer.	noun	a logical connection between two things
	The bridge **links** the two towns.	verb	to join or connect
minor	A 17-year-old is still a **minor**.	noun	a person under the age of 18
	That point is just a **minor** detail.	adjective	less important or serious
	In college I think I'll **minor** in Spanish.	verb	to study as a secondary course in college
monitor	My new computer has a big **monitor**.	noun	computer screen
	The **monitor** measured the amount of air pollution.	noun	a tool for collecting data
	The nurse will **monitor** the patient's breathing throughout the night.	verb	to observe or check
odd	My younger brother looks **odd** in his blue suit.	adjective	strange or unusual
	The dresser is full of **odd** socks.	adjective	mismatched
	We used **odd** scraps of fabric to make a quilt.	adjective	leftover
	One and three are examples of **odd** numbers.	adjective	not able to be divided by two
prime	Clothing is a **prime** export of China.	adjective	first in importance
	We had **prime** seats at the play.	adjective	great, wonderful
	At age 34, Joon was in his **prime**.	noun	the time of life when a person is at his or her best
	I **primed** the group for the mission.	verb	to make ready or prepare

Word	Sample Sentences	Part of Speech	Possible Meanings
quote	I **quoted** a line from my favorite poem.	verb	to repeat information from a text or person
	The plumber **quoted** the repairs at $110.	verb	to give an estimate
range	These shoes come in a **range** of colors.	noun	variety, or number of different things in the same category
	The age **range** of students is from 15 to 18 years old.	noun	complete group included between two points on a scale
	The radar has a **range** of ten miles.	noun	maximum distance that something can reach
	The Himalayas are the tallest **range** in Asia.	noun	a series of connected mountains
	The cows grazed on the **range**.	noun	a large area of open land
source	We did not know the **source** of the problems.	noun	the cause of something
	My **source** for the article was reliable.	noun	a person who provides information
	The **source** of the river is farther north.	noun	the spring or lake where a river begins
stress	She's under a lot of **stress** to make the swim team.	noun	suffering from worries and tension
	The skater's ankle bone broke from too much **stress**.	noun	pressure that pushes on an object
	I want to **stress** the importance of daily exercise.	verb	to emphasize an important point
volume	The can has a smaller **volume** than the box.	noun	amount of space that something occupies
	I need to find the first **volume** of the encyclopedia.	noun	one of the books in a set of books
	Turn down the **volume** of the radio.	noun	loudness

Jargon

Listen to two people speaking. How can you tell a car mechanic from a football coach? Or a surfer from a computer engineer? It may be the **jargon**, or specialized and technical words they use. If you're not part of their group, the words they use may sound like *technobabble* or just plain *gobbledygook*.

How to Figure Out Jargon

When you're reading and come across jargon, follow these steps:

1. Look for clues in the text—in the same sentence and in the sentences that come before and after.

2. Predict the meaning and test it in the sentence to see if it makes sense.

3. You may not have enough information to figure out what the jargon means. In that case, check a dictionary or ask someone.

What do the highlighted words in the magazine article mean?

NOT ALL RIDES ARE ALIKE

Henry Ford invented the world's first affordable family car in 1908. It was called the Model T. The only problem with Model Ts was that they all looked alike. Drivers wanted their cars to be special. They looked for ways to trick out their rides to make them stand out.

In the 1930s, ragtops, also called convertibles, were first available. Ragtops are cars with a top that can be removed or retracted. In the 1960s, pony cars were very popular. They were small and sporty, with very large engines and special exhaust systems. Pony cars could go really fast, but they used a lot of gas.

Today, you can find hundreds of different kinds of cars. For instance, you might see low riders cruising down the highway. These cars sit as close to the ground as possible. There are countless other ways to make a ride, or car, special. What's yours?

> If you're not sure what *pony cars* are, read on and you'll find clues in the next sentences.

Jargon

Often, everyday words take on new meanings when they're used by athletes, business people, musicians, or computer scientists. Do you want to sound like an expert, or maybe a fanatic? Study the jargon that appears on the next four pages.

Music Jargon

action *noun*
the distance of guitar strings from the fretboard. *The **action** made the strings hard to press.*

bridge *noun*
the section that connects two parts of a song. *We added a **bridge** to make the last part of the song sound smoother.*

cover *verb*
to record a new version of a song originally recorded by someone else. *At the concert, Max's band **covered** a Jimi Hendrix song.*

dynamics *noun*
changes in volume. *The **dynamics** in this song go from very soft to very loud.*

gig *noun*
a musical performance, often paid. *Her band has four **gigs** this weekend!*

phrase *noun*
a short portion of a song. *I couldn't get that **phrase** out of my head!*

pitch *verb*
to set an instrument to a certain key. *The **pitch** was too high for me to sing along.*

rest *noun*
the silence between two musical notes. *At the **rest**, the horn players took a deep breath.*

score *verb*
to write the music for a movie or play. *My cousin wrote the **score** for the director's new movie.*

READER'S FILE

burn *verb*
to create a CD or DVD. *He **burned** the CD for his mom.*

bug *noun*
an error in a computer program. *This program must have a **bug** because my computer keeps freezing.*

cookie *noun*
a piece of information sent from the Internet to a personal computer. *When you visit that Web site, it sends a **cookie**.*

download *verb*
to transfer data onto a computer. *I'm going to **download** some audio files from this Web site.*

emoticon *noun*
a symbol that represents human emotions such as 😊 . *A smiling face is an example of an **emoticon**.*

interface *noun*
how something on a computer looks and how easy it is to use. *I can never find what I want because the **interface** is bad.*

program *noun*
a set of directions that makes a computer do different tasks. *With this **program**, you can make charts and tables.*

surf *verb*
to explore different Web sites on the Internet. *Last night I spent two hours **surfing** the Internet.*

upload *verb*
to send data from your computer to another location. *I **uploaded** my project onto the school's Web site.*

worm *noun*
a program that damages information stored on a computer. *When a **worm** attacked his computer, he lost several files.*

Basketball Jargon

air ball *noun*
a missed shot that fails to touch the backboard, net, or rim. *Even professional players sometimes shoot* **air balls***.*

assist *noun*
a pass made by one player to another player who scores a point. *Davon had three* **assists** *in last night's game.*

break *verb*
to throw the ball down the court to a waiting teammate. *Our team scored two points on a fast* **break***.*

fake *verb*
to move in a way that makes the defender go in the wrong direction. *I* **faked** *to the left, then ran past all the other players.*

foul *verb*
to break a rule of the game. *The referee warned me about making a* **foul***.*

key *noun*
the key-hole shaped area extending from the baseline under the basket. *I practiced making baskets from the* **key***.*

man-to-man *adjective*
a type of defense when each player guards a specific opponent. *With* **man-to-man** *defense, I had to guard the same player all night.*

press *verb*
to cover the offense closely to force a turnover. *Three players* **pressed** *Shalon and she lost the ball.*

rebound *noun*
a shot that bounces off the basket and is grabbed by a player on the other team. *Scott got the* **rebound** *and ran down the court.*

travel *verb*
to move a foot without first dribbling the ball. *As soon as the whistle blew, I knew he had* **traveled** *with the ball.*

turnover *noun*
when the other team gets the ball due to a player's mistake. *They managed to score after the* **turnover***.*

Business Jargon

800-pound gorilla *noun*
the most important person involved in a business deal. *The company founder was the 800-pound gorilla in the meeting.*

bear *noun*
someone who thinks the stock market will do badly. *My mom is such a bear, she sold all her stock.*

best of breed *noun*
the best product in a category. *This car gets such good gas mileage, it is best of breed.*

bull *noun*
someone who thinks the stock market will do well. *My aunt is a bull and wants to invest more money in stocks.*

burn rate *noun*
how fast a new company spends its money before it makes any profits. *The banker warned him to control his company's burn rate.*

collar *noun*
an agreement between a buyer and a seller. *After a week of meetings, they finally came up with a collar.*

joint venture *noun*
a business project that involves two or more companies. *The baker and chef decided to start a joint venture.*

noise *noun*
changes in price and amount. *There was a lot of noise before we agreed to the deal.*

overhead *noun*
the general cost of doing business. *The company's overhead increased when it moved its offices to Los Angeles.*

poison pill *noun*
a special right given to stockholders to prevent a takeover by a different company. *The stockholders voted to swallow a poison pill when a European group tried to buy their company.*

Use Word Parts

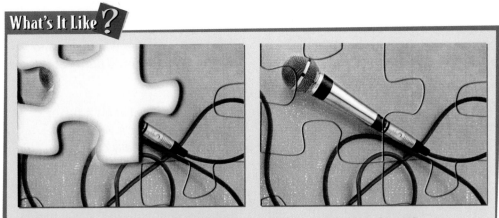

Puzzles are fun to work. Sometimes, when you fill in an important piece, the picture in the puzzle becomes clear. Words can work like that, too. If you know the meaning of an important word part, you can often figure out the meaning of the whole word.

What Are Word Parts?

Some English words are made up of parts. These parts include **base words**, **roots**, **prefixes**, and **suffixes**. You can use these parts as clues to a word's meaning.

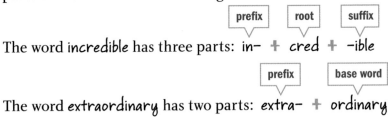

The word *incredible* has three parts: in- + cred + -ible

The word *extraordinary* has two parts: extra- + ordinary

If you don't immediately know a word, look to see if you know any of its parts. Put the meaning of the word parts together to figure out the meaning of the whole word.

FOCUS POINT Read "One Heroic Act" on the next page. How did each reader figure out a word? What word parts do you recognize in the other highlighted words?

One Heroic Act

Heroes can be ordinary people who do extraordinary things. Jarrett Patterson is this type of hero. He started a program that has had an unforgettable impact on his town.

Kids Closet originated in August 2003. Its goal is to provide clothes and shoes to less fortunate kids in the neighborhoods of Hudson, Michigan. People donate clothes. Then Jarrett delivers them to the Board of Education building. He also works with teachers to make sure that kids who need clothes get them. Kids Closet has undeniably helped countless teens and children in Michigan. Hopefully, this type of program will spread all across the United States!

Using Word Parts

The prefix *un–* means "not." So if something is *unforgettable*, you can't forget it.

The *origin* is the "beginning, or start of something." And the ending *–ed* signals a past tense verb. So *originated* must mean "started."

Compound Words

What do these words have in common?

They're all **compound words**, or words made up of two or more smaller words. English is full of compound words, and so is your classroom. Look around and you'll probably see a *textbook, backpack, bookshelf, keyboard,* and even a *sweatshirt* or two.

Compound words also appear in legal contracts and business letters. Words like *furthermore, nonetheless,* and *whereas* are part of the formal language of communication.

Looking for Word-Part Clues

When you come across a long word, it may be a compound word. Here's how you can figure out its meaning:

1. Look for smaller words inside the long word. Break the long word into parts.

2. Think about the meaning of each part. Sometimes the meaning of a compound word is the same as the sum of its parts.

everyday means "happening all the time"

3. Often you can't predict the meaning from the parts. Then you have to use your experience and the meaning of the other words to figure out what the compound word means.

highlight means "the best part of an experience," not "a light that is high"

If you're not sure, you can ask someone to explain the meaning or check a dictionary.

Review the compound words on page 119. Then read each highlighted word. Can you predict the meaning from its parts?

TEXT CHAMPION

People all over the United States do it. It's becoming a national phenomenon. What is it? Text messaging! It is common to see people standing on a street corner typing messages into their cell phones and sending them to friends and family.

Text messaging has such widespread popularity that there's even a competition held each year to see who is the fastest text messenger in the world! The world record for text messaging was set in 2006 by a Utah teen named Ben Cook. He was able to type a sentence that contained 160 characters in less than 43 seconds!

Many teens keep in touch with text messages.

Ben is no newcomer to the competition. He also won the title in 2004. Many people would not even try to take on such a challenge. However, for Ben Cook, the outcome of the competition was no surprise, and it was the highlight of his year.

Prefixes

A **prefix** is a word part that comes at the beginning of a word. It changes the meaning of the word. For example, the prefix *in-* means "not." Add it to the word *dependent*, and you get *independent*, which means "not dependent." Independent people do things on their own.

Most prefixes come from Greek, Latin, or Anglo Saxon, which is sometimes referred to as Old English. There's good news—only four prefixes show up in 58 percent of all words with prefixes.

▲ The most common prefixes

Using Prefix Clues

When you come across a word you don't know:

1. Look for word parts you do know. Break the word into parts.

2. Think about the meaning of each part. The prefix *dis-* means "not" or "the opposite of." The base word *advantage* means "something good" or "benefit."

3. Put the meanings of the word parts together. What is the meaning of the whole word?

4. Be sure the meaning makes sense.

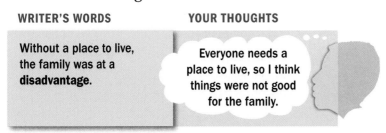

WRITER'S WORDS

Without a place to live, the family was at a **disadvantage**.

YOUR THOUGHTS

Everyone needs a place to live, so I think things were not good for the family.

Review the common prefixes on page 116. Then read each highlighted word. Can you predict the meaning from its parts?

Essay

Following the Crowd

If your friends want to go to a preview of a movie instead of doing their homework, do you join them? You're probably faced with decisions like this one all the time. You're dealing with peer pressure.

Usually peer pressure is seen as something that is negative. But when it comes to smoking, this view is inaccurate. Peer pressure can be positive, too.

Students in some schools are starting antismoking campaigns. These campaigns put pressure on both students and adults to break a habit that can kill.

Other teens are working to solve the bullying problem in their schools. These students are involved with projects that stop kids from showing disrespect to one another.

Sometimes it's OK to follow the crowd when it's leading you in the right direction!

IT'S NO JOKE DON'T SMOKE!

BE SMART DON'T START

STOP SMOKING NOW!

Suffixes

A **suffix** is a word part that comes at the end of a word. It changes a word's meaning and its part of speech. For example, when you add the suffix *-er* to the verb *teach*, you get *teacher*, a noun. The new word means "someone who teaches."

Using Prefix and Suffix Clues

When you come across a long word, it may have a prefix and/or a suffix. Follow these steps:

1. Examine the word's beginning, middle, and end. Break down the word into any meaningful parts.

| prefix | base word | suffix |

disrespectful ➡ dis + respect + ful

2. Focus on the base word or root. See if you know any related words and their meanings. For example, the base word *respect* means "to think well of" or "to honor."

3. Put the meanings of the word parts together. What is the meaning of the whole word?

| not | honor | full of | not full of honor |

dis + respect + ful = disrespectful

4. Be sure the meaning makes sense.

Review the common suffixes on page 118, then read each highlighted word. How do the suffixes change the word's meaning and its part of speech?

Fiction

Saving the Day

Leo was enjoying a day at the lake. Suddenly, a scream shattered the silence. He looked up and saw a woman frantically pointing to the icy water near the boat landing. She was holding a baby blanket and some toys. Leo rushed to her side and dove into the water. He knew that it doesn't take long for a child to drown. The mother stood motionless as she watched. A minute passed. Then another. Finally Leo came to the surface gasping for breath and holding a little boy. Within seconds, the grateful woman was thanking Leo for his incomparable bravery.

Greek and Latin Roots

Many words in English contain Greek and Latin roots. A **root** is the central word part that has meaning, but it cannot stand on its own. *Aud, ology,* and *spect* are some examples of roots.

Using Word Roots

When you come across a long word, it may have a Greek or Latin root.

1. Break down the word into meaningful parts.

2. Focus on the root. Do you know other words that have the same root? For example, you may know *structure* and *construction* and realize that *struct* has to do with "building."

3. Put the meanings of the word parts together.

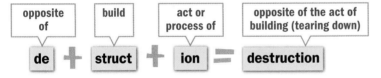

4. Be sure the meaning makes sense.

Use the meanings of the roots *ped*, *hydro*, *cred*, *tele*, *photo*, and *port* to predict the meanings of the highlighted words.

Journal Entry

August 22, 2007
Day 5: Anza-Borrego Desert State Park

Today we completed the toughest hike yet in our week-long expedition through California. We were in the Anza-Borrego Desert State Park. The trail was not that difficult, but because of the extremely hot temperatures, we struggled to complete the 6.5-mile trek. By noon the temperature was 110° F. We all felt the effects of the heat. To avoid dehydration, we guzzled water as often as we could. Our hike leader had excellent credentials so we followed her suggestions. We took frequent rests in any shade we could find. I was grateful for my sunglasses and hat. I wasn't so happy about the weight of my telephoto lens and my portable cook stove!

▼ Borrego Badlands, California

Prefixes

Many long words begin with a **prefix**, or short word part like *re-* and *un-*. Sometimes knowing the meaning of the prefix can help you predict the meaning of the word. Since many prefixes have multiple meanings, it's always a good idea to confirm what the word means.

Prefixes That Mean "Not"	Key Words	Sample Sentence
il-	illegal, illegible, illogical	Driving without a license is **illegal**.
im-	impossible, imperfect, immature	It's **impossible** to walk to the moon.
in-	inattentive, independent, insane	The **inattentive** parent didn't see her child fall.
ir-	irrational, irreplaceable, irregular	His sudden decision seemed **irrational**.
non-	nonsense, nonsmoker, nonfat	It's **nonsense** to spend all your money.
un-	unhappy, unimportant, unclear	The coach is **unhappy** when her team loses.

Prefix	Meaning	Key Words	Sample Sentence
anti-	against	antisocial, antifreeze	Breaking windows is an **antisocial** act.
de-	opposite	defrost, deactivate	He will **defrost** the frozen meat before cooking it.
dis-	opposite of	dishonest, disagree	If I say I like raw fish, I would be **dishonest**.
en-	cause to	enforce, endanger	The airlines will **enforce** new rules for travelers.
fore-	before	forehead, forecast	A large cat is in the **foreground** of the picture.
im-	in	imprison, immigrate	The judge wants to **imprison** him for ten years.
inter-	between	international, interracial	The **international** flight stopped in three countries.
mis-	wrongly	misspell, misjudge	I **misspell** words, so I always proofread my work.
over-	over	overreact, overestimate	This reviewer always **overrates** the horror films.
pre-	before	prehistoric, preschool	Dinosaurs were **prehistoric** creatures.
re-	again	reelect, rebuild	We want to **reelect** Carlos for class president.
	back	repay, return	I promise to **repay** the money I borrowed.
sub-	under	submarine, subway	The **submarine** explored the ocean depths.
	less than	substandard, subhuman	The condition of the building was **substandard**.
trans-	across	transcontinental, transplant	The **transcontinental** railroad crossed the country.

Spelling Tip   When you add a prefix to a base word, never change the spelling of the base word.

Useful But Not Perfect

Breaking words into parts is a great way to figure out the meaning of new words. But watch out for these pitfalls.

Pitfall 1

Letters at the beginning of a word may look like a prefix, but they aren't. For example, the *un* in *under* doesn't function as a prefix. If you take away the *un*, you won't see a helpful base word or root. Try it with these other words to see if *un* is really a prefix:

uncle   undo   unhappy   united

Pitfall 2

Even when you find a word with a prefix, the meaning of the word parts may not be clear. For example, the meaning of *increase* has nothing to do with the word *crease*. *Increase* comes from the Latin word *crescere*, which means "to grow."

Pitfall 3

A prefix can have different meanings. For example, the prefix *re-* can mean "again" or "back." In the word *rewrite*, the prefix means "again," but in the word *return*, it means "back."

When you predict the meaning of a new word, always try that meaning in the sentence to see if it makes sense. If you're not sure, you can ask someone to explain the meaning, or check the meaning in a dictionary.

Suffixes/Compound Words

Suffixes

Many English words end with a **suffix**, or a short word part. The suffixes shown below change the meaning of words and their part of speech. Recognizing these suffixes can help you figure out a new word's meaning.

Suffix	Meaning	Changes...	Key Words	Sample Sentence
-able	can be done	a verb to an adjective	predictable, lovable	I wasn't surprised by the **predictable** ending.
-al, -ial	having characteristics of	a verb to a noun	refusal, denial	We didn't understand their **refusal** to help.
-en	cause to become	an adjective to a verb	weaken, darken	The heat will **weaken** the climbers.
-er, -or	one who	a verb to a noun	teacher, actor	My **teacher** asks good questions.
-ful	full of	a noun to an adjective	resourceful, hopeful	The **resourceful** boy survived in the desert.
-ion, -tion	act, process	a verb to a noun	progression / celebration, translation	I see a **progression** from low to high costs. / Everyone brought food to the **celebration**.
-ious	having the qualities of	a noun to an adjective	spacious, mysterious	The **spacious** room can seat 200 people.
-ity	state of	an adjective to a noun	popularity, similarity	His **popularity** grew after he gave a speech.
-ive	adjective form	a verb to an adjective	creative, active	**Creative** people often have the best ideas.
-less	without	a noun to an adjective	careless, clueless	I try to avoid **careless** mistakes.
-ly	in a certain way	an adjective to an adverb	slowly, probably	She drove **slowly** because there was so much traffic.
-ment	action or process	a verb to a noun	payment, movement	The landlord expects **payment** by Tuesday.
-ness	state of	an adjective to a noun	happiness, kindness	The baby squealed with **happiness**.
-y	characterized by	a noun to an adjective	dirty, icy, funny	Playing football got my clothes **dirty**.

Compound Words

Many long words are compound words, or words made up of two or more words. Some compound words, such as *know-it-all*, are hyphenated.

childlike
The man's interest in cartoons seemed **childlike**.

earache
The baby cried in pain from the **earache**.

guideline
I need a **guideline** for the number of people to hire.

handwriting
His **handwriting** is so bad that I can't read his signature.

heart-stopping
Seeing the alligator was a **heart-stopping** moment.

heavy-duty
The hiker wore **heavy-duty** boots.

highlight
The **highlight** of the concert was the band's last song.

keyboard
She can type much faster on her new **keyboard**.

know-it-all
It's really annoying when someone acts like a **know-it-all**.

masterpiece
The essay I wrote for English is a **masterpiece**.

mix-up
I lost my luggage because of a **mix-up** at the airport.

network
The **network** of tunnels was confusing.

newspaper
The game's final score was on page 16 of the **newspaper**.

notebook
In your **notebook** make a list of compound words.

part-time
I was glad to get the **part-time** job.

rainforest
The **rainforest** is home to many amazing birds.

secondhand
Even though they were **secondhand** clothes, they looked new.

self-defense
She learned judo as a method of **self-defense**.

softball
The girls' **softball** team won the state championship.

straightforward
I liked his **straightforward** manner of speaking.

tablecloth
For the party, he set the table with a green **tablecloth**.

teammate
My selfish **teammate** hogged the ball.

textbook
The **textbook** contains helpful pictures.

trade-off
Missing the dance was a **trade-off** for going to the game.

waterfall
There is a beautiful **waterfall** at the end of the trail.

widespread
The musician enjoys **widespread** fame.

Greek and Latin Roots

A **root** is a central word part that has meaning but cannot stand on its own in English. Roots appear in all subject areas. For example, *bio* appears in social studies (*biography*), science (*biology*), and medicine (*antibiotic*). The charts below show some common roots and sample words from certain subject areas.

Communication

Root(s)	Origin	Meaning	Key Words
aud	Latin	hear	audible, audience, audio
dict	Latin	say, tell	dictate, dictionary, predict
gram, graph	Greek	write	diagram, graphic, paragraph
manu	Latin	hand	manual, manuscript
phon	Greek	sound	microphone, phonetic, telephone
scrib, script	Latin	write	describe, scribble, transcription
voc	Latin	speak, call	advocate, vocal, vocabulary

Medicine and Anatomy

Root(s)	Origin	Meaning	Key Words
cardi, cardio	Latin	heart	cardiac, cardiology
dent, dont	Latin	tooth	dental, dentist
derm	Greek	skin	dermatology, epidermis
ortho	Greek	straighten	orthopedics, orthodontist
path	Greek	suffer, disease	empathize, pathology, pathogen

Mental and Physical Action

Root(s)	Origin	Meaning	Key Words
cog	Latin	know	cognition, recognize, incognito
cred	Latin	believe	credential, incredible, credit
fract, frag	Latin	break	fraction, fracture, fragile
ject	Latin	throw	eject, object, reject, project
port	Latin	carry	portable, report, import, deport
rupt	Latin	break	bankrupt, erupt, interrupt

READER'S FILE

Science

Root(s)	Origin	Meaning	Key Words
aqua	Latin	water	aquarium, aquatic
aster, astr	Greek	star	astronaut, astronomy
bio	Greek	life	biology, biodegradable
corp	Latin	body	corpse, incorporate, corps
geo	Greek	earth	geography, geology, geometry
hydro	Greek	water	hydroelectric, dehydrate
meter	Greek	measure	barometer, thermometer
ology	Greek	study of	sociology, technology
ped, pede, pod	Latin	foot	pedal, pedestrian, tripod
photo	Greek	light	photograph, photography
phys	Greek	nature	physical, physics
sect	Latin	cut	bisect, insect, section
tele	Greek	far	telescope, telephoto, telephone
terra	Latin	earth	terrain, territory
zo	Latin	animal	protozoa, zoology, zoo

Social Studies

Root(s)	Origin	Meaning	Key Words
chron	Greek	time	chronic, chronological
cycl	Greek	cycle, circle	cyclone, encyclopedia
dem	Greek	people	democracy, demographic
jud	Latin	judge	judgment, misjudge, prejudice
liber	Latin	free	liberate, liberty
loc, local	Latin	place	local, locate, location
migr	Latin	move	immigrate, migrate
poli, polis	Greek	city	metropolis, police, politician
pop, pub	Latin	people	populate, population, public
stru, struct	Latin	build	construct, destruct, instruction

Beyond the Literal Meaning

At first, this may look like a photo of a bee. But look again. It's a flower. Words can fool you, too. Sometimes you have to look beyond what they seem to mean.

How Writers Make Language Rich

What's the difference between a great read and a boring one? Often it comes down to the language writers choose. They can add interest by using words and phrases that have meanings beyond their literal, or usual, definitions.

- Two words—like *bad* and *sinister,* may have similar meanings. But when you read these words they trigger different feelings, or **connotations**.

- An **idiom** is a colorful way to say something. Usually a few words work together to create a new meaning. For example, *pie in the sky* means "something you wish for."

- A **simile** uses *like* or *as* to compare two things. Example: "That runner took off *like a rocket!*"

- **Metaphors** compare two things without using *like* or *as.* Example: "The football player *is a machine.*"

- **Personification** gives human qualities to things that aren't human. Example: *"Lights danced on the wall."*

FOCUS POINT Read "Beastly Weather" on the next page. Look beyond the literal meaning to tell what the highlighted phrases really mean.

Beastly Weather

SUPPOSE YOU WERE planning to meet some friends for a basketball game. Then you hear that it's raining cats and dogs. You'd probably be pretty unhappy. Playing in the rain is no fun, especially when it's raining hard. But what if you saw actual cats and dogs raining down from the skies? You might say, "Give me a break!" However, in some places people really have seen it rain animals!

In 1953 people reported a downpour of frogs and toads in Leicester, Massachusetts. The town residents froze like frightened deer when they saw amphibians covering their streets! Frogs and toads aren't the only animals that have rained down from above. In Louisiana, hundreds of fish came tumbling from the sky. Many of the fish were dead, but some were still alive. That was a nightmare!

Scientists believe that it rains animals when a particularly strong windstorm passes over a lake or pond. The storm sucks the animals out of the water and drops them someplace else. So, the next time the winds begin to scream and howl, beware. They may be preparing to drop some unsuspecting animals on your town!

Denotation and Connotation

Think about the meanings of these words: *hard, challenging, overwhelming.* They all have similar dictionary definitions, or **denotations**. All three words can mean "difficult." But each one has a different **connotation**, or feeling, associated with it.

A connotation can be positive, negative, or neutral.

- A *challenging* job is a job that's difficult to do, but it is usually a positive learning experience. So, *challenging* has a positive connotation. It's a "feel-good" word.

- An *overwhelming* job is unpleasant and may even cause physical pain or mental stress. So, *overwhelming* has a negative connotation. It stirs up bad feelings.

- A *hard* job can be difficult but it is not necessarily challenging or overwhelming. So *hard* creates neither positive nor negative feelings. The word is neutral.

Exploring the Connotations of Words

Writers choose words with certain connotations to make readers react and feel a certain way. Compare how you feel when you read the three phrases in each column.

Compare Connotations	
inexpensive shoes	**refreshing** air
reduced shoes	**cool** air
cheap shoes	**frigid** air

Read "The Quest for El Dorado" on the next page. Compare each pair of highlighted words. What feelings does each word suggest?

THE QUEST FOR EL DORADO

▼ Gold breastplate, Colombia, c. 600-1600 A.D.

With great care, Gonzalo Jiménez de Quesada checked the last supplies that were being loaded. The conquistador then eyed his fleet of ships and smiled. He had been on many journeys before. He had conquered many new lands for the king and queen of Spain. However, this time Gonzalo hoped the journey would be different. He finished checking the supplies and looked over at his First Mate.

"For years we have searched for El Dorado—the land of gold. I vow that in the year 1569 my search will be successful!" Gonzalo proclaimed.

"Gonzalo, you are already a very wealthy man, and this journey will be difficult," the first mate replied.

"That's true, but I will not be satisfied until I find El Dorado!" Gonzalo said. Within hours he set sail for the dense jungles and high mountains of South America.

Two years later, Gonzalo and his men returned from their grueling journey. They were penniless, exhausted, and defeated. His team of 500 men had dwindled to only 25. Gonzalo's quest for riches had cost him dearly.

Idioms

If your friend tells you, "I'm down in the dumps" you know she doesn't mean that she's standing in a place filled with trash. She means, "I'm feeling very sad." *Down in the dumps* is a special kind of phrase called an **idiom**.

In an idiom, the phrase as a whole means something different from what the words mean by themselves. Writers use idioms to make language fun and colorful, and to grab your attention.

How to Figure Out Idioms

An idiom often sounds puzzling and maybe even silly at first. You won't always be able to figure it out, but try these tips:

1. Look for other words and phrases that give clues about its meaning.

2. Make a guess about its meaning and see if it fits the sentence.

3. If the meaning doesn't make sense or if you're unsure, ask someone or check a dictionary or the Internet.

WRITER'S WORDS

Gil backed the car right into a telephone pole and dented the trunk. He knew his parents would be **bent out of shape.**

SAMPLE EXPLANATION

Hmmm, this makes no sense—the trunk is bent and so are his parents? It's logical that they'd be angry, but I'll look this one up just to check!

What clues in the text on the next page can help you figure out the highlighted idioms?

It had been a long, dusty ride in the desert. Emmett and Joe left their motorcyles next to the neon Bixby Café sign and went inside for a bite. Tired, they looked over their maps.

Two locals sat on stools at the far end of the counter. They were talking excitedly in hushed tones. One pointed out the window toward the horizon. Emmett heard the second person say "U…."

"U… something," Emmett told Joe. "That dude must have said UFO!" But when Emmett started to question the waitress about flying saucers and aliens, she gave him the cold shoulder.

"Guess she doesn't like us," Joe said.

That night, they kept their eyes peeled for a UFO. All they saw were a few shooting stars and a small airplane. No mysterious lights. No hovering saucers. And no eerie sounds.

The following morning they heard the news on the radio. A UAV—Unmanned Aerial Vehicle—from the local airforce base had been missing. That morning it had crashed in the desert nearby. So a U-something was out there after all—just not the kind they hoped for.

Joe told Emmett, "It's a good thing. I figured at the first sign of a real UFO, you'd get cold feet and be too afraid to examine it."

Idioms

An **idiom** is a phrase that taken as a whole means something different from what the individual words mean. Many idioms include animal names or body parts. Check the lists on the following pages.

Where Did That Come From?

Bad hair day was first used in 1992 in a movie. The main character tells a one-armed vampire, "I'm fine but you're obviously having a *bad hair day*." The phrase has taken on the meaning of having a "really terrible day"—a day when everything goes wrong.

Idiom	Meaning	Sample Sentence
all ears	very eager to hear	If you have a good idea, then I am **all ears**.
beat around the bush	to avoid the question or point	He **beat around the bush** before finally asking me to go to the movies.
by the skin of one's teeth	just barely	She passed the test **by the skin of her teeth**.
down in the dumps	feeling sad	Roy was **down in the dumps** after his team lost.
drive one up the wall	to irritate or frustrate	It **drives me up the wall** when my brother whines.
get cold feet	to feel hesitant or afraid	She wanted to ask him to dance but got **cold feet** and didn't.
in a pinch	in an emergency	Manuel always helps his friends out **in a pinch**.
keep a straight face	to avoid laughing or smiling	When he tripped, I couldn't **keep a straight face.**
keep one's eyes peeled	to watch out for	The police **kept their eyes peeled** for the robber.

Where Did That Come From?

The idiom **learn by heart** dates back to the time of the ancient Greeks. They believed that thought and memory took place in the heart. So, when someone memorized something, people said they *learned it by heart*.

It sure is hard to memorize this speech!

Idiom	Meaning	Sample Sentence
laugh one's head off	to laugh very hard	I **laughed my head off** at the comedy show.
learn the ropes	to become familiar with	To do well at a new job, you have to **learn the ropes**.
let the cat out of the bag	to reveal a piece of information	She **let the cat out of the bag** about DeLisa's surprise party.
make ends meet	to have enough money to pay bills	Mrs. Charles works hard to **make ends meet**.
one's John Hancock	signature	Put **your John Hancock** on this contract.
play up to	to try to gain the favor of	He **played up to** the teacher so that she would give him a passing grade.
pop the question	to ask someone to get married	Mike loves Amy and wants to **pop the question**.
pull one's leg	to joke or kid	My brother told me that he was fired, but he was just **pulling my leg**.
put one's best foot forward	to try to make a good impression	I tried to **put my best foot forward** at the interview.

Where Did That Come From?

To **shell out** means "to give someone something of value." Hundreds of years ago in the American colonies, it meant "to make a payment." When there was a shortage of paper money and coins, people paid their bills with corn kernels. The event where people removed the kernels from the cob was called a *shell out*.

Idiom	Meaning	Sample Sentence
quake in one's boots	to feel very afraid	I left the horror movie **quaking in my boots**.
see eye to eye	to agree with someone completely	My cousin and I **see eye to eye** on everything.
see red	to become very angry	**I see red** when my friend uses my things without asking.
skirt around	to avoid something	Stop **skirting around** the facts and get to the point.
sleep on it	to think something over before making a decision	I had a job offer, but I wanted to **sleep on it** before I officially accepted it.
something up one's sleeve	a secret plan to be used at the right time	The coach always seems to have **something up her sleeve** when the team is in trouble.
steal the spotlight	to take attention away from someone else	My friend likes to **steal the spotlight** from others.
take five	to take a break during work	The workers **take five** every few hours.
think outside the box	to think in a new, creative way	To solve this problem, I am going to have to **think outside the box**.
tie in knots	to make someone nervous	The thought of going to the dentist **tied him in knots**.

Where Did That Come From?

When you say **thumbs down**, you mean that you "don't like or approve of something." This expression goes back to the gladiator contests of ancient Rome. The people watching would decide whether the loser should live or die. To show a vote for death, they would make the "thumbs down" sign.

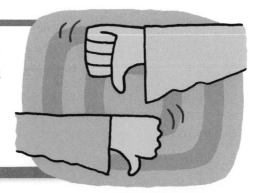

Idiom	Meaning	Sample Sentence
toe the line	to follow the rules	She **toes the line** so that her parents will loan her their car.
turn up one's nose	to not accept something	Carlos felt badly when Linda **turned up her nose** at his birthday gift.
24-seven	constantly; all the time	Kaysar and Will are together **24-seven**.
under the weather	feeling tired or ill	The flu made Danielle feel **under the weather**.
up the creek	in trouble	Lupe was **up the creek** when he lost his ID.
veg out	to relax and not think	I've finished my work and just want to **veg out**.
the walls have ears	people might be listening secretly	Don't say too much because **the walls have ears**.
wrack one's brain	to think hard to solve a problem	I **wracked my brain** for a way to save more money.
you said it	to agree with someone strongly	"It sure is hot today," Jan commented. "**You said it**," Rene replied.
zip it	to keep quiet	John wanted to tell his secret, but decided to **zip it**.

Similes

The sentence "Your hands are like ice" is an example of a **simile**. A simile compares two things that are alike in some way. It uses the word *like* or *as* to connect the two things being compared.

Writers use similes to make you think about things in new ways and to create pictures in your mind. When you read a simile, ask yourself:

- What two things are being compared?
- How are the two things alike?

Identifying Similes

Read the article on page 133 and try out the strategy. You may want to use a chart like the one below.

Simile	Two Things Being Compared	How They're Alike
the stones stand like museum guards	stones and museum guards	They're both powerful and commanding.
each as heavy as two large SUVs	stones and SUVs	They're both extremely heavy.

► The Stonehenge monument is made up of large standing stones set in a circle.

THE MYSTERIES OF STONEHENGE

Archaeologists believe that Stonehenge was built around 3200 B.C.

STONEHENGE in southern England is two mysteries in one. No one knows who built it or why. Today, the stones stand like museum guards, still protecting the secrets of the site.

Builders began constructing Stonehenge about 5,000 years ago. The work probably lasted for about one thousand years. The builders carved and shaped nearly 100 giant stones. Without the help of modern cranes, the workers set the stones—each as heavy as two large SUVs— in a circle. They placed stones across the tops of upright stones, forming structures like enormous doorways.

Modern experts believe the builders arranged these stones in special ways. Some believe that Stonehenge is like a giant calendar. The positioning of the stones tracks the midsummer sunrise and midwinter sunset. But we will probably never know for sure all the secrets of the stones.

The words *like* and *as* signal a **simile.**

133

Metaphors

The sentence "María is an eagle on the tennis court" includes a **metaphor**. A metaphor compares one thing to another without using the word *like* or *as*. One thing *is* another thing. So, María is an eagle when she plays tennis. She has an eagle's power, speed, and sharp eyesight.

Writers of fiction, nonfiction, and poetry use metaphors to create vivid images in your mind. By comparing two unlike things, they make you think about things in fresh, new ways.

When you read, look for comparisons of two things that seem quite different.

When you find a metaphor, ask yourself:

- What two things are being compared?
- How are they alike?

Identifying Metaphors

It's easy to miss metaphors because they don't have the signal word *like* or *as*. Read the article on page 135 and try out the strategy. You may want to use a chart like this one:

Metaphor	Things Compared	Meaning
Earhart was a force to be reckoned with.	Earhart & a force	Earhart's efforts were significant.

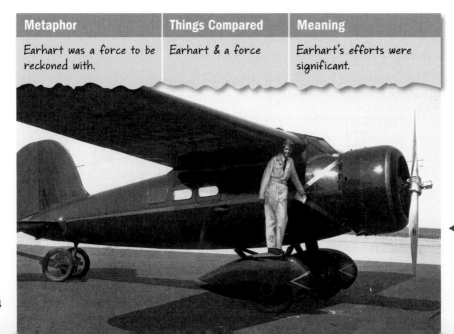

◄ Amelia Earhart preparing for a coast-to-coast race

THE DISAPPEARANCE OF AMELIA EARHART

Amelia Earhart, 1931

After her first ride in an airplane in 1920, Amelia Earhart knew she would learn to fly. By age 40, she had already become the first woman to fly solo across the Atlantic Ocean. She had also flown nonstop across the U.S. Earhart was a force to be reckoned with.

In 1937 Earhart set off on her fateful around-the-world flight. In those days, danger and risk were a pilot's constant companions. On this flight, she planned to fly 2,200 miles from New Guinea to Howland Island. The longest part was over the Pacific Ocean. The aircraft never arrived. After a long search, neither her plane nor her body was found. Before radar and satellite navigation systems, the ocean was a vast desert and an airplane, a grain of sand.

Some people think that Earhart may have flown past tiny Howland Island by mistake and crashed at sea. Some think that she was on a secret spy mission for the United States. No proof of either theory exists. To this day, her disappearance remains a mystery.

A **metaphor** often uses the word *was*, *were*, *is*, or *are*.

Personification

The sentence "The empty house wanted a family" is an example of **personification**. When writers use personification they give human qualities to nonhuman things. So, the house has the ability to wish for a family.

Writers of poetry, fiction, and nonfiction use personification to make their writing more colorful and powerful. When you come across personification, try this strategy:

• Picture the image in your mind.

• Think about the meaning the writer is trying to convey.

Identifying Personification

Read the article on page 137 and use the strategy. You may want to use a chart like this one:

Object	Human Quality
distress flag	is able to beg for help
cheerless ship	is able to feel happy or sad

► Engraved whale's tooth, known as **scrimshaw**, c. 1830

THE MYSTERY OF THE Mary Celeste

Mary Celeste, 1870, Rudolph Ruzicaka. Wood engraving.

Photo © Keystone/Getty Images

In 1872 the captain of a passing ship noticed a vessel drifting in the waters ahead. Coming closer, he noted its name, the *Mary Celeste*, but saw no crew aboard. No distress flag begged for help.

Climbing aboard, sailors found the cheerless ship abandoned. Tools used for navigation were broken or missing, and its lifeboat was gone. The captain and crew, including the captain's wife and daughter, were never found.

What happened? The *Mary Celeste* offered few clues. It could tell its story to no one. Mutiny and yellow fever were two possible suspects, but no one could prove either cause. All that is known is that an abandoned ship steered itself, changing course with the wind, until another ship's crew found it. The lonely ship was 600 miles from its last stated position.

When writers use **personification,** they give human qualities or feelings to objects or animals.

▶ A sextant used by sailors to find their position at sea

137

Figurative Language

Similes

Similes are comparisons that use the signal words *like* or *as* to show how two unlike things are similar.

Hooper

Hooper came twice within a step of dying.
Once was in Brooklyn while working as a hodcarrier,
fifty stories up.
The people below small as insects
when the scaffolding teeter-tottered under him suddenly.
The second time was in the Nam,
bullets whispering violently by
as he pushed himself as deeply as he could
against the ground.
Here, the smallest of insects
large as automobiles
darting on blades of grass.

—Leroy Quintana

Harlem (2)

"What happens to a dream deferred?

Does it dry up
Like a raisin in the sun?
Or fester like a sore—
And then run?
Does it stink like rotten meat?
Or crust and sugar over—
like a syrupy sweet?

Maybe it just sags
like a heavy load.

Or does it explode?"

—Langston Hughes

Metaphors

Metaphors compare two unlike things without using signal words.

"The dawn came quickly now, a wash, a glow, a lightness, and then an explosion of fire as the sun rose out of the Gulf. Kino looked down to cover his eyes from the glare."

—John Steinbeck
from *The Pearl*

Personification

Personification gives human qualities to nonhuman things.

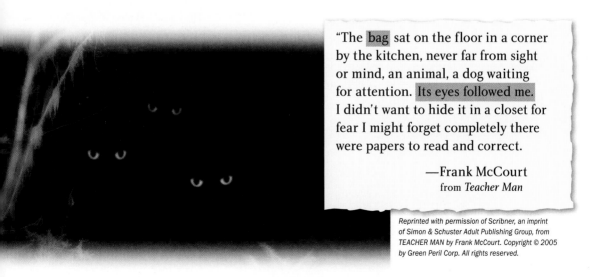

"The bag sat on the floor in a corner by the kitchen, never far from sight or mind, an animal, a dog waiting for attention. Its eyes followed me. I didn't want to hide it in a closet for fear I might forget completely there were papers to read and correct.

—Frank McCourt
from *Teacher Man*

Build Word Knowledge

Once you figure out a meaning of a new word, what can you do to understand it fully and remember it in the future? How can you make a new word your own?

- Read, read, and read some more.

- Get to know a word up close. Say it, record it, get clear on its meaning, and figure out your own way to remember it. Look at it, listen to it, and use it as many times as you can.

- Consult a reference such as a glossary, dictionary, or thesaurus.

- Link the new word to words you already know.

- Collect more data about a word. The more you know about a word, the easier it is to remember it.

How Do You Make New Words Your Own?

" Sometimes I look them up in a dictionary. Then I write them down in a notebook that I keep especially for new words. "

—Raquel

" I try to connect them to words I already know. So when I want to learn a word like *dexterity*, I think of how it's like the word *skill*. "

—Shondra

" I think of all the places I've heard or seen the word. And I ask myself: *Does the meaning change?* "

—Ammad

" When I want to learn new words, I test them out. I use them when I'm talking and writing. Then they become my own! "

—José

You can download more Readers Talk tips. hbgoodreaders.com

Get to Know a Word

Make New Words Your Own

To really get to know a new word you have to spend time with it.

- Notice when you come across a new word and learn to say it correctly.

- Get clear on its meanings. Many words have more than one meaning.

- Come up with a way to remember it.

- Look and listen for it.

- Use it as many times as you can when you write and talk.

FOCUS POINT How much do you really know about words like *fuel* and *hybrid*? Find out by taking the survey on the next page. In this chapter, you'll learn how to make words like these your own. Then you can retake the survey to see how much your knowledge of the words has grown.

VOCABULARY SURVEY

Directions: Download the survey at hbgoodreaders.com and complete it twice—once **before** you've read this chapter, and once **after** you've read it. Compare your answers and ratings.

Word	Do you know how to say the word correctly?		Do you know more than one way to use it?		Use the scale* to rate your word knowledge.			
	✔ Yes	✔ No	✔ Yes	✔ No				
fuel					1	2	3	Before
					1	2	3	After
hybrid					1	2	3	Before
					1	2	3	After
gauge					1	2	3	Before
					1	2	3	After
accelerate					1	2	3	Before
					1	2	3	After
performance					1	2	3	Before
					1	2	3	After
traction					1	2	3	Before
					1	2	3	After
transmission					1	2	3	Before
					1	2	3	After

*Rating Scale

1 = I don't know what this word means.

2 = I have an idea of this word's meaning, but I need more help.

3 = I know what this word means and could teach it to someone.

Make a Word Your Own

Readers who do well inside and outside of school know thousands of words. Of course, some words are known better than others. It's a lot like knowing cars. Spending time with them and paying attention to them helps you know them well.

Read, Read, and Read Some More

Suppose you want to learn what *torque* means. A dictionary definition would tell you it's a "measure of the effectiveness of a rotational force and the perpendicular distance from the line of action to the axis of rotation." Not too helpful, is it?

Now suppose you read a few car magazines that compare the torque of different cars' engines and how it affects the way the cars perform. You might actually have some idea of what *torque* really means. The best way to learn new words is to read materials in which they come up again and again. There's another benefit to wide reading—the more you read, the more words you'll learn and the better you'll read.

Get Up Close and Personal

To really get to know a word, you have to spend some time with it.

- **Learn to say the word correctly** If you're not sure how to say it, check the pronunciation in a print or online dictionary.

- **Record it** Make word cards or keep a vocabulary notebook. Record words you come across that you want to learn. Review and practice their meanings.

- **Use it** Want to really master new words? Use new words as much as possible in speaking and writing.

Get Clear on Its Meanings

Here are some ways to get clear on the meanings of new words and make them "stick."

- Think about where you may have seen or heard the word. If you come across the word *hybrid* in your reading, you might think: **I heard the word *hybrid* in a TV ad for a car and in biology class.**

- Ask yourself some questions about the word: **Why are people interested in *hybrid* cars? How is a *hybrid* different from a regular car?**

  Then try to answer your questions.

- Think of a sentence that will help you get clear on the meaning: **If I drive a *hybrid*, I can save money on gasoline because the car can run on electricity, too.**

- Use your own words to tell what the word means: **A *hybrid* is something that combines two or more things. Cars can be hybrids; plants that come from different cuttings can be hybrids, too.**

Use Memory Tips to Remember the Word

You've done all the right things. You've read about hybrid cars and learned how to say *hybrid* correctly. You've used the word in speaking and writing and even used your own words to tell what it means. But how are you going to remember it days or weeks from now? See the next page for some memory tips.

Use Memory Tips

You may think you understand a word on Friday, but will you remember it on Monday? Try these tips to help you remember words and build your storehouse of word knowledge.

Memory Tip: Store It!

Make a word map for each new word you want to learn.

1. Write the word in the center. Write what it means in the top box. Give an example and a non-example in the boxes below.

2. Use a dictionary to check the information in your map.

3. Write where you heard or saw the word and the date. Keep your word map in a vocabulary notebook.

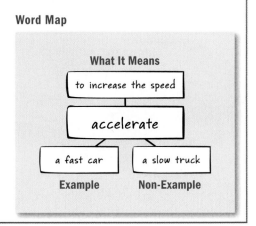

Word Map

Memory Tip: Explore the Word Family

Just like people, words have families, too.

1. Write the word you want to learn. Circle the base word or root.

2. Make a list of words that share the base word or root.

3. Write a sentence for each word in the family.

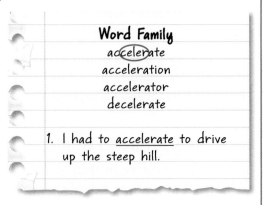

Memory Tip: Picture It!

Suppose you are trying to learn the word **traction**. You can use a key word and picture to remember its meaning.

1. Think about the meaning of the new word: **Traction is what happens when a moving object rubs against or grips the surface.**

2. Think of a key word that sounds like the new word: **My key word is tractor.**

3. Make a picture in your mind that links the meanings of the two words.

4. Whenever you hear or see the new word, think of the key word and the matching picture.

YOUR PICTURE   **YOUR LINK**

A tractor's wheels grip the soil. That's **traction.**

Memory Tip: Self-Check Spelling

Learning to spell a word correctly is part of making it your own.

1. Say the word.   accelerate

2. Write the word, syllable by syllable: ac-cel-er-ate.

3. Read what you've written. Does it sound right? Does it look right? If not, check the spelling in a dictionary.

4. Repeat steps 1 and 2 three more times.

Consult a Reference

Where you go for information depends on what you need to know. Suppose you're going on a job interview. Who is more likely to know what an interview will be like—your mom or your little brother? When you have questions about a word, it's also important to know where you can get the information you need.

What Are Some Useful References?

References are books—and people—you go to when you want information. Different types of references give different information about words. Sometimes, you may decide to look up a word in more than one type of reference.

Here are four types of useful references:

1. glossary   **2.** thesaurus
3. dictionary   **4.** well-informed person

FOCUS POINT Each reference source described on the next page gives different information about words. What are the differences between a glossary, a thesaurus, and a dictionary? Which reference should you use to find out the meaning of *summit*? Where can you go to find its synonyms? When should you ask someone?

What Is a Glossary?

A **glossary** is a list of key words and their definitions. It is found at the end of books such as science and social studies textbooks. Each word is defined as it's used in the book, and the pronunciation of the word may be included.

> **S**
>
> **summit** (sum'·it) the highest point of a mountain or hill (234)

What Is a Thesaurus?

A **thesaurus** is a book that lists synonyms, or words with related meanings. Sometimes, a sentence is included to give you an example of the different ways a word can be used. For many words, the thesaurus also lists antonyms.

> **summit** noun *We climbed to the mountain's summit.* PEAK, tip, top, crest. ANTONYMS bottom, base.

What Is a Dictionary?

A **dictionary** is a reference book that gives <u>all</u> the meanings of a word and its pronunciation. It also tells you whether the word is a noun, verb, and so on. Often information about what language a word came from, or its origin, is also given.

> **summit** \sum'·ət\ *n* **1** : The highest point or part **2** : a meeting between heads of government [ME *somete,* from Anglo-French *sumet,* diminutive of *sum* top, from L *summus* highest]

Who Is a Well-Informed Person?

A **well-informed person** is someone, such as a scientist or researcher, who knows a lot about a certain subject. Parents, teachers, and friends can be well-informed, too.

Glossaries

Have you found a word that you want to make your own, that you want to understand and remember for a long time? Turning to a **glossary** ensures that you get a clear and precise meaning of the word.

A glossary is a list of the important terms used in the book, along with their definitions. The terms are in alphabetical order. In a glossary, you'll find:

• technical words used only in that subject area

• common words that have a special meaning in the book

Predict and Check the Meaning

Suppose you came across the following sentence in your science textbook:

The canopy blocks sunlight from getting to the forest floor.

Now suppose you aren't sure what *canopy* means. You can use a prediction chart to figure it out:

1. First, you predict, or decide upon a logical meaning.

2. Then, use a glossary to see if your prediction is correct. Read the predicted definition of *canopy* in the chart below.

Prediction Chart

What I think it means	What it means
something with a dark color that blocks light	

Read these entries, or listings, from a page in a glossary.

Glossary

C

canopy (ka'·nə·pē) the spread of treetops that make up the top layer in a forest (258)

capillary (ka'·pə·ler·ē) small vessel, or tube, that carries nutrients to different parts of a plant (98)

carbon cycle (kär'·bən sī'·kəl) the movement of carbon dioxide and oxygen through the Earth's ecosystem (100)

chaparral (shap'·ə·ral) a thick growth of shrubs and trees found in areas with hot, dry summers and mild, wet winters (162)

> Some glossaries include a **respelling** that tells you how to pronounce the word.

> Some glossaries show the **page number** where the word appears in the book.

Once you know the correct meaning of *canopy*, you can write it in the chart next to your prediction. Look at the completed prediction chart below. How close was the prediction to the glossary definition?

Prediction Chart

What I think it means	What it means
something with a dark color that blocks light	the spread of treetops that make up the top layer in a forest

▼ The canopy of a rainforest in Costa Rica

The Thesaurus

The name *thesaurus* comes from a Latin word that means "storehouse or treasury." And in this case, the treasures are words. A **thesaurus** is a storehouse of synonyms, or words that have almost the same meanings. Sometimes it also shows antonyms, or words that have opposite meanings of the entry word.

What's the Difference Between Synonyms?

Walk, pace, strut. What do these synonyms have in common? They all describe an action—to move along by putting one foot in front of the other. But how are these synonymous terms different?

Two words almost never mean exactly the same thing. They have shades of meaning—slight differences—that make each one special. For example:

- When you hear the word *walk,* you think of someone simply moving from one place to another.

- When you hear the word *strut,* you think of someone walking proudly and showing off.

walk   pace   strut

Some synonyms differ in their level of intensity. For example, think about words related to *rain*: *drizzle, storm,* and *hurricane.* All these words have to do with wet weather, but each word in the list describes stronger, more intense weather conditions.

Build Your Storehouse

Unlike a glossary or dictionary, a thesaurus doesn't provide definitions. When you look up a new word, you may find a synonym that you know well. If so, you're on the right track to the new word's meaning. Read these entries from a thesaurus.

Thesaurus

camouflage noun *The men wore dark pants for camouflage.* CLOAK, disguise, mask, screen.

▶ verb *Some frogs have colors that camouflage them from enemies.* CONCEAL, disguise, cover, mask. ANTONYMS expose, reveal, show.

canopy noun *The canopy helped shield us from the sun.* SHADE, awning, cover, sunshade, marquee, tilt.

compound verb **1** *Having a bad attitude will compound the problem.* INCREASE, intensify, worsen, complicate. **2** *The scientists compounded two plants to make a new medicine.* MIX, blend, mingle, combine, devise, make.

A **sample sentence** shows how to use the word. Then the **synonyms** are shown. Sometimes, the first synonym is written in all capital letters.

Antonyms also clarify meaning by showing opposite meanings for the entry word.

Compare the synonyms for *compound*. Which words have a negative meaning?

Using a Thesaurus

Look at the synonyms for the word *canopy.* Do you see any words you know? Use the synonyms to get a deeper understanding of the meanings of *canopy.*

"I know the word *awning* because we have one that covers our porch. So a *canopy* shades and covers something.

If you need more information about the differences between the synonyms, you'll probably need to check a dictionary.

You can use a thesaurus to add zing to your writing. By having a choice of synonyms, you don't have to repeat the same words again and again. Also, you can choose the word with just the right shade of meaning to get across your ideas and feelings.

Dictionaries

A **dictionary** is a terrific reference to use if you want lots of information about a word. Here are just some of the things you can find in a print or online dictionary:

- how to pronounce the word

- all the different meanings of the word

- how to use the word in a sentence. Some words can be more than one part of speech. *Canopy,* for example, is both a noun and a verb.

- the origin, or history, of the word

▲ A dictionary

By permission. From Merriam-Webster's School Dictionary ©2004 by Merriam-Webster, Incorporated (www.Merriam-Webster.com).

How to Use a Print Dictionary

Follow these steps to find the information you need:

1 Look Up the Base Word

Dictionaries usually don't define words with endings like *-ing, -ed,* or *-es*. So, take off the ending to figure out the base word, and look for that word in the dictionary.

2 Use the Guide Words to Quickly Locate a Word

Dictionary entries are arranged in alphabetical order. Two guide words are printed at the top of each page. They tell you the first word and last word defined on that page.

3 Find the Meaning

In some dictionaries, the most common meaning of an entry word is listed first. In other dictionaries, the oldest meaning is shown first. Learn how the meanings in your dictionary are organized to help you find a meaning more quickly.

When you look up a new word that has more than one meaning, skim the whole entry to get the big picture. Think about all the ways the word can be used. This helps you own all of it.

Dictionary

¹**canopy** \ka'-nə-pē\ *n* **1** : a covering placed over a bed or a throne, or carried on poles over a person **2** : covering; shelter; shade **3** : the spread of treetops that make up the top layer in a forest **4** : the see-through enclosure over an aircraft's cockpit **5** : the part of a parachute that opens and catches the air [<F *canapé* sofa <L *conopeum* mosquito net <Gk. *Konopeion* bed with mosquito net < *kɔnʊps* mosquito] *plural* **canopies**

> **Synonym** *awning*

²**canopy** (1594) *v* to cover over with a canopy

canopied, canopying, canopies

When used as a **noun,** *canopy* has five different meanings.

This **word history** shows that *canopy* first came from a Greek (Gk.) word, then a Latin (L) word, and finally a French (F) word before it became an English word.

Choosing the Right Definition

Which meaning of *canopy* is used in each of these sentences?

No one could see the princess under the silk canopy.

The pilot sat in the canopy waiting for the storm to end.

To protect the children from mosquitoes, she canopied the entire campsite.

> The first sentence says that a princess sat under a canopy. In this sentence, *canopy* means "a covering over a throne."

Special Purpose Dictionaries

Special purpose dictionaries give information on specific topics, such as geographical places, film and music history, gemstones, and even people's names.

Geographical Dictionary

Do you want to know the highest mountain in Peru or the state flower of Delaware? Check a geographical dictionary. You'll find descriptions of natural features like mountain ranges and rivers as well as information about cities and countries across the globe.

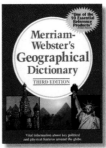

▲ A geographical dictionary has thousands of entries and includes maps.

Here's part of an entry for New York City:

> **New York**
>
> **3.** *or* **New York City.** City, SE New York, at mouth of the Hudson River; pop. (1990c) 7,322,564; largest city in the U.S. and important seaport; comprises five boroughs coextensive with five counties: Bronx (Bronx co.), Brooklyn (Kings co.), Manhattan (New York co.), Queens (Queens co.), and Staten Island (Richmond co.)

By permission. From Merriam-Webster's Geographical Dictionary, Third Edition ©2001 by Merriam-Webster, Incorporated (www.Merriam-Webster.com).

Dictionary for English Language Learners

Some English dictionaries are designed for students whose home language isn't English. These dictionaries give clear, easy-to-understand definitions and also explain how each word is used.

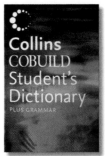

▲ An ESL dictionary gives tips for the words used most frequently in English.

Here's an entry for the word *tale*:

> ★ **tale** /teil/ **tales.** ☐1 COUNT NOUN
> A **tale** is a story, especially one involving adventure or magic. ☐2 COUNT NOUN
> You can refer to an interesting, exciting, or dramatic account of a real event as a **tale.** ...*tales of horror and loss resulting from Monday's earthquake.* ☐3 See also **fairy tale.**

Dictionary of Names

What does your name mean? *Morning dew*? *Fierce warrior*? *Talks too much*? You can learn the history of your name and of many other names in a dictionary of names.

These entries come from a dictionary of African names:

ETHIOPIA • FEMALE NAMES			
Name	Pronunciation	Meaning	Origin
Amira	Ah-meer-rah	Princess	Arabic
Yenee	Yay-nay	Mine	Ethiopian
Tenagne	Ta-non-ya	Gold	Amharic

▲ A dictionary of names is often organized by female and male names.

KENYA • MALE NAMES				
Name	Pronunciation	Meaning	Origin	Region
Onkwani	OHN-kwah-nee	He talks a lot	Kisii	East Africa
Onyango	OHN-yah-goh	Born about midday	Luo	East Africa
Otieno	OH-tee-eh-noh	Born at night	Luo	East Africa

Biographical Dictionary

A biographical dictionary gives you a snapshot of the lives and accomplishments of famous people. Do you want to know more about a favorite author or actor? Check the information in a biographical dictionary.

Here's part of an entry from a biographical dictionary of film:

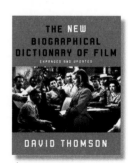

▲ A biographical dictionary lists names in alphabetical order.

Danny Glover

b. San Francisco, California, 1947

Glover has worked steadily for over two decades now, balancing box-office action movies with some genuinely adventurous explorations of the black experience.

Relate Words

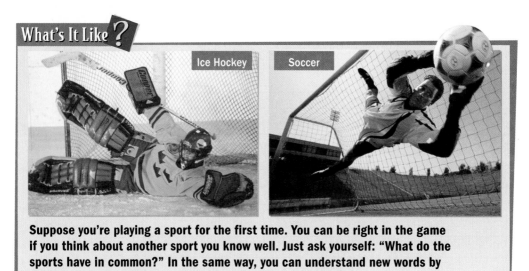

Ice Hockey

Soccer

Suppose you're playing a sport for the first time. You can be right in the game if you think about another sport you know well. Just ask yourself: "What do the sports have in common?" In the same way, you can understand new words by thinking about how they connect to words you already know.

Connect New Words to Words You Know

When you come across a new word, connect it to words you know. Suppose you're reading a sports story about ice hockey and you see these sentences:

> At yesterday's game, the goaltender displayed amazing **skill and dexterity**. How many people can actually catch a puck that's moving 90 miles per hour?

Think about the description of the goaltender and the meaning of the word *skill*. Where does the word *dexterity* fit in? You can use what you know to figure out that *dexterity* means "a skill that involves using your hands."

FOCUS POINT Do you know all the terms used in soccer and ice hockey? Look at the word web on the next page. How does the reader make a connection? Find a word or phrase you don't know. Can you figure it out by linking it to a sports term you do know?

Equipment

Ice Hockey	Soccer
puck	ball
skates	cleats
knee pads	shin guards

Location

Ice Hockey	Soccer
rink	pitch

ICE HOCKEY AND SOCCER

Positions

Ice Hockey	Soccer
center	striker
goaltender	goalkeeper
defense	defenders
left wing	wingers
right wing	

Make Connections

What's a *goaltender*? In soccer the *goalkeeper* defends the goal. So a *goaltender* must do the same thing in a hockey game.

Two in One

One way to remember new words is to do a "two in one."
Use two new words in the same sentence so that you can make
connections between them. Here's an example, using two soccer
words that may be new to you. This sentence will help you
remember the connection between a **striker** and a **goalkeeper**:

The striker kicked
the ball past
the goalkeeper
to score a point.

A *goalkeeper* guards
the goal. A *striker* must be
the player whose job it
is to score.

Map It!

Another way to connect words is to make a word map. It shows
words that belong to the same group, or category. Looking at
words in categories is a good way to see how they are connected.

big
huge
gigantic

Use a Synonym Scale

You can use a synonym scale to help you think about how words relate to each other. *Big* describes something large that could still fit through your door, but *gigantic* describes something larger than a house. So, you could put the words *big* and *gigantic* at opposite ends of a synonym scale for words describing size.

Where does *massive* fit in? Is it closer to the meaning of *big* or *gigantic*?

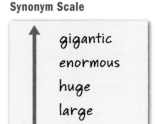

Synonym Scale

gigantic
enormous
huge
large
big

▲ As you move up the list, each word suggests a bigger size.

Use an Antonym Scale

Antonyms are words with opposite meanings. The antonyms *cold* and *hot* would be at the opposite ends of a scale of temperature words. Other words, such as *cool* and *warm* also describe temperature and fall in between *cold* and *hot*.

This antonym scale explores another pair of antonyms: *bored* and *thrilled*. Compare the meanings of the words on the scale. Where on the scale would you put the word *interested*?

Antonym Scale

bored   eager   thrilled

▲ The words at the opposite ends of the scale are antonyms.

Collect Data

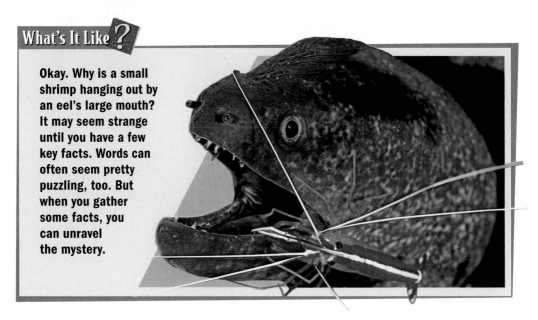

Okay. Why is a small shrimp hanging out by an eel's large mouth? It may seem strange until you have a few key facts. Words can often seem pretty puzzling, too. But when you gather some facts, you can unravel the mystery.

Why Collect Data About Words?

Have you heard the expression "Information is power"? Well, gathering data, or information, about words gives you the power to understand them, use them, and remember them. Here are some tips for building your word knowledge:

- Useful information about a word comes in many forms, including its pronunciation, definition, synonyms and antonyms, and origin, or history.

- Graphic organizers can help you gather and make sense of data.

- Use a notebook, set of cards, or computer folder to store your words in one place. Then you can review them, checking your knowledge and adding new information.

FOCUS POINT Do you know how to say *inharmonious* and when to use it? Or, do you need some additional data? How does the information on the next page build your word knowledge?

inharmonious

PRONUNCIATION	in·här·mō·nē·əs
PART OF SPEECH	adjective
BASE WORD	*harmony* "a pleasing combination of musical notes or sounds"
WORD PART	prefix *in-* "not"
WORD PART	suffix *-ous* "having the qualities of"
WORD HISTORY	from the Greek, *harmonia,* *"agreement of sounds"*
WORD FAMILY	*harmony, harmonize, harmonious, disharmony*
SYNONYMS	*harsh, unmusical, unpleasant*
ANTONYMS	*tuneful, musical, pleasant*
SAMPLE SENTENCE	The band's **inharmonious** music made me cover my ears.

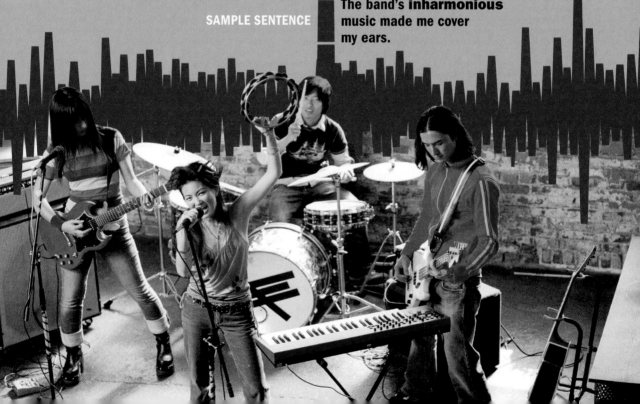

Use a Definition Map

"What does that mean again?" Have you said that after looking up a word in a dictionary? Instead of trying to memorize a definition in a dictionary, sometimes the best way to get to know a word is to gather data for your own definition.

1 **Select a Word to Study**

Write the word in large letters in the center box. The definition map on the next page has been completed for the word *cacophony*.

2 **Answer the Question: "What Is It?"**

Think about the general category to which the word belongs. A *cacophony* is a mix of sounds. If you recognize any meaningful word parts, record them and their meaning. *Cacophony* contains the root *phon*, which means "sound."

3 **Answer the Question: "What Is It Like?"**

Use the boxes on the right to describe what the word is like. What makes it different from other words in the category? A *cacophony* isn't just any mix of sounds. It's a mix of sounds that's loud and annoying.

4 **Record Examples of the Word**

Think about when you would use the word. If you can give examples of a word, then you have really "got" its meaning. The best examples come from your own life. Where have you heard a *cacophony*? Were you stuck in traffic, or volunteering at a daycare center?

5 **Read Your Completed Definition Map**

Think about how all the data fits together to give you a clear idea of the word's meaning. Use your map to teach someone what the word means. Now that's word power!

What Is It?

a mix of sounds
phon = sound

What Is It Like?

loud

annoying

makes my
ears hurt

cacophony

car horns
blaring

fans
shouting at
a baseball
game

out-of-tune
instruments
playing
together

ten babies
crying

What Are Some Examples?

Compare and Analyze Features

How are pianos and guitars alike? What's the difference between a vibraphone and a marimba? You can answer questions like these by using a vocabulary grid. Here's how:

1 **Select a Category and Examples**

You might be interested in learning about types of instruments, types of amplifiers, or even types of music. Label your grid with the category name. Then write examples of things in that category.

Instruments ◁ Category				
piano				
guitar ◁ Example				
vibraphone				
marimba				
saxophone				

2 **Add the Key Features**

What are the different features, or characteristics, of the things you listed in the grid? Add these across the top.

Instruments	wood body	metal body	strings	pedals
piano			Feature	
guitar				
vibraphone				
marimba				
saxophone				

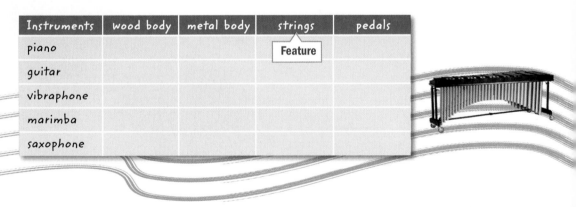

marimba

3 Show the Similarities and Differences

Start with the first thing you listed. Decide if it has each feature. For example, does a piano have a wood body?

- If so, write a plus sign (+) under "wood body."
- If not, write a minus sign (−).

Continue until you have filled each cell. Look for items that share the same sign. What do they have in common?

Instruments	wood body	metal body	strings	pedals
piano	+	−	+	+
guitar	+	−	+	−
vibraphone	−	+	−	+
marimba	+	−	−	−
saxophone	−	+	−	−

4 Expand and Explore the Grid

Expand the grid by adding more things in the category or more features. Fill in the new cells. Then discuss your findings with a partner. How are the things you listed similar? What is unique about each one?

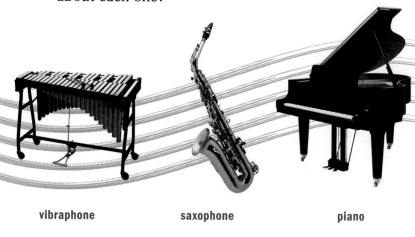

vibraphone   saxophone   piano

electric guitar

Make a Five-Senses Web

Writers use sensory images to help you imagine what they're describing as in *Her voice sounded like scratchy sandpaper.* In the same way, you can use a Five-Senses Web to build your knowledge of a word.

1 **Select a Word to Study**

Words for study come from many sources. When you're reading, a word may catch your eye, or ear. Other words may be assigned for study by your teachers.

2 **Link the Word to Sensory Images**

Now comes the interesting part. Write the word in the center of a web. Then imagine what the word smells like, tastes like, feels like, sounds like, and looks like.

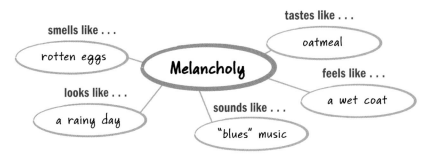

3 **Refine Your Ideas**

Make the images more memorable by adding or replacing words. For example:

> bland
> ~~tastes like~~ oatmeal

4 **Put Your Ideas in Writing**

Use your completed web to update your Vocabulary Notebook. Write an entry for each word you are studying.

Use a Denotation and Connotation Chart

Would you rather listen to *cool* music or *new* music? *Cool* music probably sounds better if you associate good things with the word *cool*. All words have a **denotation**, or dictionary definition. But often, words also have a **connotation**, or feelings that are associated with them. Compare the two sentences below:

> The song had a **steady** beat.

> The song had a **monotonous** beat.

Both sentences say that the song had a constant, even beat. However, *steady* and *monotonous* suggest two different feelings. What kind of feeling do you get when you read each sentence? Not sure? Then use a denotation and connotation chart.

Follow these steps:

- Use a dictionary to find the denotation of each word.

- Think of an example that illustrates the word.

- Think about the feeling the word suggests. Is it positive, negative, or neutral (neither positive nor negative)?

Denotation and Connotation Chart

Word	Denotation	Example from My Life	Connotation
steady	"not changing; constant"	when the beat in a song stays the same	☐ positive ☑ neutral ☐ negative
monotonous	"not changing; repetitious and dull"	when the beat in a song is boring	☐ positive ☐ neutral ☑ negative

Make a Vocabulary Study Card

Study cards are a great way to build your word power. Make a card for every word you want to learn. As you collect new data about the word, you can add it to the card. Here's how:

1. **Select a word.** It may come from your reading or from a discussion.

2. **Make a word map.** On the front of the card, write
   - the word in the center
   - what it means at the top
   - an example and a non-example

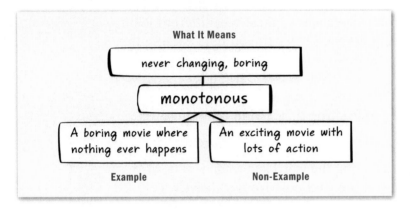

3. **Collect more data.** On the back of the card, add the data.

Pronunciation	mə • no′ • tə • nəs
Synonyms	unchanging, boring
Antonyms	changing, exciting
Connotation	negative
Words in Its Family	monotony, monotone
Sentence	The concert was so monotonous I almost fell asleep.

> Check a dictionary for the pronunciation.

Be a Word Detective

Usually, there is more to a word than meets the eye or ear! By using a dictionary to do a bit of detective work, you can collect some "hidden" facts about words. Here's what you can uncover in a dictionary entry:

- the word's history, or origin
- if it has been borrowed from another language
- if it was created from two words, or "blended"
- if it is "clipped," or a shortened form of a longer word

Word Histories

A word's history is like its life story. It tells what words and languages a word originally came from, and how it changed over time. It may also tell the year when the word first started being used in English. Word origins, also called **etymologies**, can appear at the beginning or end of a dictionary entry.

Dictionary Entries

guitar \gə-tär'\ *n* (1668) a musical instrument with a long neck and usually six strings that are played by using the fingers or a pick [<F *guitare* <Sp *guitarra* <Ar *qitar* < Gk *kithara* cithara, a stringed instrument like a lyre]

> This is the **year** the word was first used in English.

> The **abbreviations** tell you that the word first came from Greek, then Arabic, Spanish, and French before becoming an English word.

scale \skāl\ *n* (1597) a series of musical notes that go up or down in pitch in a certain order [ME, from Late L *scala* ladder, staircase, from L *scalae*, plural, stairs, rungs, ladder; akin to L *scandere* to climb]

> For this word, the connection between the **current meaning** and its **origin** are very clear.

Be a Word Detective, continued

How Old is Old English?

The word *skin* dates back to a time between 500 and 1100 A.D. when people were speaking what we today call Old English. A conversation in Old English might sound like German. That's because three groups who spoke Germanic languages invaded England. Many everyday words, like *skin* and *sky,* and *they* and *make* come from Old English.

Caught in the Middle

In the years between 1100 and 1485, Old English changed to what we now call Middle English. And it sounded a little like French. That's because French-speaking invaders, the Normans, conquered England. So thousands of words with French origins such as *forest* and *courage* date to this period. Many words related to law and government such as *jury* and *court* can be traced back to Middle English as well.

▲ Words like *joust, chivalry,* and *honor* come from French words.

The Age of Science

There's a good chance you'd understand a conversation spoken in English after 1485. Thousands of words you use today date back to ideas and scientific discoveries that were "new" in the 1500s and 1600s. People created words like *microscope, astronomy,* and *autopsy* borrowing from ancient Greek words and roots.

What Are Borrowed Words?

What do *zero* and *karaoke* have in common? They are both **borrowed words**, or English words taken from another language. Borrowed words keep the same meaning and sounds from their original language, no matter what language they end up in. Knowing that words like *memoir* and *ballet* come from French can help you pronounce and spell them.

As contact between cultures increased and communities became more multicultural, more and more words from other languages were borrowed and became part of English. Such words become so familiar that no one even thinks of them as foreign words. Can you imagine English without *pizza*, *shampoo*, or *zombies*?

Here are some borrowed words we use to talk about two popular topics: animals and the weather.

Animals

English Word	Borrowed From	English Word	Borrowed From
cobra	Portuguese	panda	Nepali
cheetah	Hindi	penguin	Welsh
elephant	Hebrew	pony	Gaelic
gerbil	Arabic	poodle	German
giraffe	Arabic	racoon	Algonquin
iguana	Arawak	tiger	Farsi

Weather

English Word	Borrowed From	English Word	Borrowed From
breeze	Portuguese	monsoon	Arabic
fog	Danish	tornado	Spanish
hurricane	Taino	tsunami	Japanese
maelstrom	Dutch	typhoon	Mandarin

Be a Word Detective, continued

What Are Blended Words?

Did you know that *webcast* was made up by combining two other words? It's a **blended word** created from *web* and *broadcast*. People needed a name for the technology that allows listeners to download digital files from a radio broadcast. Since a name didn't exist, they made up, or coined, a new word!

Read the dictionary entries below. What language does the word *tempo* come from? From which two words was *saxophone* coined?

saxophone \saks'-ə-f ō n\ *n* (1851) a wind instrument with a curved metal body and a reed mouthpiece [The word *saxophone* was created from the name of its Belgian inventor, Antoine-Joseph **Sax** and the Greek word *phonos* meaning "sound."]

> Saxophone came from blending two words.

tempo \tem'-pō\ *n* (ca. 1724) **1** : the rate of speed of a musical piece **2** : the rate of movement or activity [Italian, literally meaning *time* < L *tempus*] *plural* **tem-pos**

> Like many music words, *tempo* was borrowed from Italian.

What Are Clipped Words?

Clipped words are like nicknames—they are shortened forms of words. You probably use them all the time, but don't realize it. Do you talk about TV ads or having the flu? *Ad* is short for *advertisement,* and *flu* is short for *influenza.* Clipped words are made by cutting off the beginning of a word, its end, or both its beginning and end.

Read these dictionary entries for two clipped words. Where does the word *fan* come from? What part of *telephone* was clipped?

³**fan** *n* [prob. short for *fanatic*] (1682) a person who is very interested and excited about something such as a sport

²**phone** [shortened form] *n* **1** : TELEPHONE **2** : EARPHONE

▼ An old-fashioned telephone

Boost Your Reading Power

Learn Academic Vocabulary

Becoming familiar with the meanings of the words on the following pages will increase your understanding of just about any subject. But how can you learn and remember these "power words"? Here are three tips to try:

Explore the Family Tree

Can't remember what *achievable* means? Try listing other words in its word family. For example, if you know the meaning of *achieve* and *achievement*, it'll be a snap to figure out the meaning of *achievable*.

Map the Word's Meaning

Another way to help you learn a word is to map it. Add your map to a personal vocabulary file.

▲ When something is **achievable**, you can make it happen.

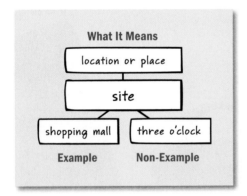

What It Means

location or place

site

shopping mall | three o'clock

Example | Non-Example

Use the Word a Lot!

Just like practicing a sport or musical instrument, you'll get better and better at remembering what words mean if you use them a lot.

- Collect sentences or phrases you read that use the word— and add your own as you think of them.

- Use the word in your writing and in conversation with classmates, friends, and family. That way you'll make the power words your own.

How many of the words in the following list have you read in your textbooks or used in your classwork? Study their meanings and you'll be sure to boost your reading power.

achieve

v. When you **achieve** something, you succeed in completing something.

synonym accomplish   *antonym* fail

   I will **achieve** my goal of buying a car if I work hard.

EXAMPLE: winning a contest
NON-EXAMPLE: losing a contest
WORD FAMILY: achievable, achieved, achievement, achieving

affect

v. To **affect** means to cause change in something or someone.

synonym influence

   Low rainfall will **affect** a plant's growth.

EXAMPLE: blowing out a candle
NON-EXAMPLE: watching a lit candle
WORD FAMILY: affected, affecting, affective, affectively, unaffected

acquire

v. When you **acquire** something, you get it or take hold of it.

synonym obtain   *antonym* lose

   At cooking school, he will **acquire** many skills.

EXAMPLE: getting new jeans
NON-EXAMPLE: giving away old jeans
WORD FAMILY: acquired, acquiring, acquisition

alternative

n. When you have an **alternative**, you have more than one choice.

synonyms option, choice

   Her **alternative** was to leave the dog at home.

EXAMPLE: choosing among three ice cream flavors
NON-EXAMPLE: having only one ice cream flavor
WORD FAMILY: alternate, alternatively, alternatives

administrate

v. To **administrate** means to run or manage something.

synonym control

   His daughters **administrate** the family business.

EXAMPLE: to direct what a company does
NON-EXAMPLE: to get a job as a waitperson
WORD FAMILY: administrates, administration, administrative, administrator

analyze

v. To **analyze** is to examine something closely.

synonym study

   Detectives **analyze** the evidence.

EXAMPLE: reading a document carefully
NON-EXAMPLE: quickly skimming a document
WORD FAMILY: analyses, analysis, analytical, analyzed

approach

n. An **approach** is the way you deal with a situation.

synonym method

The doctor's **approach** was to chat with the patient first.

EXAMPLE: how you solve a math problem
NON-EXAMPLE: your best subject in school
WORD FAMILY: approachable, approached, approaches, approaching

appropriate

adj. Something **appropriate** is right for the situation.

synonym proper   *antonym* unsuitable

It is not **appropriate** to wear jeans to a wedding.

EXAMPLE: paying attention in class
NON-EXAMPLE: interrupting someone
WORD FAMILY: appropriately, appropriateness, inappropriate

area

n. An **area** is a part of a city, country, or the world.

synonyms region, place

Parrots live in a tropical **area**.

EXAMPLE: a neighborhood
NON-EXAMPLE: a house
WORD FAMILY: areas

aspect

n. An **aspect** is one of the parts or characteristics of something.

synonyms feature, trait

The best **aspect** of instant messaging is its speed.

EXAMPLE: a building's shape
NON-EXAMPLE: a building's owner
WORD FAMILY: aspects

assess

v. When you **assess** something, you rate it or judge it.

synonyms rate, evaluate

The fire inspector will **assess** the damage.

EXAMPLE: researching an item before buying it
NON-EXAMPLE: buying an item on a whim
WORD FAMILY: assessed, assessment, reassess

assist

v. When you **assist** someone, you help.

synonym aid   *antonym* hinder

Parents sometimes **assist** their children with their homework.

EXAMPLE: clearing the table after a meal
NON-EXAMPLE: leaving your dishes on the table
WORD FAMILY: assistance, assistant, assisted, unassisted

assume

v. When you **assume** something, you think it is true.

synonym suspect   *antonym* know

Lisa **assumed** the long-distance calls were free.

EXAMPLE: thinking that you have permission to borrow your friend's car
NON-EXAMPLE: your friend telling you that you can borrow her car
WORD FAMILY: assumed, assuming, assumption

authority

n. If you have **authority**, you have the power to give orders or make decisions.

synonym power

The Senate has the **authority** to pass laws.

EXAMPLE: a police officer
NON-EXAMPLE: a prisoner
WORD FAMILY: authoritative, authorities

available

adj. If something is **available**, you can use it or get it.

Tickets are **available** for the concert.

EXAMPLE: a book on your bookshelf
NON-EXAMPLE: a book that is no longer in print
WORD FAMILY: availability, unavailable

benefit

n. A **benefit** is something that helps or improves your life.

synonym advantage   *antonym* harm

One **benefit** of the job is a good paycheck.

EXAMPLE: feeling healthy from exercising
NON-EXAMPLE: catching a cold
WORD FAMILY: beneficial, beneficiary, benefited, benefits

category

n. A **category** is a group of things that have something in common.

synonym type

Rap is a **category** of music.

EXAMPLE: heavy metal
NON-EXAMPLE: music
WORD FAMILY: categorize, categorizable, categorization

chapter

n. A **chapter** is one of the main parts of a book.

The first **chapter** of *Huckleberry Finn* is my favorite.

EXAMPLE: chapter 17 in a science textbook
NON-EXAMPLE: the index in a science textbook
WORD FAMILY: chapters

circumstance

n. A **circumstance** is a fact or an event that makes a situation the way it is.

synonym condition

Under certain **circumstances**, the students can have lunch off campus.

EXAMPLE: a snowfall that cancels school
NON-EXAMPLE: a school team
WORD FAMILY: circumstantial

comment

v. When you **comment** on something, you give a written or spoken opinion about it.

synonym remark

I will **comment** on the new dress code for school.

EXAMPLE: telling what you think about a CD
NON-EXAMPLE: telling the name of the CD
WORD FAMILY: commentary, commentator, commented, comments

commission

v. To **commission** is to ask people to do certain work.

synonym order

The mayor will **commission** a design for the new library.

EXAMPLE: asking someone to do a job
NON-EXAMPLE: someone volunteering to do a job
WORD FAMILY: commissioned, commissioner, commissions

community

n. A **community** is a group of people who live in a place or are alike in some way.

synonyms residents

The **community** organized a Labor Day picnic.

EXAMPLE: your neighbors
NON-EXAMPLE: your house
WORD FAMILY: communities

compensate

v. To **compensate** is to provide something in place of something lost, damaged, or missing.

He offered to **compensate** me for denting the wheel on my bike.

EXAMPLE: replacing your friend's CD after you lost it
NON-EXAMPLE: telling your friend you lost his CD
WORD FAMILY: compensated, compensation, compensatory

concept

n. A **concept** is a general idea.

synonym belief

My **concept** of fairness means treating everyone with respect.

EXAMPLE: the idea that all people deserve to be free
NON-EXAMPLE: a speech about freedom
WORD FAMILY: conception, concepts, conceptual

complex

adj. Something **complex** is difficult or has many parts.

synonym complicated   *antonym* simple

A **complex** problem is not easily solved.

EXAMPLE: a 1,000-piece jigsaw puzzle
NON-EXAMPLE: a 10-piece jigsaw puzzle
WORD FAMILY: complexities, complexity

conclude

v. When you **conclude** something, you think about it carefully to form an opinion.

synonym decide

The judge **concluded** that the young man was innocent.

EXAMPLE: to make a decision after careful thought
NON-EXAMPLE: to make a decision without thinking about it first
WORD FAMILY: concluded, conclusion, conclusive

component

n. A **component** is a part of something.

synonym piece   *antonym* whole

The rudder is one **component** of a ship.

EXAMPLE: a computer monitor
NON-EXAMPLE: the entire computer system
WORD FAMILY: components

conduct

n. Someone's **conduct** is the way that person acts.

synonym behavior

Their good **conduct** was rewarded.

EXAMPLE: being polite to others
NON-EXAMPLE: a person's clothes
WORD FAMILY: conducted, conducting, conducts

compute

v. When you **compute** something, you use math to figure out an answer or result.

synonyms calculate, determine

I **computed** the distance to be 50 miles.

EXAMPLE: to use arithmetic to arrive at an answer to a math problem
NON-EXAMPLE: to guess the answer to a math problem
WORD FAMILY: computation, computed, computer

consent

n. When you give your **consent**, you give your permission or approval.

synonym agreement   *antonym* refusal

May I have your **consent** to leave the room?

EXAMPLE: your dad saying "yes" to a request
NON-EXAMPLE: your dad saying "no" to a request
WORD FAMILY: consensus, consented, consenting

consequent

adj. **Consequent** means following as a result.

synonym resulting   *antonym* preceding

My illness and **consequent** absence from school lasted one week.

EXAMPLE: a lamp breaking after falling off a table
NON-EXAMPLE: a lamp staying on a table
WORD FAMILY: consequence, consequences, consequently

constitute

v. To **constitute** means to form or make up something.

synonym equal

Ten years **constitute** one decade.

EXAMPLE: twelve people make a jury
NON-EXAMPLE: trials held in the courthouse
WORD FAMILY: constituent, constituting, constitution, constitutional

considerable

adj. Something that is **considerable** is large in size, amount, or importance.

synonym large   *antonym* small

It took **considerable** effort to clean up all the trash on the beach.

EXAMPLE: the number of cars in the U.S.
NON-EXAMPLE: the number of tigers in the U.S.
WORD FAMILY: considerably

constrain

v. To **constrain** something is to hold it back or restrict it in some way.

synonym limit   *antonym* free

They used a rope to **constrain** the wild horse.

EXAMPLE: to keep an animal in a cage
NON-EXAMPLE: to open the door of a cage
WORD FAMILY: constrained, constraints, unconstrained

consist

v. To **consist** is to be made of.

synonyms include, contain

The walls **consist** of brick and stone.

EXAMPLE: making purple paint from red and blue paint
NON-EXAMPLE: using red paint
WORD FAMILY: consisted, consistent, consistently, inconsistent

construct

v. When you **construct** something, you build it.

synonym build   *antonym* destroy

We will **construct** the house in one month.

EXAMPLE: to build a new house
NON-EXAMPLE: to tear down an old house
WORD FAMILY: constructed, construction, constructive, reconstruct

constant

adj. Something that is **constant** is always the same.

synonym steady   *antonym* irregular

The kitchen faucet had a **constant** drip.

EXAMPLE: the speed of light
NON-EXAMPLE: the speed of a car
WORD FAMILY: constancy, constantly

consume

v. When you **consume** something, you use it all.

synonym spend   *antonym* save

The engine **consumes** a lot of fuel.

EXAMPLE: using all the water in a bottle
NON-EXAMPLE: saving water to drink later
WORD FAMILY: consumed, consumer, consuming, consumption

context

n. The **context** is the place and time in which something happens.

synonyms situation, setting

> They made the new theater fit the **context** of the neighborhood.

EXAMPLE: New York in 1900
NON-EXAMPLE: a map of New York
WORD FAMILY: contexts, contextual, contextualize

coordinate

v. To **coordinate** means to organize something or make the parts work together.

synonyms organize, manage

> The league manager **coordinates** twenty different games.

EXAMPLE: putting together a school newspaper
NON-EXAMPLE: writing an article
WORD FAMILY: coordinated, coordinating, coordination, coordinator

contract

n. A **contract** is a formal, legal agreement.

synonym deal

> The students signed a **contract** promising to complete the mural.

EXAMPLE: a paper signed by a boss and her employee
NON-EXAMPLE: a conversation between a boss and her employee
WORD FAMILY: contracted, contracts, contractor

core

n. The **core** is the central or most important part of something.

synonym center

> Poverty is at the **core** of the homelessness problem.

EXAMPLE: the middle of an apple
NON-EXAMPLE: the skin of an apple
WORD FAMILY: cores, coring, cored

contribute

v. When you **contribute** something, you give it to another person or group.

synonym donate *antonym* take

> Volunteers **contribute** time to the homeless shelter.

EXAMPLE: giving ten dollars to a charity
NON-EXAMPLE: taking ten dollars for allowance
WORD FAMILY: contributed, contributes, contribution, contributor

corporate

adj. Something that is **corporate** belongs to a business or large company.

synonym commercial

> The **corporate** headquarters are in Dallas, Texas.

EXAMPLE: a large computer company
NON-EXAMPLE: a child-owned lemonade stand
WORD FAMILY: corporation, corporations

convene

v. To **convene** means to come together for a meeting.

synonym gather *antonym* scatter

> The board will **convene** to discuss the budget.

EXAMPLE: meeting with a group of people
NON-EXAMPLE: taking a break from a meeting
WORD FAMILY: convention, convened, conventional, unconventional

correspond

v. For one thing to **correspond** to another, it has to be similar or closely related.

synonym connect

> The amount of fruit the tree makes **corresponds** to the amount of rain.

EXAMPLE: doing a good job and being praised
NON-EXAMPLE: doing a good job and eating lunch
WORD FAMILY: corresponded, correspondence, corresponding

create

v. If you **create** something, you make it or form it.

synonym produce   *antonym* destroy

The dancers **create** a mood of joy.

EXAMPLE: writing a first draft of a story
NON-EXAMPLE: tearing up a draft of a story
WORD FAMILY: created, creation, creative, creator, recreate

credit

n. **Credit** means praise or recognition for something you have done.

synonym praise   *antonym* blame

The players gave **credit** to the coach for the win.

EXAMPLE a trophy
NON-EXAMPLE: a warning
WORD FAMILY: credited, crediting, creditors, credits

criteria

n. **Criteria** are the standards used to judge or choose something.

synonym guidelines

What **criteria** do you use when choosing which car to buy?

EXAMPLE: a rubric a teacher uses to grade a paper
NON-EXAMPLE: making up the rules of a game as you play
WORD FAMILY: criterion

culture

n. **Culture** is the arts, customs, beliefs, and activities of a certain group of people.

synonym traditions

Respect for nature is an important part of Cherokee **culture**.

EXAMPLE: Swahili language spoken by Tanzanians
NON-EXAMPLE: mountains of Tanzania
WORD FAMILY: cultural, culturally, cultures, uncultured

data

n. **Data** are facts, figures, or other information.

synonym information

Scientists collected **data** about the volcano.

EXAMPLE: information in reference books
NON-EXAMPLE: fiction and poetry
WORD FAMILY: datum

deduce

v. When you **deduce** something, you use information to figure out an answer.

synonym interpret

These clues may help us **deduce** the boy's age.

EXAMPLE: determine word meanings by looking at their parts
NON-EXAMPLE: find word meanings in a dictionary
WORD FAMILY: deduces, deducing, deduction, deductive

define

v. To **define** something, you tell the meaning of it.

synonym explain

I **define** friendship as "always being willing to listen."

EXAMPLE: telling someone what a word means
NON-EXAMPLE: asking someone to guess what a word means
WORD FAMILY: definable, defined, definition, redefine, undefined

demonstrate

v. **Demonstrate** means to show how to do something.

synonyms teach, show

The teacher will **demonstrate** how to do the experiment.

EXAMPLE: showing how to strum a guitar
NON-EXAMPLE: telling how to strum a guitar
WORD FAMILY: demonstration, demonstrative, demonstrator

derive

v. When you **derive** something, you get it from a particular source.

synonym extract   *antonym* contribute

Scientists **derive** many medicines from tropical plants.

EXAMPLE: making gasoline from crude oil
NON-EXAMPLE: filling your car with gas
WORD FAMILY: derivation, derivative, derived, deriving

design

v. When you **design** something, you make or draw plans for it.

synonym develop

I will **design** the building by using a blueprint.

EXAMPLE: drawing a sketch of a doghouse
NON-EXAMPLE: building a doghouse without planning it first
WORD FAMILY: designed, designing, designs

distinct

adj. Something **distinct** is different from others.

synonym separate   *antonym* identical

The class sat in two **distinct** groups of girls and boys.

EXAMPLE: a person wearing orange in a crowd of people wearing purple
NON-EXAMPLE: a crowd of people wearing orange
WORD FAMILY: distinction, distinctive, distinctly, indistinct

distribute

v. When you **distribute** something, you spread it out over an area.

synonym give   *antonym* collect

He **distributes** newspapers to all the shops on Main Street.

EXAMPLE: handing out flyers to classmates
NON-EXAMPLE: picking up flyers dropped on the floor
WORD FAMILY: distributed, distribution, distributor

document

v. When you **document** something, you make a record of it.

synonym record

Every year, scientists **document** the phases of the moon.

EXAMPLE: taking notes during an experiment
NON-EXAMPLE: watching someone do an experiment
WORD FAMILY: documentation, documented, documents

dominate

v. When you **dominate** something, you control it or rule over it.

synonym overpower

Jill talked constantly in order to **dominate** the conversation.

EXAMPLE: winning a soccer game 6-to-0
NON-EXAMPLE: tying a soccer game
WORD FAMILY: dominance, dominant, dominated, domination

economy

n. A country's **economy** is the system it uses to manage resources, products, and money.

The U.S. **economy** keeps growing.

EXAMPLE: people earning and spending money
NON-EXAMPLE: people playing sports for fun
WORD FAMILY: economic, economical, economics, economist

element

n. An **element** is a part of a whole.

synonym piece

Surprise is an important **element** in a mystery story.

EXAMPLE: the stem of a plant
NON-EXAMPLE: the entire plant
WORD FAMILY: elements

emphasis

n. **Emphasis** is special importance or attention.
synonym stress

   The report put **emphasis** on health care.
EXAMPLE: the accented syllable in a word
NON-EXAMPLE: the unaccented syllable in a word
WORD FAMILY: emphasize, emphasizing, emphatic, emphatically

ensure

v. To **ensure** means to make sure of something.
synonym confirm   *antonym* neglect

   Hard work will **ensure** a good grade.
EXAMPLE: to copy your work on a disc
NON-EXAMPLE: to erase your work
WORD FAMILY: ensured, ensures, ensuring

environment

n. The **environment** is everything around you that affects the way you live.
synonym habitat

   Pollution harms the **environment**.
EXAMPLE: where you live, play, and work
NON–EXAMPLE: what you buy
WORD FAMILY: environmental, environmentalist, environmentally

equate

v. To **equate** means to think of something as equal to something else.
synonym compare

   People **equate** sunny days with happiness.
EXAMPLE: converting inches to centimeters
NON-EXAMPLE: using a ruler to measure inches
WORD FAMILY: equated, equating, equation, equations

establish

v. When you **establish** something, you set it up or start it.
synonym create *antonym* eliminate

   The bank will **establish** a branch nearby.
EXAMPLE: beginning a new company
NON-EXAMPLE: closing a business
WORD FAMILY: disestablish, established, establishing, establishment

estimate

v. To **estimate** something, you come up with a rough idea about its amount or worth.
synonym guess

   I **estimate** that the car repairs will cost about $350.00.
EXAMPLE: getting enough cash for groceries
NON-EXAMPLE: paying the grocery bill
WORD FAMILY: estimated, estimation, overestimate, underestimate

evaluate

v. When you **evaluate** something, you study it to decide its worth or value.
synonyms assess, rate

   To **evaluate** a Web site, look for useful information.
EXAMPLE: choosing which movie to see
NON-EXAMPLE: finding the movie theater
WORD FAMILY: evaluated, evaluating, evaluation, re-evaluate

evident

adj. If something is **evident**, it is very clear to see or understand.
synonym apparent   *antonym* unclear

   The crack on the mirror was **evident** to everyone.
EXAMPLE: a black glove lying in the snow
NON-EXAMPLE: a white glove lying in the snow
WORD FAMILY: evidence, evidential, evidently

exclude

v. When you **exclude** something, you leave it out.

synonym remove   *antonym* include

Pets are **excluded** from entering some restaurants.

EXAMPLE: a "Keep Out!" sign
NON-EXAMPLE: a welcome sign
WORD FAMILY: excluded, excluding, exclusion, exclusionary, exclusive

export

v. To **export** is to send things for sale or trade to another country.

synonym ship overseas   *antonym* import

Many Asian countries **export** goods to the United States.

EXAMPLE: the United States selling fish to China
NON-EXAMPLE: the United States buying sugar from Ecuador
WORD FAMILY: exported, exporter, exports

factor

n. A **factor** is something that causes an event to happen.

synonym influence

Bad weather was a **factor** in the team's loss.

EXAMPLE: weather causes school to close
NON-EXAMPLE: school opens as usual
WORD FAMILY: factored, factoring, factors

feature

n. A **feature** is a distinct part or quality of something.

synonym characteristic

One **feature** of a story is the characters' dialogue.

EXAMPLE: a girl's large brown eyes
NON-EXAMPLE: a girl's whole face
WORD FAMILY: featured, featuring, features

final

adj. Something that is **final** happens at the end.

synonym last   *antonym* first

We left the theater after the **final** scene.

EXAMPLE: the last act of a play
NON-EXAMPLE: the opening act of a play
WORD FAMILY: finalize, finalized, finalizing, finality, finally, finals

finance

n. **Finance** is the act of managing money.

synonym economics

Business majors can study **finance** in college.

EXAMPLE: keeping a budget
NON-EXAMPLE: spending money without thought
WORD FAMILY: financed, finances, financial, financier, financing

focus

n. The **focus** is the center of attention or activity.

The rock star was the **focus** of all the photographers.

EXAMPLE: a spotlight on a stage
NON-EXAMPLE: the curtains on a stage
WORD FAMILY: focused, focuses, focusing, refocus

formula

n. A **formula** is a plan or method of doing something.

synonym procedure

There is no easy **formula** for success.

EXAMPLE: 2 parts hydrogen + 1 part oxygen = water
NON-EXAMPLE: a breath of fresh air
WORD FAMILY: formulae, formulas, formulate, formulation

framework

n. A **framework** is the structure that holds something together.

synonym support

The building's **framework** was solid steel.

EXAMPLE: an outline for an essay
NON-EXAMPLE: an essay's conclusion
WORD FAMILY: frameworks

illustrate

v. When you **illustrate** something, you make it clear by using pictures or examples.

synonym clarify

To **illustrate** his recipes, the cook made a video.

EXAMPLE: drawing a map to your house
NON-EXAMPLE: telling someone directions
WORD FAMILY: illustrated, illustrates, illustration, illustrative

function

n. The **function** of an object is what it is used for.

synonym purpose

The **function** of that switch is to start the fan.

EXAMPLE: using a wrench to tighten bolts
NON-EXAMPLE: using a wrench to hammer nails
WORD FAMILY: functional, functionally, functioned, functions

immigrate

v. To **immigrate** is to go to a new country to live.

synonym resettle

People from around the world **immigrate** to the United States.

EXAMPLE: moving from the United States to Peru
NON-EXAMPLE: moving from an apartment into a house
WORD FAMILY: immigrant, immigrated, immigrates, immigration

fund

n. A **fund** is a sum of money saved for a specific purpose.

synonym savings

We started a **fund** that will help kids go to college.

EXAMPLE: money saved to buy a gift
NON-EXAMPLE: a gift that you buy
WORD FAMILY: funded, funder, funding, funds

impact

n. An **impact** is the striking of one thing against another with great force.

synonym collision

The **impact** of the rock broke the window.

EXAMPLE: two cars crashing into each other
NON-EXAMPLE: bumper-to-bumper traffic
WORD FAMILY: impacts

identify

v. To **identify** is to figure out who someone is.

synonym recognize

The police could not **identify** the person in the photograph.

EXAMPLE: picking out a person you know in a crowded room
NON-EXAMPLE: forgetting a person's name
WORD FAMILY: identifiable, identification, identified, identity

imply

v. When you **imply** something, you suggest it without actually saying it.

synonym hint   *antonym* state directly

The teacher's smile **implied** that she thought the class had done well.

EXAMPLE: giving clues about a gift you'd like
NON-EXAMPLE: stating exactly what gift you'd like
WORD FAMILY: implied, implies, implying

income

n. Your **income** is the money you earn from working.

synonym salary   *antonym* expenses

Working a second job raised her **income**.

EXAMPLE: money received from babysitting
NON-EXAMPLE: money spent on food and clothes
WORD FAMILY: incomes

injure

v. To **injure** means to hurt or harm someone or something.

synonym wound   *antonym* heal

People can slip on ice and **injure** themselves.

EXAMPLE: cutting your finger with a knife
NON-EXAMPLE: bandaging your cut finger
WORD FAMILY: injured, injures, injury, uninjured

indicate

n. When you **indicate** something, you point it out.

synonym show

The teacher will **indicate** which problem to do.

EXAMPLE: showing someone the correct road to take
NON-EXAMPLE: asking for directions
WORD FAMILY: indicated, indication, indicative, indicator

instance

n. An **instance** is an example of a specific situation or event.

synonym moment

One **instance** of pollution is toxic waste.

EXAMPLE: one particular win of a team
NON-EXAMPLE: all the wins of the team
WORD FAMILY: instances

individual

n. An **individual** is a single human being, separate from others in a group.

synonym person   *antonym* crowd

Each **individual** must buy his or her own lunch.

EXAMPLE: one player on a track team
NON-EXAMPLE: an entire track team
WORD FAMILY: individualized, individuality, individualist, individualistic

institute

v. When you **institute** something, you set it up or get it started.

synonym launch   *antonym* stop

The school will **institute** a new dress code.

EXAMPLE: starting a new program
NON-EXAMPLE: ending a program
WORD FAMILY: instituted, institutes, institution, institution

initial

adj. **Initial** means happening at the beginning.

synonym first   *antonym* last

The **initial** step is to preheat the oven.

EXAMPLE: starting a research paper
NON-EXAMPLE: handing in a research paper
WORD FAMILY: initially

interact

v. When you **interact**, you become involved with or communicate with others.

synonym socialize

Group members must **interact** with one another to complete the project.

EXAMPLE: to work with a partner
NON-EXAMPLE: to work independently
WORD FAMILY: interacting, interaction, interactive, interact

interpret

v. If you **interpret** something, you explain its meaning.

synonym clarify

I **interpret** your smile to mean you agree with me.

EXAMPLE: telling about the events in a photo
NON-EXAMPLE: taking a photo
WORD FAMILY: interpretation, interpretative, interpreted, interprets

invest

v. To **invest** means to use money to buy something that will produce a profit.

synonym spend

Some people **invest** money in the stock market.

EXAMPLE: to put your money into a new company
NON-EXAMPLE: to take your money away from a new company
WORD FAMILY: invested, investment, investor, reinvest

involve

v. To **involve** means to include someone or something.

synonym include   *antonym* exclude

The final scenes **involve** all the actors.

EXAMPLE: asking someone to join a game
NON-EXAMPLE: leaving someone out of a game
WORD FAMILY: involved, involvements, involving, uninvolved

issue

n. An **issue** is a topic or a subject people are concerned about.

synonym problem

Minimum wage was an important **issue** at the debate.

EXAMPLE: teen drinking
NON-EXAMPLE: playing sports
WORD FAMILY: issued, issues, issuing

item

n. An **item** is a separate thing or article.

synonym object

Every **item** in the store is on sale.

EXAMPLE: one of the products on a store shelf
NON-EXAMPLE: all the products on a store shelf
WORD FAMILY: itemize, itemizing, items

journal

n. A **journal** is a written record of someone's thoughts and experiences.

synonym diary

She kept a daily **journal** while she was at camp.

EXAMPLE: an explorer's field notes
NON-EXAMPLE: writing on a chalkboard
WORD FAMILY: journals

justify

v. When you **justify** something, you give good reasons for why it's the way it is.

synonym support

Nothing can **justify** the high price of this car.

EXAMPLE: explaining the reasons for your friend's actions
NON-EXAMPLE: blaming your friend for his actions
WORD FAMILY: justifiable, justification, justified, unjustified

labor

n. **Labor** is hard work performed for money.

synonym work   *antonym* rest

Repairing the fence took a day's **labor**.

EXAMPLE: building a wall
NON-EXAMPLE: lying in a hammock
WORD FAMILY: labored, laboring, labors

layer

n. A **layer** is something spread over a surface.
synonym coating

One **layer** of paint will not cover the spots.

EXAMPLE: icing on a cake
NON-EXAMPLE: a piece of cake
WORD FAMILY: layered, layering, layers

locate

v. When you **locate** something, you find it.
synonym discover

You can use the Internet to **locate** a good hotel.

EXAMPLE: arriving at the place you were looking for
NON-EXAMPLE: getting lost in a neighborhood
WORD FAMILY: located, locating, location, relocate, relocation

legal

adj. If something is **legal**, it is allowed under the law.
synonym lawful   *antonym* illegal

Legal papers proved the couple was married.

EXAMPLE: parking in marked spaces
NON-EXAMPLE: parking next to a fire hydrant
WORD FAMILY: illegal, illegality, legality, legally

maintain

v. When you **maintain** something, you keep it in good condition.
synonym care for   *antonym* neglect

The new owner will **maintain** the house.

EXAMPLE: changing the oil in your car
NON-EXAMPLE: running the car with dirty oil
WORD FAMILY: maintained, maintaining, maintains, maintenance

legislate

v. To **legislate** means to create laws.

The town will **legislate** laws to stop noise pollution.

EXAMPLE: to make rules for skateboarding on public streets
NON-EXAMPLE: to decide if skaters are following the rules
WORD FAMILY: legislated, legislation, legislative, legislature

major

adj. Something that is **major** is greater in importance than something else.
synonym main   *antonym* minor

Winning the state championship was a **major** event in her life.

EXAMPLE: a final exam
NON-EXAMPLE: a practice quiz
WORD FAMILY: majorities, majority

link

n. A **link** is anything that joins or brings together two things.
synonym connection   *antonym* separation

There is a **link** between exercise and good health.

EXAMPLE: each ring in a chain
NON-EXAMPLE: a long rope
WORD FAMILY: linkage, linkages, linked, linking, links

maximize

v. When you **maximize** something, you make it as large as possible.
synonym increase   *antonym* decrease

They use ads to **maximize** their profits.

EXAMPLE: using the full screen to view your work on the computer
NON-EXAMPLE: viewing your work in a tiny corner of the screen
WORD FAMILY: max, maximize, maximized, maximum

method

n. A **method** is a way of doing something or carrying out a plan.

synonym system

What **method** will you use to conduct the experiment?

EXAMPLE: how you study for a test
NON-EXAMPLE: your best subjects
WORD FAMILY: methodical, methodological, methodology, methods

minor

adj. Something **minor** is small in size or importance.

synonym unimportant   *antonym* major

A **minor** delay only cost us a few minutes.

EXAMPLE: a member of the chorus in a play
NON-EXAMPLE: the leading actor in a play
WORD FAMILY: minorities, minority, minors

negate

v. When you **negate** something, you undo it or make it useless.

synonym cancel out   *antonym* support

My vote for the plan **negates** your vote against the plan.

EXAMPLE: eating sweets after running
NON-EXAMPLE: running and drinking water
WORD FAMILY: negative, negated, negates, negatively, negatives

normal

adj. Something **normal** is usual or common.

synonym typical   *antonym* unusual

Seeing a UFO is not a **normal** event.

EXAMPLE: a 98.6-degree body temperature
NON-EXAMPLE: a 105-degree body temperature
WORD FAMILY: abnormal, normalize, normality, normally

obtain

v. When you **obtain** something, you get it or gain it.

synonym get   *antonym* lose

He has to pass the driving test to **obtain** a license.

EXAMPLE: buying a car
NON-EXAMPLE: selling a car
WORD FAMILY: obtainable, obtained, obtains, unobtainable

occur

v. To **occur** means to come about or to take place.

synonym happen

When will the next assembly **occur**?

EXAMPLE: presenting a concert
NON-EXAMPLE: cancelling a concert
WORD FAMILY: occurred, occurrence, occurs, reoccur

outcome

n. An **outcome** is the result or consequence of something.

synonym effect

The **outcome** of the rainstorm was a flood.

EXAMPLE: a team's score at the end of a game
NON-EXAMPLE: a team's score at halftime
WORD FAMILY: outcomes

participate

v. When you **participate** in something, you take part in it.

synonym join in

I won't have time to **participate** in the meeting.

EXAMPLE: joining a club in your school
NON-EXAMPLE: not joining a club in your school
WORD FAMILY: participant, participation

partner

n. A **partner** is someone who does an activity with you.

synonym ally

Each dancer had to find another **partner**.

EXAMPLE: your best friend
NON-EXAMPLE: a group of friends
WORD FAMILY: partners, partnership

perceive

v. When you **perceive** something, you notice or understand it in a special way.

synonym comprehend   *antonym* misunderstand

Some say that dogs can **perceive** people's feelings.

EXAMPLE: solving math problems quickly
NON-EXAMPLE: struggling with solving math problems
WORD FAMILY: perceived, perceives

percent

n. A **percent** is one part or unit of each hundred.

Sixty-three **percent** of all high school students go to college.

EXAMPLE: half of a pizza
NON-EXAMPLE: two pizzas
WORD FAMILY: percentage, percentages

period

n. A **period** is a portion of time during which certain things happen.

synonym span

For a **period** of 35 years after WWII, many countries were distrustful of one another.

EXAMPLE: the Victorian Age
NON-EXAMPLE: all of recorded history
WORD FAMILY: periodic, periodical, periodically, periods

philosophy

n. A **philosophy** is a set of beliefs that a person has and always follows.

synonym thinking

His **philosophy** is that people should always help one another.

EXAMPLE: the beliefs that guide your life
NON-EXAMPLE: rules set by others you must follow
WORD FAMILY: philosopher, philosophical, philosophize, philosophizing

physical

adj. **Physical** means relating to the body.

He built up his **physical** strength by running everyday.

EXAMPLE: working out at a gym
NON-EXAMPLE: thinking about a poem
WORD FAMILY: physically

policy

n. A **policy** is a plan or set of guidelines used to make decisions about certain actions.

synonym procedure

It is a good **policy** to listen before you act.

EXAMPLE: your school's dress code
NON-EXAMPLE: your school's location
WORD FAMILY: policies

positive

adj. Something **positive** is favorable or helpful.

synonym good   *antonym* negative

Forgiving someone is a **positive** act.

EXAMPLE: helping a child who falls
NON-EXAMPLE: ignoring at a child who falls
WORD FAMILY: positively

potential

adj. **Potential** means likely to happen.
synonym possible *antonym* unlikely

The broken glass is a **potential** hazard.

EXAMPLE: a drama student becoming an actor
NON-EXAMPLE: a drama student winning the lottery
WORD FAMILY: potentially

proceed

v. To **proceed** means to move forward or keep on following a course of action.
synonym continue *antonym* stop

Proceed to the next block and then turn left.

EXAMPLE: walking through a park
NON-EXAMPLE: resting on a bench
WORD FAMILY: proceeded, proceeding, proceeds

previous

adj. **Previous** means happening before or earlier than something else.
synonym prior *antonym* following

The fishing was better in **previous** summers.

EXAMPLE: the person who had a job before you
NON-EXAMPLE: the person who you ask for a job
WORD FAMILY: previously

process

n. A **process** is a series of steps that occur in order to bring about a specific result.
synonym procedure

The digestive **process** can take several days.

EXAMPLE: following a recipe
NON-EXAMPLE: eating dinner
WORD FAMILY: processed, processes, processing

primary

adj. Something **primary** is first in importance.
synonym main *antonym* minor

The **primary** goal of fire drills is to learn how to get away from a fire safely.

EXAMPLE: a leader of a group
NON-EXAMPLE: a member of a group
WORD FAMILY: primarily

proportion

n. A **proportion** is a part of a whole.
synonym piece

A small **proportion** of people liked the concert.

EXAMPLE: a family in a neighborhood
NON-EXAMPLE: an entire neighborhood
WORD FAMILY: disproportionate, proportional, proportionally, proportions

principle

n. A **principle** is a basic law or truth behind something.
synonym rule

Everyone should believe in the **principle** of fairness.

EXAMPLE: equality
NON-EXAMPLE: enthusiasm
WORD FAMILY: principled, principles

publish

v. **Publish** means to prepare printed or electronic material to share with others.
synonym make public

The newspaper will **publish** her article.

EXAMPLE: copying your story for classmates to read
NON-EXAMPLE: keeping your story private
WORD FAMILY: published, publisher, publishing, unpublished

purchase

v. When you **purchase** something, you pay for it.

synonym buy   *antonym* sell

   I will **purchase** a cake for the party.

EXAMPLE: paying for a shirt
NON-EXAMPLE: making a shirt
WORD FAMILY: purchased, purchaser, purchases, purchasing

range

v. A **range** is a set of all the possible activities or topics in the same category.

synonym scope

   She felt the role was well within her **range** as an actress.

EXAMPLE: courses you can take in college
NON-EXAMPLE: one course
WORD FAMILY: ranged, ranges, ranging

react

v. When you **react**, you respond or act in response to something.

synonym answer

   Firefighters must **react** quickly to an alarm.

EXAMPLE: removing your hand from a hot stove
NON-EXAMPLE: ignoring something or someone
WORD FAMILY: reacted, reaction, reactionary, reactivate, reactor

region

n. A **region** is a large space or area.

synonym territory

   The polar **region** is extremely cold.

EXAMPLE: your surrounding states
NON-EXAMPLE: your backyard
WORD FAMILY: regional, regionally, regions

register

v. When you **register**, you sign up for something.

synonym enroll

   When you are 18, you can **register** to vote.

EXAMPLE: entering a raffle
NON-EXAMPLE: signing a check
WORD FAMILY: deregistration, registered, registering, registration

regulate

v. When you **regulate** something, you control it.

synonym govern

   These valves **regulate** the flow of water.

EXAMPLE: setting a thermostat to 70 degrees
NON-EXAMPLE: installing a thermostat
WORD FAMILY: regulated, regulates, regulating, regulation

revelant

adj. Something that is **relevant** is related to the topic being discussed.

synonym significant   *antonym* unrelated

   Shoe prints at the crime site are **relevant** facts.

EXAMPLE: a science class talking about chemistry
NON-EXAMPLE: an English class talking about math
WORD FAMILY: irrelevance, irrelevant, relevance

rely

v. To **rely** on something is to trust or count on it.

synonym depend

   People **rely** on watches and clocks to tell time.

EXAMPLE: leaning on someone's shoulders
NON-EXAMPLE: working independently
WORD FAMILY: reliability, reliable, reliance, relies, relying, unreliable

remove

v. To **remove** something, you take it off or take it away from a person or place.

synonym eliminate   *antonym* add

No one should **remove** this sign from the wall.

EXAMPLE: weeding the garden
NON-EXAMPLE: planting flowers
WORD FAMILY: removable, removal, removed, removes, removing

resource

n. A **resource** is something useful that can be depended upon when needed.

synonym asset

Oil is an important natural **resource**.

EXAMPLE: a librarian
NON-EXAMPLE: a "Quiet" sign
WORD FAMILY: resourceful, resources, unresourceful

require

v. When you **require** something, you need it or insist on having it.

synonym demand

Some schools **require** students to wear uniforms.

EXAMPLE: taking a driver's test for a license
NON-EXAMPLE: driving a car with a stick-shift
WORD FAMILY: required, requirement, requires, requiring

respond

v. When you **respond** to something, you answer it.

synonym reply

I will **respond** to your questions when I have all the facts.

EXAMPLE: explaining why you are late
NON-EXAMPLE: remaining quiet
WORD FAMILY: responded, response, responsive, unresponsive

research

v. When you **research** something, you look for information about it and gather all the facts.

synonym investigate

Scientists **research** different kinds of cancer to try to find a cure.

EXAMPLE: looking for the best tickets for a concert
NON-EXAMPLE: listening to a concert
WORD FAMILY: researched, researcher, researches, researching

restrict

v. To **restrict** means to keep something within certain limits.

synonym limit

Parents **restrict** the amount of candy their children eat.

EXAMPLE: having a curfew
NON-EXAMPLE: not having a curfew
WORD FAMILY: restricted, restricting, restriction, unrestricted

reside

v. When you **reside** in a place, you live or stay there.

synonym live

People who **reside** near coastal areas should be aware of hurricanes.

EXAMPLE: living in a house
NON-EXAMPLE: traveling from place to place
WORD FAMILY: resided, resident, residential, residents, residing

role

n. A **role** is a part played by someone or something.

synonym job

My favorite actor was cast in the starring **role**.

EXAMPLE: a character in a play
NON-EXAMPLE: the title of the play
WORD FAMILY: roles

scheme

n. A **scheme** is a sneaky plan.

synonym plot

> The **scheme** to get back at Russ was to put all his CDs in the wrong cases.

EXAMPLE: a plan to hide your brother's shoes
NON-EXAMPLE: a plan to build a treehouse
WORD FAMILY: schematic, schemed, schemes, scheming

seek

v. When you **seek** something, you try to get it.

synonyms search for, pursue

> I had to **seek** a doctor's advise about my cut.

EXAMPLE: asking for a job
NON-EXAMPLE: not looking for a job
WORD FAMILY: seeking, seeks, sought

section

n. A **section** is a part of something.

synonym piece   *antonym* whole

> A **section** of the path was worn away.

EXAMPLE: part of an orange
NON-EXAMPLE: the whole orange
WORD FAMILY: sectioned, sectioning, sections

select

v. When you **select** something, you choose it.

synonym pick

> Which fabric did the designer **select**?

EXAMPLE: deciding who to include on a team
NON-EXAMPLE: asking who the team captain is
WORD FAMILY: selected, selection, selective, selector

sector

n. A **sector** is a part or portion of an area or society.

synonym zone

> Citizens monitored the **sector** of town with the most crime.

EXAMPLE: the French Quarter in the city of New Orleans
NON-EXAMPLE: the whole city of New Orleans
WORD FAMILY: sectors

sequence

n. The **sequence** is the order in which things happen or follow each other.

synonym order

> The next number in the **sequence** 1-2-3 is 4.

EXAMPLE: the chain of events in a story
NON-EXAMPLE: a list of random events
WORD FAMILY: sequenced, sequences, sequential, sequentially

secure

v. When you **secure** something, you make sure it's safe.

synonym protect   *antonym* harm

> I will **secure** the jewelry in a safe.

EXAMPLE: to keep poison away from children
NON-EXAMPLE: to let children play near a pool
WORD FAMILY: insecure, secures, securities, security

sex

n. A person's **sex** describes whether he or she is male or female.

synonym gender

> What is the **sex** of their first child?

EXAMPLE: boy or girl
NON-EXAMPLE: tall or short
WORD FAMILY: sexes, sexism, sexual, sexuality, sexually

shift

v. When you **shift** something, you change its position.

synonym relocate   *antonym* keep

Let's **shift** our seats so we can see better.

EXAMPLE: moving a plant from a table to a window
NON-EXAMPLE: keeping a plant on the table
WORD FAMILY: shifted, shifting, shifts

source

n. A **source** is the original place something began.

synonym beginning   *antonym* end

The **source** of the argument was forgotten in time.

EXAMPLE: a well
NON-EXAMPLE: a glass of water
WORD FAMILY: sourced, sources, sourcing

significant

adj. Something **significant** is important.

synonym important   *antonym* unimportant

Cars are a **significant** part of modern life.

EXAMPLE: graduating from high school
NON-EXAMPLE: buying your lunch at school
WORD FAMILY: insignificant, significance, significantly, signifies

specific

adj. If something is **specific**, it is exact.

synonym precise   *antonym* vague

Because her directions were **specific**, we arrived right on time.

EXAMPLE: a beagle
NON-EXAMPLE: any dog
WORD FAMILY: specifically, specification, specifications, specificity

similar

adj. If things are **similar**, they are alike.

synonym alike   *antonym* different

Brothers and sisters often look **similar**.

EXAMPLE: Mars and Earth
NON-EXAMPLE: Earth and the sun
WORD FAMILY: dissimilar, similarity, similarly

specify

v. When you **specify** something, you name it or state it clearly.

synonym indicate   *antonym* generalize

Please **specify** your date of birth.

EXAMPLE: telling a friend your sister's name
NON-EXAMPLE: telling a friend that you have a sibling
WORD FAMILY: specified, specifies, specifying, unspecified

site

n. A **site** is a location or place.

synonym place

The treaty was signed at this **site**.

EXAMPLE: a shopping mall
NON-EXAMPLE: three o'clock
WORD FAMILY: sites

strategy

n. A **strategy** is a careful plan for reaching a goal.

synonym plan

The coach had a new **strategy** for winning the next game.

EXAMPLE: how to make money over the summer
NON-EXAMPLE: driving to the mall
WORD FAMILY: strategic, strategically, strategies, strategize

structure

n. The **structure** is the way different parts are put together to build or organize something.

synonym arrangement

In a story's **structure**, the characters and the setting are described in the beginning.

EXAMPLE: the frame of a house
NON-EXAMPLE: a single plank of wood
WORD FAMILY: structural, structures, restructure, unstructured

technical

adj. **Technical** relates to special and scientific skills.

synonym specialized   *antonym* general

Electronics is a highly **technical** field.

EXAMPLE: using a calculator
NON-EXAMPLE: counting on one's fingers
WORD FAMILY: technically

sufficient

adj. If something is **sufficient**, it is enough for the purpose.

synonym adequate   *antonym* unsatisfactory

To make an apple pie, two pounds of apples are **sufficient**.

EXAMPLE: eight hours of sleep every night
NON-EXAMPLE: three hours of sleep every night
WORD FAMILY: sufficiency, insufficient, insufficiently, sufficiently

technique

n. A **technique** is a particular way of doing something.

synonym procedure

Her **technique** is to microwave the chicken two minutes before putting it on the grill.

EXAMPLE: taking piano lessons
NON-EXAMPLE: plinking on a piano
WORD FAMILY: techniques

survey

n. A **survey** is a broad or general look at a subject or situation.

synonym overview

The article included a **survey** of some of the most popular spy movies.

EXAMPLE: an encyclopedia entry about a musician
NON-EXAMPLE: an entire book about one musician
WORD FAMILY: surveyed, surveying, surveys

technology

n. **Technology** is the study and use of science for gathering and applying information.

Computer **technology** is constantly changing.

EXAMPLE: using the Internet
NON-EXAMPLE: taking notes in a notebook
WORD FAMILY: technological, technologically

task

n. A **task** is a certain job that needs to be done.
synonym job

One **task** of a geologist is to identify types of minerals.

EXAMPLE: counting supplies in a lab
NON-EXAMPLE: looking at supplies in a lab
WORD FAMILY: tasks

text

n. **Text** is the words in something you read.
synonym content

The full **text** of the article is available online.

EXAMPLE: the words in a book
NON-EXAMPLE: the pictures in a book
WORD FAMILY: texts, textual

theory

n. A **theory** is an idea or belief based on facts.

synonym hypothesis

> Scientists perform tests to see if a **theory** is true.

EXAMPLE: Darwin's ideas about human evolution
NON-EXAMPLE: the number of primate species
WORD FAMILY: theoretical, theoretically, theories, theorists

tradition

n. A **tradition** is a belief or a custom handed down from generation to generation.

synonym custom

> It is a family **tradition** to eat turkey on Thanksgiving.

EXAMPLE: celebrating a birthday
NON-EXAMPLE: learning how to play guitar
WORD FAMILY: traditional, traditionally, traditions

transfer

v. When you **transfer** something, you move or carry it from one place to another.

synonym transport

> His friend might **transfer** money from one bank to another.

EXAMPLE: moving a desk from one office to another
NON-EXAMPLE: keeping a desk in one place
WORD FAMILY: transferable, transference, transferred, transfers

valid

adj. Something that is **valid** is usable and acceptable under the law.

synonym lawful   *antonym* invalid

> The check was not **valid** after 90 days.

EXAMPLE: an unexpired driver's license
NON-EXAMPLE: an expired license
WORD FAMILY: invalidate, validate, validated, validating, validity

vary

v. When you **vary** something, you change it to make it different.

synonym differ

> The amount of daylight will **vary** by season.

EXAMPLE: to eat something different for lunch everyday
NON-EXAMPLE: to always eat the same lunch
WORD FAMILY: invariably, variables, variant, variation, varied

volume

n. The **volume** is the size or amount of something.

synonym amount

> A fire hose pumps out a great **volume** of water.

EXAMPLE: 10 L of water
NON-EXAMPLE: a bunch of grapes
WORD FAMILY: volumes

Chapter 4 · READING STRATEGIES

Your Job as a Reader

"**I**n the case of books, the point is not to see how many of them you can get through, but rather how many can get through you—how many you can make your own."

—MORTIMER ADLER

Be an Active Reader

Good readers know that they need different tools at hand to open up the meaning of different texts. Often, you use more than one. It all comes down to knowing which tools to use to help you be an active reader.

- Know what tools help you hold your thinking. Sometimes you may want to mark the text or use self-stick notes. Other times you may want to make and use a graphic organizer.

- Know what strategies you have in your mental toolbox.

- Know what you are reading. Some tools are better than others for different texts.

- Be flexible. Sometimes you need to drop one tool for another—switching or adding strategies gets easier the more you read.

How Are You an Active Reader?

" I ask myself questions and then look for answers when I read. This gets me thinking a lot. "

—Ahote

" As I'm reading I highlight things I want to remember. Then I can find them later. When I can't write directly in the book, I put a self-stick note beside the important ideas and information. "

—Alondra

" I like to use a graphic organizer while I read. Then I can keep track of information and see how things fit together. "

—James

" When I read nonfiction, I think about the information the writer gives and how it fits with what I know about the topic and other things I've read. "

—Danielle

You can download more Readers Talk tips.  hbgoodreaders.com

Step Into Reading

Where do you take charge? Is it on the basketball court? In the science lab? On the dance floor? Good readers step into reading ready to take charge. They know what tools to use to get the most out of what they read.

How to Be an Active Reader

Good readers know they have to keep thinking while they're reading. Here's how to read actively:

- **Get in the Driver's Seat** Take charge even before you start reading. Look through the text quickly to get an idea of what it will be about and what you might learn. Then decide on your purpose, or reason, for reading.

- **Stay in Control** While you're reading, stop now and then to ask yourself: *Does this make sense?* Write questions and comments on self-stick notes or mark up the text. Use a graphic organizer to group important information.

- **Pause and Reflect** Use ideas from the writer, along with your responses, to decide what you're going to take away from the text.

- **Choose the Right Strategy** Use the strategies in your mental toolbox. Be flexible and add or switch strategies.

FOCUS POINT Are you an active reader? Find out by taking the survey on the next page.

ARE YOU AN ACTIVE READER?

Directions: Download the survey at hbgoodreaders.com and complete it twice—once **before** you've read this chapter, and once **after** you've read it. Compare your answers and ratings.

Before you read a text, do you . . .	✔ Yes	✔ No
look at it quickly to get an idea of what it will be about?		
decide why you are going to read it?		
choose a graphic organizer (outline, Venn diagram, etc.)		
While you're reading, do you . . .	✔ Yes	✔ No
use a graphic organizer?		
write questions and comments on self-stick notes?		
highlight or underline the parts you want to remember?		
read with your purpose in mind?		
check in with yourself to make sure you're understanding the text?		
reread parts that are unclear?		
put the writer's ideas in your own words?		
think about the main ideas?		
pause to sum up what you've read?		
ask questions about the text?		
use your senses to imagine what the writer is describing?		
try to figure out things the writer doesn't say directly?		
think about what the text reminds you of?		
put together new information with old information to come up with new ideas?		
After you read, do you . . .	✔ Yes	✔ No
feel as though you've met your purpose for reading?		
go back and review your questions and comments?		
think about what you've learned and if it has changed your thinking?		

There are many ways to be an active reader. On the lines below, write some other things you do to take charge when you step into reading.

_____   _____

_____   _____

Get in the Driver's Seat

You have something to read, and your job is to understand it. You know that pronouncing the words one at a time is not enough. What do you do? Get in the driver's seat. Here's how.

THE MONARCH'S LONG JOURNEY

FEBRUARY: Nuevo León, México
When I think of paradise, I envision thousands of monarch butterflies resting in trees. So here I am in paradise. The ovamel trees have been covered for months with wintering monarchs, wings overlapping wings. Here, I wait for them to begin their annual migration north. I'm studying one of nature's great mysteries: How do the monarchs find their way back?

MARCH: Stephenville, Texas
We spotted larvae on the milkweed plants today. We always have lots of butterflies, but it's the first time we spotted larvae, or eggs!

APRIL: Baton Rouge, Louisiana
Monarch butterflies are migrating near our trailer park right now. I counted 14 monarchs during a picnic yesterday. Their journey north continues.

MAY: Florissant, Missouri
My biology students and I are tracking a spectacular migration that's moving through Missouri right now. No other species migrates like the monarchs of North America. This two-way journey covers 3,000 miles. They are the only type of butterfly to make this long, annual migration. How do they do it?

Plan Your Reading

Preview and Tap Into What You Know

" I know that some butterflies migrate long distances. "

Preview and Predict

" This looks like someone's observation log, so maybe the writer is studying the butterflies' migration. "

Preview and Set a Purpose

" I want to find out where the butterflies go and how long it takes them. "

Stay in Control

Just like any good driver, you need to be in control. You drive the car; the car doesn't drive you. The key to controlling your reading is to keep thinking and reading actively. Here's how:

Check in With Yourself

- Stop from time to time to make sure you're getting the most out of the text—that you're achieving your purpose.

- As you're reading, ask yourself: *Does this make sense?* Try explaining the writer's ideas in your own words. If the text is confusing, stop and clear up the confusion.

Science Report

Where Did the Martian Water Go?

What happened to the water on Mars?

The more that scientists learn about the Red Planet, the more eager they are to solve the mystery: *Where did all the water go?* The question matters. If there once was water on Mars, then the planet might have supported life. To find the answer, scientists ask other questions.

At one time did Mars have a warmer climate, with a thicker atmosphere? In the late 1980s and early 1990s, scientists discovered features that appeared to be river valleys and ancient lakeshores on the planet's surface. Water could have once existed in those locations.

Could reservoirs of water be out of sight, maybe deep below the planet's surface? Scientists theorize that water might exist in the form of liquid or ice underneath the planet's surface. In December, 2006, photographs from a Mars rover showed that the landscape had changed since earlier photographs. Are those changes proof that water sometimes flows on the planet?

Check In With Yourself

" I want to know where all the water went. I'm going to look for the answer as I read."

" At first I wasn't sure what *features* meant. So I read on and saw the clues *river valleys* and *lakeshores*."

" Where did the water go? I didn't find a definite answer—just theories."

Stay in Control, continued

Use Self-Stick Notes

When you write about what you are reading, it's as if you and the author are having a private conversation. You can't always write in the book and, sometimes, you might not want to. Stay in control by using self-stick notes.

Magazine Article

NATURE'S MARVELS: ANIMAL COMMUNICATION

Elephants hear through their feet.

Humans may depend on wires, cables, screens, transmitters, and satellites to send messages across the miles. Not so with animals. Creatures who roam the land and seas have developed streamlined methods of communication.

Hearing Sounds With Feet

In the African bush a female elephant rumbles a greeting. Her message travels to a mate six miles away. Elephants use both low frequency and high frequency sounds. They communicate warnings, greetings, mating calls, food location, excitement, and fear. The low frequency sounds, called stomach rumbles, actually come from an elephant's throat.

Amazingly, elephants "hear" other elephants' rumbles through their feet. The sounds pass through the air and travel even farther through the ground. Elephants feel the sounds coming up the ground through their feet. They can detect tremors from rainstorms or sense stampeding animals. They also identify the calls of other elephants.

Write questions and comments.

What does the writer mean by "streamlined"?

Trap what you want to remember.

Elephants can communicate many things.

Able to feel low frequency sounds with their feet

Review Your Notes

Try to answer your questions. What will you remember?

Use a Graphic Organizer

You're reading actively and focusing on your purpose. But how do you keep track of all the important ideas and information you come across—especially when you're reading a long text? One way is to use a graphic organizer.

When to Use a Graphic Organizer Graphic organizers group information in a visual way. They let you see how ideas from one or more texts are related to each other. Use a graphic organizer when you need to analyze, organize, and keep track of how things fit together.

How to Choose a Graphic Organizer Choose a graphic organizer that matches both the type of text you're reading and your purpose. (See pages 230–237 to find a variety of graphic organizers for different texts and purposes.)

Suppose you're reading a long nonfiction text about how animals communicate. You preview and notice many paragraphs, facts, and details. Your purpose is to answer your own question: *How do animals communicate?* So, you decide to use a Main Idea Diagram like the one shown below.

Main Idea and Details Diagram

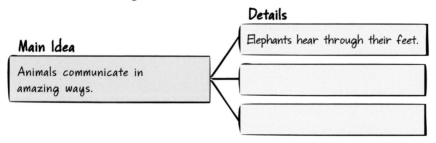

How to Use the Organizer After Reading Review the graphic organizer to produce your own conclusions and new ideas from what you read.

Stay in Control, continued

Mark the Text

Marking the text is a good way to read actively. When you're allowed to write on the book pages, use pens, pencils, and markers. Try these techniques:

- **Highlight Important Ideas**
  Highlight words, phrases, and sentences that you think are important. After you highlight, you can easily spot those key ideas and jog your memory. This is a great way to review when you study for a test.

- **Underline Phrases That Spark a Question**
  Underline words or phrases that bring up questions in your mind. Run that line right into the margin and add a question. Then read on. Later, check back and try to answer your questions.

- **Keep Track of What You Want to Remember**
  While you are reading, ask yourself: *What is worth remembering?* You react by summarizing the main idea, asking questions, and making personal connections. Write notes in the margin as you read. Look back at your notes to keep track of what's important to you.

Thumbprint

—EVE MERRIAM

In the heel of my thumb
are whorls, whirls, wheels
in a unique design:
mine alone.
What a treasure to own!

These are what thumbprints look like.

My own flesh, my own feelings.
No other, however grand or base,
can ever contain the same.
My signature,
thumbing the pages of my time.

She repeats "my" over and over. Important idea = Each person is unique.

How is time like pages?

My universe key,
my singularity.
Impress, implant,
I am myself,
of all my atom parts I am the sum.
And out of my blood and my brain
I make my own interior weather,
my own sun and rain.
Imprint my mark upon the world,
whatever I shall become.

I make my own good and bad moods. I need to remember this!

Does this have more than one meaning?

Stay in Control, continued

Expand the Conversation

You can expand your conversation with the author by bringing another reader into the picture. Here's how to exchange marked texts or notes with a classmate:

1 Mark Your Page

Read a selection, such as a poem, on your own. Be in control by marking the text with questions, comments, and other connections.

2 Exchange Pages and React

Exchange pages with a classmate. Read and build on your classmate's notes. Answer his or her questions. Add your own comments. Confirm and challenge his or her ideas.

3 Read Your Classmate's Reponses

Now trade pages again to see what your classmate has written. Did you get some answers to your questions? Did your classmate react to the text in the same way you did? Talk with your partner about your responses to expand the conversation even more.

Thumbprint

—EVE MERRIAM

In the heel of my thumb
are whorls, whirls, wheels
in a unique design:
mine alone.
What a treasure to own!
My own flesh, my own feelings.
No other, however grand or base,
can ever contain the same.
My signature,
thumbing the pages of my time.
My universe key,
my singularity.
Impress, implant,
I am myself,
of all my atom parts I am the sum.
And out of my blood and my brain
I make my own interior weather,
my own sun and rain.
Imprint my mark upon the world,
whatever I shall become.

These are what thumbprints look like. They all start with the same sound, too!

She repeats "my" over and over. Important idea = Each person is unique.

I agree.

How is time like pages?

Your life is like your story.

Blood and brain—ugh! I make my own good and bad moods. I need to remember this!

Yes, it's important.

Does this have more than one meaning?

Your mark is the print on your thumb and the effect you have on people.

Pause and Reflect

While you were reading, you were in control. You read with a purpose, wrote comments and questions, and used graphic organizers to group important information. Now it's time to pause and reflect on what you've read.

Decide What to Think

Use ideas from the text, along with your responses, to decide what you're going to take away from the reading. Review your notes and graphic organizers as you answer these questions:

- How do the ideas fit together?

- What did the text remind you of?

- Were all your questions answered? What new questions, if any, do you have?

- How will you use the writer's ideas in the future? Do they change your thinking in any way?

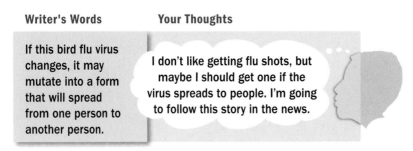

Writer's Words

If this bird flu virus changes, it may mutate into a form that will spread from one person to another person.

Your Thoughts

I don't like getting flu shots, but maybe I should get one if the virus spreads to people. I'm going to follow this story in the news.

Read the passage on the next page. Then pause and reflect. Tell your classmates what you decide to think.

HEALTH WATCH The Flu Pandemic

Microscopic Assassins

Virus, in Latin, means "poison." And poisons they are. Viruses cause untold suffering throughout the world. They cause colds and diseases like rabies and AIDS. Yet their origin remains a mystery.

Viruses are invaders and parasites. They cannot reproduce alone. They must occupy another living cell to reproduce. Scientists suspect they evolved like all parasites do, with their hosts.

Unfortunately, viruses can mutate quickly. While the human body tries to fight back, the cunning virus changes. Like a defenseless soldier in a bewildering battleground, the human body doesn't recognize this ever-changing enemy. The results have been devastating. Flu epidemics occur three or four times each century. Millions of people die.

The Bird Flu

Now scientists are preparing for a new battle. A simple virus that infects birds has also infected

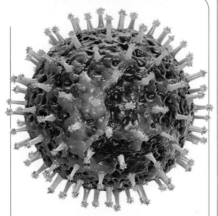

Scientific illustration of bird flu virus known as "H5N1"

some humans. People have no natural defense against viruses that contaminate animals. Right now, people get sick when they come into contact with an infected bird. If this bird flu virus changes, it may mutate into a form that will spread from one person to another person. The toll will be heavy. Estimates reach as high as 2,000,000 deaths if such an epidemic occurs.

Scientists prepare for battle, hoping to arm the population with its best weapons: vaccines against the changing bird flu virus. In time, the battle may be won.

Pause and Reflect, continued

Keep a Journal or Log

Logs and journals are another good way to reflect on your reading. You can use them to record the writer's words and your own thoughts and feelings, page-by-page or part-by-part. See how one reader uses a double-entry journal.

What the Text Says	What I Think, Feel, and Know
"Estimates reach as high as 2,000,000 deaths if such an epidemic occurs."	I didn't realize that a virus would be able to kill so many people. Now I realize how serious preventing an epidemic is.
"Scientists prepare for battle, hoping to arm the population with its best weapons: vaccines against the changing bird flu virus. In time, the battle may be won."	I heard that scientists are having trouble making enough of the vaccine for everyone in the U.S. Maybe that's why the writer says the battle may be won.

Talk It Through

Different readers bring different experiences to a text. They also have different reactions to it. After reading, discuss the text with other readers. Use these questions to guide your discussion:

- How would you briefly describe the text to someone who hasn't read it?

- What are the most important ideas or events?

- Were any parts confusing? How did you clear up the confusion?

- What will you remember most from reading the text?

Choose the Right Strategy

Good readers have a whole set of strategies to choose from when they read. Learn these strategies in the rest of this chapter. Then, choose the strategies that work best for you.

▶ Plan and Monitor Your Reading

You preview the text so you know what to expect. While you're reading, you read with a purpose in mind and make sure you understand what the writer is saying.

▶ Determine Importance

You focus on what matters—what the writer wants you to take away from the text and what you want to remember. You sum up what you've read and make the ideas your own.

▶ Ask Questions

You wonder about the characters and events in a story or ideas and information in nonfiction texts. To answer some questions, you bring in your own experience.

▶ Visualize

You use your five senses to experience what the author is describing.

▶ Make Inferences

You put together what the text says, with what you know, to figure out things the author doesn't tell you directly.

▶ Make Connections

You think about what the text reminds you of and use it to form new knowledge. You link different texts by the ideas, author's style, and genre.

▶ Synthesize

You put together information from different places and come up with new understandings. You decide what you want to believe and take a position.

Plan and Monitor Your Reading

Suppose you're taking a road trip with your two best friends. You've been planning for weeks—which routes to drive, where to stop, and what music to take. Then you hit the road. You keep track of where you are and check the gas tank. Before long, you see that the road you wanted to take is closed. So you have to figure out an alternate route.

Reading is a lot like traveling. You have to plan and think about what's ahead of you. While you're reading, you keep track of where you are and deal with any confusions or new conditions that you meet along the way. Look at the next page to see how some teens navigate the roads of reading.

How Do You Plan and Track Your Reading?

" Even before I start to read, I try to figure out what the text is about. I look at the title, headings, pictures, and captions. "

—Michelle

" Before I start reading something, I think about why I'm reading it. What do I hope to get from this particular selection? "

—Antonio

" Sometimes when I read, I realize I'm a little mixed up. So then I go back and reread the parts that confuse me. That helps me understand what I'm reading. "

—San

" When I come across a word I don't know, I keep on reading to see if I really need to know the word. Sometimes I do, so I look it up. But a lot of the time I can just keep going and still understand what I'm reading. "

—Iman

You can download more Readers Talk tips.  hbgoodreaders.com

Make Your Own Road Map

What's It Like?

When you're driving, road signs help you plan for what lies ahead. You decide to slow down or watch the road more carefully. When you read, it's also important to plan for what lies ahead.

Plan for What Lies Ahead

Doing some planning before you read gives you an idea of what lies ahead. Here's how to plan for your reading:

- **Preview** Look ahead at what you're about to read. Quickly scan, or look over, the title and any headings, photos, captions, or words in boldface. These will give you an idea of what the selection is about. Also, skim the first few paragraphs to determine whether it's fiction or nonfiction.

- **Make predictions** Use the preview information to decide what you might learn about the topic and the kind of things you'll be reading about. For example, are the events real or made-up?

- **Think about your purpose** Ask yourself: *Why am I reading this selection? What do I hope to get from it?*

FOCUS POINT Read the passage on the next page and each reader's plan. How do they preview the selection? Which reader makes a prediction? Which one sets a purpose for reading?

BESSIE COLEMAN:
AVIATION PIONEER

She was a woman, and she was black. And in 1919, no aviation school in the U.S. would accept her. That did not stop Bessie Coleman. As the world's first female African American pilot, she was a true pioneer.

Realizing Her Dream

The air war in Europe during World War I inspired Coleman to learn how to fly. But realizing her dream in the United States proved difficult.

So, in 1919, Coleman turned to Robert S. Abbott. He had started the most influential newspaper in the U.S. for African Americans. He urged her to apply to a school outside of the U.S. Coleman followed his advice. The French school of aviation accepted her.

After taking French lessons, Coleman sailed to France in November. Her dream came true a few years later on June 15, 1921. She earned her pilot's license. For fifteen years, she worked as a stunt and exhibition flier.

Bessie Coleman in 1922

The Reader's Plan

> From the title, heading, and photo, I think this is going to be about a real person. I think it's going to tell the true story of someone's life in the 1920s.

> I read the title and the first paragraph. Now I'm going to keep reading to find out how an African American woman became a pilot so long ago.

Preview

When you **preview**, you take a quick look at what you're about to read. Previewing gets you in the right frame of mind for your reading.

What's the Topic?

Before reading, ask yourself: *What is this going to be about?* You can get a pretty good idea about the **topic** by scanning, or looking at, features in the text: the title, headings, pictures, and boldfaced words. Skimming, or glancing quickly, through a few paragraphs will give you some hints, too.

What's the Genre?

To get an idea about the major **genre**, or type of writing, ask yourself: *What kind of writing is this—fiction or nonfiction?* When you get an idea about genre, you know what to expect. If something is fiction, for example, you'll be ready to read about made-up characters and events. If something is nonfiction, you'll expect facts about real people and events.

Let's use this checklist to figure out the major genre of the passages on the next page.

Fiction	Nonfiction
Look for these elements:	Look for these elements:
☐ plot with events that lead up to characters solving a problem	☐ mainly factual information about real people and events; may include dates and statistics
☐ made-up characters, actions, and dialogue	☐ headings, subheadings, and words in bold type
☐ a setting—where and when the story takes place—could be real or imaginary	☐ key information in photos, captions, maps, graphs, diagrams, and time lines
☐ illustrations or photographs	

Which of these elements appear in the texts on page 223?

Spain's New World Conquests

Spanish explorers arrived in America in 1521. They conquered Native Americans and called the region *New Spain*.

New Spain once included Mexico and most of the western United States.

Exploring Northward

In 1540, the ruler of New Spain wanted to expand his power. He sent Francisco Vázquez de Coronado north to find the legendary "Seven Golden Cities of Cíbola."

GOLD, BLOOD, AND TEARS   17

By seven in the morning, the heat was already unbearable. A pink haze covered the sky. Sand and stone glistened. Some animals gathered around a small spring. They were just as thirsty as the poor fools who had slept in the canyon. They awoke tired and feeling defeated.

García, López, and Mondragón had walked for days, dreaming of the riches that awaited them in Cíbola. Yet, they had found nothing. Other pioneers had heard the stories and were sure to search for the gold. "The map is worthless," García grumbled.

"If you go back, it will be more gold for us," López replied.

Make Predictions

After you preview, make some **predictions** before you start reading. A prediction is a thoughtful guess about what's to come. Making predictions gets you to think ahead before you jump into your reading.

How Do You Make a Prediction?

- Start with what you know from your preview. Think about the **topic** and **genre**. For example, I can tell that "Seward's Dream" is a nonfiction selection about a real person named Seward and the purchase of Alaska.

- Add your own experience and what you already know.

- Then decide what the selection will be like. Ask yourself: *What do I think this selection will tell me about the **topic**? What does this **genre** tell me about the kind of content I'll be reading?*

How Do You Confirm a Prediction?

As you read, look for information that tells if your prediction is correct. You may come across new information and have to rethink your original prediction. Or the information may confirm your prediction.

As you get new information, keep reading. Keep making new predictions and look for information to see if your prediction is correct.

Seward's Dream

Expanding the Nation

William H. Seward had a dream. He had been U.S. Secretary of State during the Civil War. He had seen how the terrible war had almost split the United States into two weaker countries.

Now that the war was over, he wanted to strengthen and expand the nation. He believed it was the nation's right to claim land throughout North America. Like Seward, many people believed in this idea of **Manifest Destiny**, or the right to expand.

Seward dreamed of expanding U.S. borders northward into Alaska, which was Russian territory. If the United States owned Alaska, pioneers would settle the land. More land meant a stronger nation, Seward believed.

Secretary of State
William H. Seward

Facing Ridicule

In 1867, Seward found a way to achieve his dream. He met with Russian leaders and came away with an agreement to purchase Alaska for $7.2 million.

Most citizens, including members of Congress, thought Seward was a maverick—out of step with the rest of the country. Seward wanted the U.S. government to spend millions of dollars on land that wasn't connected to any of the states. The disbelievers joked that no one would travel that far to reach a vast "icebox."

Many people opposed the purchase of Alaska, calling it "Seward's Folly."

How to Make a Prediction

1. Figure out the topic.

2. Figure out the major **genre**.

3. Think about what you know and make a prediction.

" The topic seems to be Alaska. The first two paragraphs talk about a person named Seward who wants to make the U.S. bigger. I predict that Seward will buy Alaska. "

How to Confirm a Prediction

Look for information as you read.

" Here's where the text says Seward bought Alaska. I was right! "

Keep Making New Predictions

" This part sounds like not everyone agreed. But I think in the end, it will be a good deal. "

Alaska's Resources

As Seward had predicted, pioneers began to settle in Alaska. Fur trading became successful. Later miners discovered gold. The **Klondike Gold Rush** in 1896 brought about 30,000 people to Alaska. The population nearly doubled in the following years. By then, everyone realized that Alaska was worth far more than the two cents per acre that the U.S. had paid for it. Unfortunately, Seward had died in 1872 and didn't see his predictions come true.

Today Alaska still provides key natural resources such as oil and fish. "Seward's Icebox" proved its value many times over.

Keep Confirming Your Predictions

" Yes, here it tells how valuable Alaska is. "

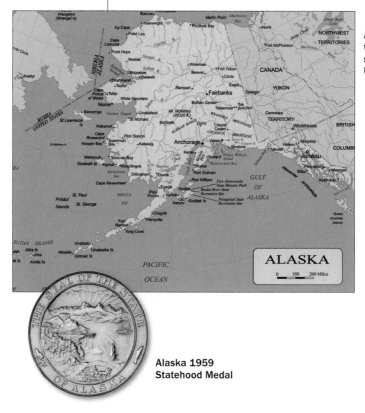

Alaska is now the largest state in the U.S.

Alaska 1959
Statehood Medal

Set a Purpose

Having a purpose, or reason, for reading is another way to keep your mind on the text. To set a purpose, ask yourself: *Why am I reading this?* Here are some general purposes for reading.

Major Genre	Purpose for Reading
Fiction Examples: short stories, novels	• To be entertained, to enjoy
Nonfiction Examples: biographies, textbooks, how-to articles	• To learn and remember information • To find out how to do something like tune a car engine

- **Purpose for Fiction** When you read fiction, preview to set a specific purpose.

Short Story

TOP SPEED   51

"You're good to go," Rafael shouted as he hit the hood. Cassie nodded and screeched back onto the raceway.

"I'm going to win," she told herself over and over. She smiled thinking of all the people who had told her that women could never make it as competitive drivers. As she made the final turn, she felt the tires nearly slipping. She sped up anyway.

This was her chance to lock in her first NASCAR win. Beside her in the turn, inches from her door, she spotted Darrell's bright silver car. "I'm not going to let him beat me again!" Cassie thought, clenching her teeth. Ahead, she could see the checkered flag. She floored the gas pedal.

How to Set a Purpose

Read the title and skim the text. What do you look forward to finding out?

" I'm looking forward to finding out more about Cassie."

" I wonder if she's going to win the race."

Set a Purpose, continued

- **Purpose in Nonfiction** When your purpose is to learn new information, you're often reading nonfiction with lots of facts. After previewing, you can set a more specific purpose to narrow down what facts to look for while you read.

Magazine Article

Reinhold Messner:
A CLIMBER MAKES HISTORY

If you ask Reinhold to name his biggest accomplishments, he'll mention two. In 1984 he climbed two 8,000-meter peaks, back to back. And in 1978, he made the solo climb of his life, Nanga Parbat. But the climb that captured popular imagination was the first ascent of Everest without oxygen, in the spring of 1978.

The very idea was revolutionary. In the 1970s, expeditions typically carried 50 kilos of oxygen per person, for use above 7,200 meters. According to physiologists, to attempt the biggest 8,000-meter peaks, such as Everest and K2, without oxygen was to risk permanent brain damage.

How to Set a Purpose

1. Turn the title into a question such as:

   " Who is Reinhold Messner and how did he make history? "

2. Look at any charts and graphs. Decide what information you want to learn.

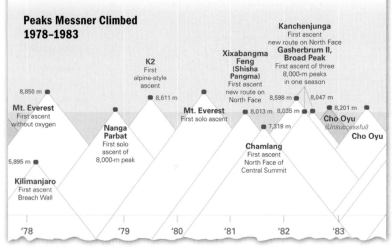

Peaks Messner Climbed 1978–1983

Kanchenjunga
First ascent
new route on North Face

Gasherbrum II,
Broad Peak
First ascent of three
8,000-m peaks
in one season

Xixabangma
Feng
(Shisha
Pangma)
First ascent
new route on
North Face

K2
First
alpine-style
ascent

8,850 m ●

● 8,611 m

8,598 m ●   ● 8,047 m

Mt. Everest
First ascent
without oxygen

Mt. Everest
First solo ascent

● 8,013 m 8,035 m ● ●   ● 8,201 m

Cho Oyu
(Unsuccessful)

**Nanga
Parbat**
First solo
ascent of
8,000-m peak

● 7,319 m

Cho Oyu

5,895 m ●

Chamlang
First ascent
North Face of
Central Summit

Kilimanjaro
First ascent
Breach Wall

'78   '79   '80   '81   '82   '83

Tap into the Text Structure

Writers decide how to organize the information they want to present. That organization is called the **text structure**. Knowing the structure before reading helps you know what to look for and how to track what the writer is saying.

Types of Text Structures

- Writers use a **narrative** structure to tell a story. The structure is based on a plot, or series of events, with a beginning, a middle, and end. Often the main character has a **goal** and the story is organized around the character's actions and the **outcome**.

- Many biographies, stories, and novels use a **time order** structure to tell about events in the order in which they happened. How-to manuals also present steps in a procedure in time order.

- Writers of history and science texts often use a **compare and contrast** structure to show how things are similar and different. The author of a story may choose to use this structure, too, to tell how two characters are alike and different, for example.

- Writers of persuasive texts present their **position** on an issue and a series of **arguments** that support that position.

- Some nonfiction texts use a **cause and effect** structure to explain why events happen and the results, or effects, of those events. Others use another kind of **logical order** to show how ideas are related. For example, a writer might start with the most important idea and move to the least important.

Graphic organizers can help you "see" how text is organized. Look at the organizers on the Reader's File pages 230-237. Which ones work for different text structures?

Text Structures

Story Structures

Plot Diagram

Fiction writers create action in a story that builds to a climax, or turning point, and then winds down to a conclusion. A Plot Diagram shows the key parts of a plot.

- The **exposition** introduces the characters and setting. It leads to a **conflict**, or **problem**, that the characters face.

- **Complications** make the conflict worse.

- The conflict worsens until something important or exciting happens. This is the turning point, or **climax**, of the story.

- After that, the action winds down because the conflict is settled. This point, at the end of the story, is the **resolution**.

Plot Diagram

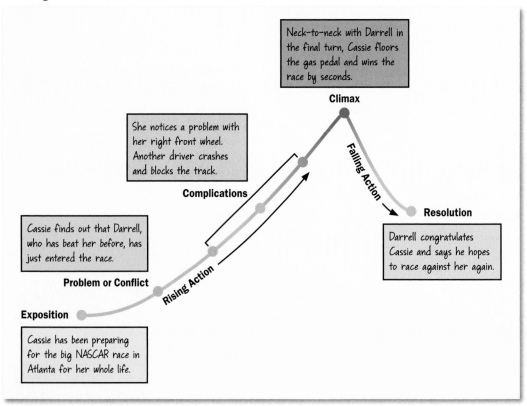

Neck-to-neck with Darrell in the final turn, Cassie floors the gas pedal and wins the race by seconds.

Climax

She notices a problem with her right front wheel. Another driver crashes and blocks the track.

Complications

Falling Action

Resolution

Cassie finds out that Darrell, who has beat her before, has just entered the race.

Darrell congratulates Cassie and says he hopes to race against her again.

Problem or Conflict

Rising Action

Exposition

Cassie has been preparing for the big NASCAR race in Atlanta for her whole life.

Goal-and-Outcome Map

Some writers start a story with the goal that a character has.
The story progresses by showing the obstacles that the character
faces and the actions taken to overcome the obstacles. The story
ends when the writer shares whether or not the character achieves
the goal.

Goal-and-Outcome Map

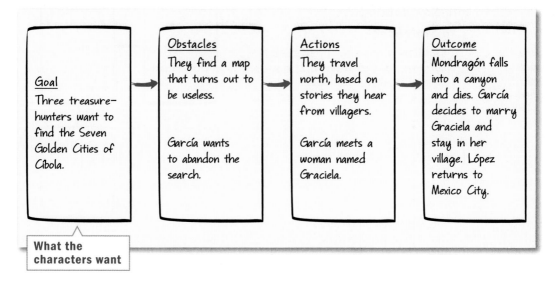

Goal
Three treasure-
hunters want to
find the Seven
Golden Cities of
Cíbola.

**What the
characters want**

Obstacles
They find a map
that turns out to
be useless.

García wants
to abandon the
search.

Actions
They travel
north, based on
stories they hear
from villagers.

García meets a
woman named
Graciela.

Outcome
Mondragón falls
into a canyon
and dies. García
decides to marry
Graciela and
stay in her
village. López
returns to
Mexico City.

Text Structures

Chronological Order

Time Line

When reading history and other nonfiction, it's easy to get confused about when things happened. A Time Line helps to track important events in the order that they happened.

Time Line

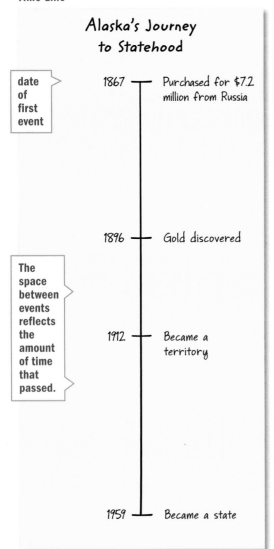

Alaska's Journey to Statehood

date of first event ▷

1867 — Purchased for $7.2 million from Russia

The space between events reflects the amount of time that passed. ▷

1896 — Gold discovered

1912 — Became a territory

1959 — Became a state

Sequence Chain

A diagram like this shows the story events in the order in which they happen, from the beginning to the ending.

Sequence Chain

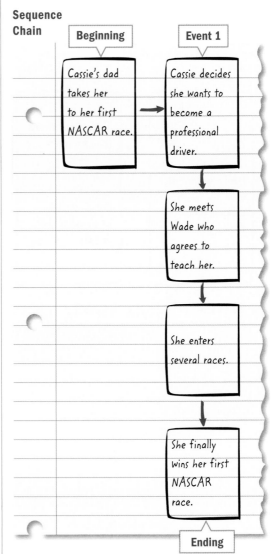

Beginning

Cassie's dad takes her to her first NASCAR race.

Event 1

Cassie decides she wants to become a professional driver.

She meets Wade who agrees to teach her.

She enters several races.

She finally wins her first NASCAR race.

Ending

Procedural Order

Steps in a Process

Many things you read explain how to do something—how to get a driver's license, bake a cake, or even conduct a science experiment. Use a Steps-in-a-Process Diagram to help you track and understand all the necessary steps.

Steps-in-a-Process Diagram

How to Get a Pilot's License

Steps

1 Meet age and language qualifications.

2 Enroll in a licensed flight school.

3 Pass a medical exam.

4 Complete a ground school course.

5 Pass a written test.

6 Complete 30-40 hours of flight time with an instructor.

7 Complete a solo flight.

8 Pass a final exam, called a "check ride."

A science writer might want to show the process for how things in the natural world happen—how hurricanes are formed or how avalanches occur, for example. Use a flow chart to track ideas in these types of texts.

Flow Chart

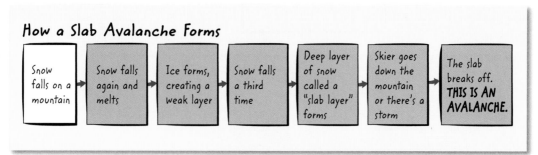

How a Slab Avalanche Forms

Snow falls on a mountain → Snow falls again and melts → Ice forms, creating a weak layer → Snow falls a third time → Deep layer of snow called a "slab layer" forms → Skier goes down the mountain or there's a storm → The slab breaks off. **THIS IS AN AVALANCHE.**

Text Structures

Comparison and Contrast

A Venn Diagram shows how things are alike and different. Use it to compare characters, ideas, and events you read about.

Venn Diagram

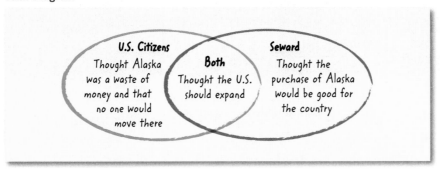

U.S. Citizens
Thought Alaska was a waste of money and that no one would move there

Both
Thought the U.S. should expand

Seward
Thought the purchase of Alaska would be good for the country

A Y Diagram is another way to show how people and things are alike and different.

Y Diagram

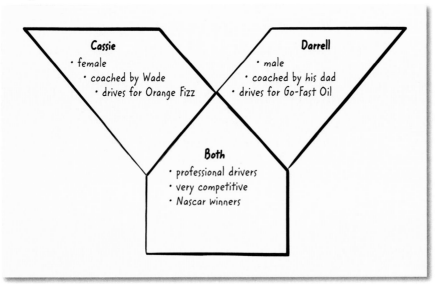

Cassie
• female
• coached by Wade
• drives for Orange Fizz

Darrell
• male
• coached by his dad
• drives for Go-Fast Oil

Both
• professional drivers
• very competitive
• Nascar winners

Position and Support

In letters to the editor, book reviews, speeches, and debates, a writer will express an opinion or try to persuade you to do something. When you read these materials, use an Argument Chart to note the writer's points and to decide what you think about the issue.

Argument Chart

ISSUE: Should Corporations Sponsor High School Sports?

What The Writer Says	What I Think
Public schools are supposed to educate young people, not convince them to buy things they don't need.	Advertisements in school stadiums don't have that much of an effect. Young people are used to seeing ads everywhere and making decisions about what to buy.
Since taxpayers' money already goes to pay for schools, taxpayers shouldn't have to see ads all over a school stadium when they watch sports.	We don't get enough money from taxes. At my school, a company paid for the stadium lights. Without those lights, we wouldn't even be able to play night games. Having corporate sponsors is better than not playing at all.

> You may agree or disagree with what the writer says.

Text Structures

Logical Order

Main Ideas and Details

A Main Idea Diagram helps you organize information when you read nonfiction texts.

Main Idea Diagram

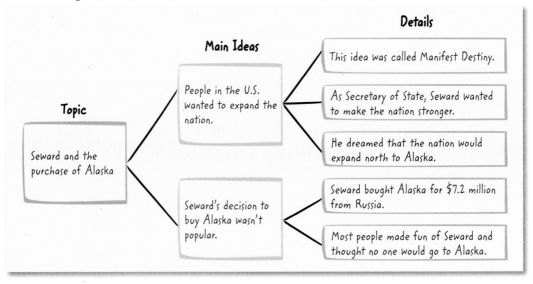

Writers of nonfiction texts, such as articles and textbooks, often present ideas logically. An outline helps you remember how the ideas go together.

Outline

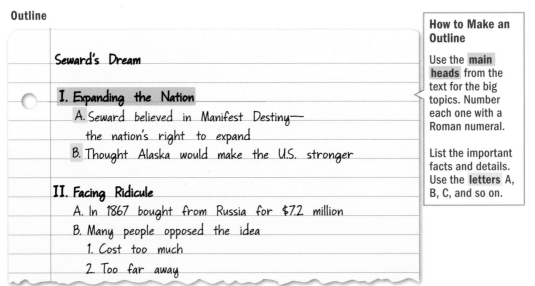

Causes and Effects

When writers want to explain how one thing affects another, they often use a cause-and-effect structure.

One Cause, Multiple Effects

This diagram shows how one event causes several other events to happen.

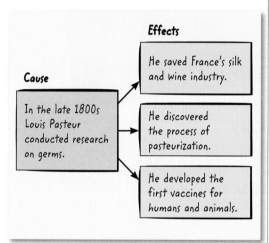

Multiple Causes, One Effect

This diagram shows how many causes lead to one result, or effect.

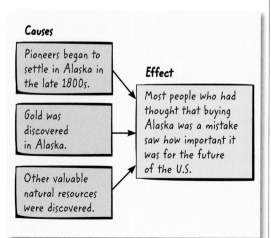

Cause-and-Effect Chain

Sometimes, one cause sets off a series of events.

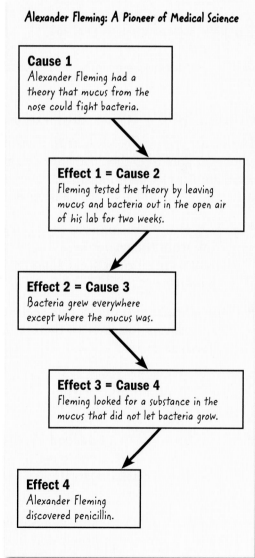

Clarify Ideas and Vocabulary

What's It Like ?

When you watch a movie at home, you're in control. If you miss something, you can press "rewind" and go back. You're in control when you read, too. If you miss something or get stuck, you can go back, clear up the confusion, and move on.

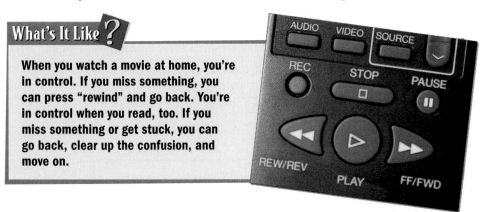

How to Clarify Ideas and Vocabulary

The whole point of reading is to understand what you read. So, whenever you're reading, be sure to check in with yourself. Ask yourself: *Do I get what I just read? Does it make sense, or am I stuck?* If you're stuck, here's what to do:

- Stop after difficult sentences or paragraphs. In your mind, picture what the writer is saying, explain it to yourself, and ask yourself questions. If you're still confused, reread those sections.

- If rereading doesn't help you, read on. You might come across information later in the text that will clear up the confusion.

- Read at the right speed. You might need to read texts with a lot of facts and information more slowly than you'd read a short story or a novel.

- When you come to a word you don't know, ask yourself: *Do I need to know this word to understand this part of the text?* If you do, use different strategies to try to figure it out. If not, keep reading.

FOCUS POINT Read the passage on the next page. How did the readers clarify vocabulary and ideas?

DECIDING MOMENTS

"Lourdes. Lourdes!"

Did someone call my name? I was walking down the hallway totally preoccupied. For the past six weeks, I had spent every waking moment preparing for the SAT. The twins, Marisol and Carmen, came into focus.

"Lourdes! Stop! You know that rock concert you've been dying to go to?" began Marisol.

Carmen continued, "We have an extra ticket for you!" Simultaneously, they looked at each other and shook their heads. "She won't go; she'll study instead," they groaned in unison.

They were right, but it wasn't an easy decision for me. I was working toward a major goal. I wanted to be the first in my family to go to college—a source of pride for my parents, grandparents, and little brother. *Are role models allowed to have fun, too?* I wondered.

Now I'm only two weeks away from my college graduation, and I've never regretted the decision I made that night. My grandmother can't stop smiling, and my little brother decided that he wants to be the "second" person in my family to go to college. All in all, it was worth passing up a few nights of fun with my friends.

How Readers Clarify

How did this reader clarify vocabulary?

I wasn't sure what the word *preoccupied* meant. But I kept reading and I figured it out since Lourdes had her mind on the SAT exam.

How did this reader clarify ideas?

I wasn't sure why Lourdes's grandmother couldn't stop smiling. So I reread the part that came before. I realized that her grandmother was proud because Lourdes was the first person in her family to go to college.

Ask Yourself Questions

Reading is like a conversation with yourself. You take in ideas from the text and then you respond with your own thoughts. When you read, think about the words on the page, and the ideas that form in your mind. To keep the conversation going:

- Think about your natural responses, such as *I get this* and *Okay, there's that name again.*

- Pause now and then to check in with yourself. Ask yourself: *What does this mean? Does it make sense?* If the answer to the second question is "no," you can reread or read on.

Reread and Read On

You've got the conversation going, and you realize there's something in the text that confuses you. When you're stuck, stop and take time to solve the problem.

- Go back to the place that's confusing. You can **reread** the confusing part and what comes before it. Sometimes reading aloud can help, too.

- If the text still isn't clear, you can **read on**. The next part you read may clear up your questions.

See the tips for monitoring the reading of the passage on the next page.

IN SEARCH OF COOL

DO YOUR OPINIONS COUNT? Well, market researchers think so. They want to know what jeans you wear, what music you listen to, and what kind of parties you like. Why? It's all about money and the spending habits of thousands of teenaged customers.

Some research companies even pay teens to be "cool hunters." They hire teen correspondents to collect information about the latest trends—from fashion and music to video games, sports, and cars. Since tastes can change fast, companies want to know what's "in" and what's "out," at least according to teens.

How do the correspondents get their information? One way is to ask their friends to fill out surveys. Another way is to photograph and videotape what's happening in their towns. Correspondents are also on the lookout for "trendsetters." They're the kids who are ahead of the crowd—they set the style and other kids want to follow. Often they get their ideas from outside their own backyards.

Once the information is gathered, research firms organize, analyze, and sell it. Who buys it? Advertising agencies, news writers, and manufacturers who want to create the new must-have sneakers and shampoo. Even though adults control the messages that come through TV, radio, newspapers, and magazines, they are definitely listening to teens.

Monitor Your Reading

Ask yourself:

Do I know what market researchers are?

If not, read on.

Ask yourself:

Who are the correspondents, and what information are they looking for?

If you're not sure, reread the previous paragraph.

Make Connections to Your Life

You've piled up thousands of experiences since you were born. You also have tons of facts and information stored away in your brain. You can rely on that background to help you understand what you read.

Use What You Know

You probably know a lot about teens and may know something about video games, too. So when you read an article about a teen who started a video game business, draw on all your background knowledge. Ask yourself: *Does this make sense with what I know about video games? How is he like teens I've read about?*

Get Involved

When a friend describes an experience, you connect by saying, "I did something like that once" or "I've been to that place before." When you read, get involved the same way by thinking of your own experiences in similar situations.

See how one good reader made connections to the passage on the next page.

CAREER FOCUS

Lessons from a Business Builder

When he was growing up, Ben Cathers seemed like an average kid. He went to school, played sports, watched TV, and enjoyed hanging out with friends. But keeping up with homework, a social life, school sports, and the New York Yankees didn't give Ben enough to do. So at age 12 he started his first business.

One hopeful teen fills out a job application.

He created a Web site, called PhatGames.com. People could get news about video games and play online games for free. By the time Ben was 15, his Web site was getting 100,000 visitors a day. Ben was offered advertising contracts from big companies. He started hiring people to work for him.

Summer jobs are a good way to learn a business.

His company hit hard times during the "dot com" crash. Then Ben went on to start a radio show aimed at teens. Now he is developing a new search engine for the Internet. He has some basic advice for other teens who want to start a business: "Analyze your skills and decide what your goals are. Work for yourself and work hard, and don't let your age stop you."

Dog-walking is a fun way to get exercise and earn money.

One Reader's Connections

" I've seen people lining up to buy video games. It must be a good way to make money."

" My friend started a business hauling trash and recyclables. Ben's Web site is another way to earn money."

Picture the Text

Another way to stay in control while you're reading is to create **mental pictures** of the text. Forming pictures in your mind helps you track the events and feel part of the action. You can picture almost anything.

Feel the Action

- When you read, use all of your senses. Try to see, hear, feel, taste, and smell what the writer is describing—whether it's the *cold, icy stare* of a character in a play or the steps involved in a complicated process like cell division.

- Use your past experiences to imagine an event or how a character feels. The following chart shows one reader's responses to a story about a plane crash in the Andes mountains.

Senses Chart

Sight	Sound	Smell	Taste	Touch
I can see the wreck of the plane and the snow-covered mountains.	I can hear the wind.	I can smell the spilled jet fuel.	My mouth is dry and numb.	Everything feels ice cold.

C1

Lake County Daily | WEEKEND EDITION

SPORTS

Extreme Mike

By FLORENCE RADER

Tandem parachute jumpers

You're flying more than two miles above the Earth in a small plane. You look down at bright white clouds and listen to the wind rushing by. Cold air comes in through the open door on the side of the plane. Do you trust the parachute? Do you jump, or do you let your fear take over?

Mike McKeller takes the jump and conquers his fear. This is why he calls himself "Extreme Mike." Mike has been facing fear, one adventure at a time. He's done land sailing, hang gliding, and flown dips, curlicues, and zigzags in a stunt plane. He's also fished for sharks. Whatever he tries, Mike is a pioneer facing extreme challenges.

What makes it more extraordinary are his physical disabilities. Since early childhood, Mike has had a painful, crippling muscle and bone condition. At one point, he couldn't even move his arms and legs. He still uses a wheelchair.

As a teenager, Mike decided not to accept his physical limits. He worked hard doing physical therapy. Though it was difficult and painful, Mike overcame his own fears. That's how he gained the self-confidence to do extreme sports.

Today Extreme Mike personally shares his story with people all over the country. He wants to help them face their fears and overcome them, just as he has done. News about Mike's achievements goes out worldwide as people see videos of his extreme feats at *www.extrememike.com.*

Monitor Your Reading

What's it like to jump out of a plane? Use your senses to feel the action.

Make a movie in your mind of Mike doing each thing the writer describes.

Explain It in Your Own Words

When you are reading, stop every so often and explain the text to yourself. This will tell you if you're really getting what the writer is saying.

How to Explain the Text

Stop at the end of a difficult sentence or paragraph. To check your understanding, put in plain words what the text is saying. If you can put the ideas into your own words in a way that makes sense, move on.

If you can't explain the text, go back to the confusing part.

• Break the sentence down into smaller parts, or meaningful chunks. Find the main part of the sentence. Use the punctuation to help you see the parts.

• Don't race over the hard parts. Read slowly to make sure you get the meaning.

• If you're still stuck, you may need to check a reference for a word's meaning or discuss the part with someone.

Read the passage on the next page. Pause to explain the ideas in your own words. Try it out with a partner.

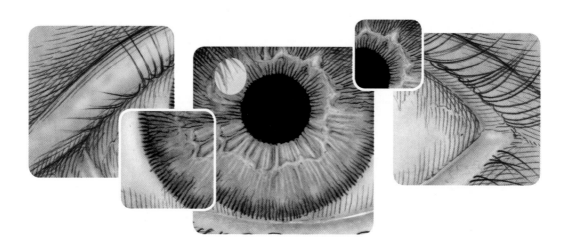

Medical Pioneers:
RESTORING SIGHT

Seeing is really a miracle, and some scientists are pioneers in using technology to cure blindness. They are developing an artificial retina that can be attached to a retina inside a blind person's eye.

Break long sentences into smaller parts. Find the **main part.**

The retina is a layer on the back of the eyeball. It is like a curved screen. Nerves in the retina respond to light and send signals to the brain. If the retina can't send those signals, a person cannot see.

The artificial retina is made of rows of electrodes that produce electrical signals. Along with the artificial retina, the blind person would wear special glasses containing a tiny video camera. The camera sees an image and sends signals to the artificial retina. There the signals become a series of tiny dots. Each dot sends a separate signal to the brain through its electrode. Then the brain uses these signals to form an image, and the blind person sees!

Scientists soon hope to have an artificial retina ready to try out in blind people. Hopefully, it will allow them to see well enough to read letters and see shapes—and perhaps even recognize faces.

Explain the paragraph in your own words.

" A blind person would wear special glasses that capture an image. Then the artificial retina would send signals to the brain."

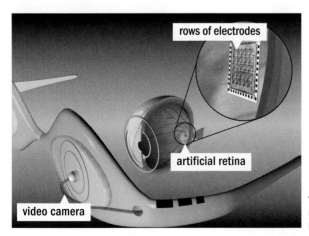

rows of electrodes

artificial retina

video camera

The artificial retina may help blind people see.

Clarify Vocabulary

Picture this—you're really into a great book. You're reading along. Then you come across a word and you have no idea what it means. Several next steps are available to you.

Should an Unfamiliar Word Stop You?

The first thing to do is to ask yourself: *Do I need to understand this word, or can I just read on?* You may be able to just keep reading. If you really need to understand the word, try these tips:

- Think of other times you may have seen the word. What do you know about it already? Do you know other words in English or another language that look like it? They could be clues to its meaning.

- Reread, looking for clues to the hard word in the words that come before and after it.

- Look for word parts you might recognize like the prefix *un-* at the beginning of a word or the suffix *-less* at the end.

- Think about who or what can help you understand the hard word right away. It could be a dictionary or someone who has a lot of knowledge about the topic.

Read the essay on the next page. Use the tips to figure out the meanings of difficult words.

WHAT MAKES A HERO?

What does the word *hero* bring to mind? What is your image of a hero? Is brawn more important than a good heart? For many people, athletes are heroes. They train, and sweat, and perform under pressure. They bring home trophies and Olympic gold medals.

Other people think that soldiers are heroes. Bronze monuments honor them. Some soldiers even sacrifice their lives. To others, heroes are firefighters or police officers. They protect fellow citizens as part of their often dangerous job.

Some people honor different kinds of heroes. Their heroes are the neighbors who showed some unexpected kindness or the parents who worked two jobs to send their kids to college. What about the person who stuck with you through tough times and never let you down? Is that person a hero?

Some heroes don't win glamorous awards. In fact, they face the real risks of being unpopular, losing friends, and possibly being harmed. These heroes speak up for what they believe in and fight against injustice in their own communities. They do not seek fame. They are just determined to do the right thing.

continued on next page

> To figure out *image,* think about other words in its family such as *imagine* and *imagination*.

> Do you know a word in your home language that looks and sounds like *injustice* ?

Clarify Vocabulary, continued

WHAT MAKES A HERO? *continued...*

Some fighters for justice do win great fame. Dr. Martin Luther King, Jr., thought that his life's work would focus on his church ministry. When he spoke out against racial injustice, people asked him to lead the civil rights movement. This hero led millions of citizens in a struggle to win their rights. Dr. King had to overcome his own fears and others' hopelessness.

He was like other heroes who courageously faced self-doubt and personal flaws. Every hero experiences failures, yet the hero struggles to keep on performing in spite of them. Struggles fortify heroes, and they go on to achieve greater goals.

Say *hero* again. Is the image in your mind *you*? You would never admit it to anyone, but you might be the greatest hero in your life. You are the only one who knows how great the challenge is that you faced last month or last week. Someone might have made fun of you or pushed you in the hallway, and you still managed to keep your composure. Your brother might have been short of cash for a car payment, and you loaned him the money. You might have walked away when everyone wanted you to break the rules. Today is another day. What challenge will make you a hero?

> To figure out *hopelessness,* break it down into its meaningful parts: *hope + -less + -ness.*

> Use context clues to figure out the meaning of *composure.*

Check Reference Sources

Sometimes you can't figure out a word from clues in the text or from reading on. Find help to learn the definition of a word you need to know. Stop and use resources, even if a word seems familiar. Many words have more than one definition. When you investigate a word, you learn that some words have richer meanings and you learn interesting ways you can use a word.

Sources for a Word's Meaning

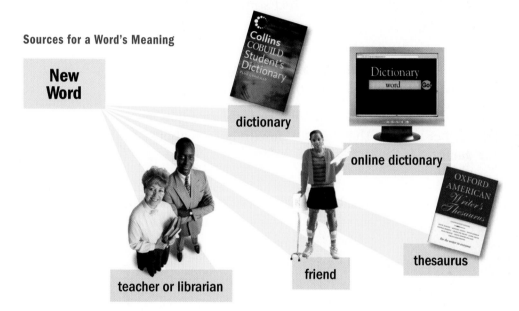

New Word

dictionary

online dictionary

thesaurus

teacher or librarian

friend

Learn About a Word—Use It and Reuse It

• Mark the page with a self-stick note so that you can find the word easily.

• Make a Vocabulary Study Card and keep it in your notebook.

• Practice saying the word.

• Use the word in a conversation and in your writing.

See Chapter 3 for more ideas about how to figure out the meanings of words as you read and how to make those words your own.

Strategy Summary

When you plan, you get ready for what's ahead of you. When you monitor, you deal with any confusion or new words that you meet while reading. This helps you stay in control of your reading.

- Prepare before you start reading. **Preview and make predictions** or **set a purpose** for reading. Think about the genre and the structure of the text so that you'll know what to expect.

- Make sure you understand what you read by checking in with yourself. Go back and **clear up confusing ideas and vocabulary** before you move on.

See how one good reader gets through a story. Notice how she gets ready for her reading then checks in with herself about confusing parts.

Fiction

FAMILY VALUES

"You will dishonor your family!" Mrs. Lee raged when Mao returned to the apartment. Two hours earlier Mrs. Lee had stopped for a gallon of milk at the Quik Shop where Mao worked. It had been the exact moment when she was hugging Ryan. But Mao was ready to face this storm.

It wasn't the first time that Mao and her mother had a fight about Mao's friends. "Mom, Ryan is a good kid," she said quietly. "You'd like him, if you gave him a chance."

Her mother snapped back, "Why can't you find Hmong friends? Besides, you are too young to date!"

> " What type of writing is this? A quick skimming tells me it is fiction. "

> My purpose—to find out why Mrs. Lee thinks dishonor is coming to her family.

> "Face this storm"? The next sentence mentions fights, so this must mean Mao will stand up to her mom's anger.

Now look at how another reader plans and then monitors when he reads nonfiction.

Magazine Article

A MAVERICK
FINDS HIS VOICE

Benjamin Zephaniah is an award-winning writer.

" I previewed and saw facts and details about a real person. This is nonfiction. "

My purpose—to find out how he uses the power of words.

"Honorary doctoral"? Clue words before— "the power of words." Clue word after— "degrees"

Benjamin Zephaniah knows the power of words. He has three honorary doctoral degrees to prove it. In his poetry, novels, plays, and music, he speaks out against racism, war, and animal cruelty. On top of that, his work is often funny.

Growing up in England and Jamaica, Zephaniah had tough experiences. He turned to street gangs for a sense of family. His gang involvement landed him in jail. He didn't learn to read until he was 21 years old.

So what's next for this voice of the people? According to Zephaniah, it's you! His ambition is to inspire people to find their own voices and make poetry.

Determine Importance

When you go to a Web site to download music, you have no trouble figuring out what's important. You see a lot of information, but you focus on which bands and songs the site has and how much the downloads will cost.

When you read, you screen out the unimportant facts and details and focus on what matters. That way, you can take away what you want to remember. Look at the next page to see how some teens figure out what's important while they're reading.

How Do You Know What's Important?

" When I read, I ask myself: *Just how big is this idea? Is it big enough to be like an umbrella that covers other smaller ideas?* If it is, then I know I've found an important idea. "

—Claudia

" What does all this add up to? That's what I'm thinking while I'm reading. It's like adding together the small pieces to get to something big. "

—Max

" When I read, I look at the headings and titles that are in big print. If they're big, they usually are important ideas. I also pay special attention to the first and last sentence in every paragraph. Writers like to make their main points at the beginning or end of a paragraph. "

—Raúl

" As I'm reading, I'm thinking: *Is this what I want to remember tomorrow, or two weeks from now? Does it matter enough to write down?* That helps me decide if something is really important. "

—Yolanda

You can download more Readers Talk tips. 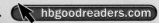 hbgoodreaders.com

Identify the Main Idea

Step back from a painting and you can see what the artist is trying to get across. Look at it close up and you can see all the small details that support that message. You do the same thing when you find the main idea and details during reading.

Get the Message

People are moved to write about many different topics, or subjects, from the agonies of war to the thrills of extreme sports. No matter what subject they choose, writers want you to get their **main idea**, or what they are mostly saying about the topic.

Often writers will directly tell you the main idea. They include a main idea statement—a sentence that states the most important thing the writer wants you to know. Then they give plenty of details to support the main idea.

FOCUS POINT Read the article and the readers' responses on the next page. Which reader focused on the main idea?

EXTREME ATHLETES CHALLENGE THE ENVIRONMENT

Volcano surfing is a risky sport.

Red, hot lava shoots high into the air. Smoke clouds hang above you. A sea of black ash covers the slope. You see someone gliding down the hill, swerving to avoid sharp rocks. This athlete is volcano surfing. Most people try to avoid live volcanoes, but some athletes seek them. Extreme sport athletes love unusual and dangerous environments.

Zoltan Istvan remembers the first time that he surfed a volcano. Lava was falling around him like bombs! Does that sound crazy?

Some athletes go to other extreme environments. Imagine climbing a frozen waterfall. Your goal is the top of a tower of ice rising thousands of feet above the ground.

Other athletes are attracted to extreme heights and dive from cliffs. Imagine being a cliff diver plunging down, down, down, and falling 85 feet at about 60 miles per hour!

There's one thing extreme athletes have in common: they love the challenge and ignore fear. Ines Papert is a champion ice climber. "During climbing I am just focused on the route and how far it is to the top—not how far it is to the ground," she says.

Which Reader Got the Main Idea?

I think the main idea is "Some athletes like to surf volcanoes."

I think the main idea is "Extreme sport athletes love unusual and dangerous environments."

Identify the Stated Main Idea

How do you know that you are getting the writer's message? Often writers make it really clear what's important for you to know. They include a main idea statement right in the text. Here's how to find the main idea:

1 Identify the Topic

The topic is what the passage is mostly about. Use the title, repeated words, and any pictures and captions as clues. Then name the topic. Ask yourself: *What is the author mostly telling about?*

2 Read for the Main Idea

Read to find the main idea of each paragraph. Remember, the stated main idea is right there in the text. Look for the sentence that states what the writer is mostly saying about the topic.

3 Check Out Details

Look at the details in the passage. Check to see that they support the main idea.

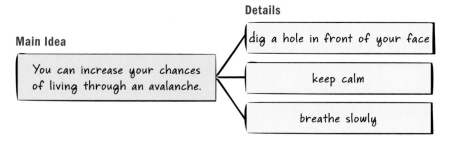

4 Make the Ideas Your Own

Look back at the topic. Ask yourself: *What did I know about surviving an avalanche before I read? What do I know now?*

Nonfiction Paragraph

Staying ALIVE in an *Avalanche*

Every second counts in an avalanche.

You are caught in an avalanche, and you're buried under heavy snow. It's dark, and you can't feel your fingers or toes. Panting hard, you're trying to catch your breath although you're feeling scared. Fifteen minutes is probably all the time you'll have left to take action. Will you survive? At least, you can increase your chances of living through an avalanche. First, you should start digging. Dig a breathing hole right in front of your face. Try to keep calm and breathe slowly. Of course your best chance for survival starts before you go outdoors. Always prepare before you go into an extreme environment.

To identify the topic

1. Read the **title** and examine the **photo and caption**. Look for repeated **key words** in the text.

2. State the topic in your own words:

" Surviving an Avalanche "

To identify the main idea

Look for a sentence that tells what the passage is mostly saying about the topic.

What If the Main Idea Isn't Stated?

When the writer doesn't tell you the main idea directly, you have to figure it out on your own. You have to **infer** it. Here's how:

1 Identify the Topic

Read the title and first sentence. Look for clues in the text to see what the selection is mostly about. Then name the topic. For example, "Women Jump to Take a Dangerous Job" is mostly about women smokejumpers.

2 Focus on Important Details

The main idea is what the writer mostly wants to say about the topic. Focus on the most important details. What idea do they add up to?

Smokejumpers parachute into forest fires. **+** There are some women smokejumpers. **+** They like the adventure and challenge.

3 Combine the Details with What You Know

Since the main idea isn't stated, different readers may sum up the writer's main idea in different ways. Draw on your experience and the details provided to come up with a main idea that makes sense.

Make sure that there is evidence in the text for your main idea statement. Does it include the topic? Does it include the ideas and information that the writer emphasizes?

Two Main Idea Statements	
" Smokejumping is a dangerous job, and some women like it."	" Women smokejumpers risk their lives, but enjoy the challenge."

④ Make the Ideas Your Own

As a final step, ask yourself: *What do I know about the topic now? What do these new ideas mean to me?*

Nonfiction Paragraph

Women Jump to Take a Dangerous Job

Imagine thick clouds of black smoke and hot, blistering flames rushing toward you. Now imagine forest land so rugged that firefighters can't reach it on foot. Enter the smokejumpers—firefighters who parachute out of airplanes into forest fires. "Jumping into a fire is, of course, very appealing. It would be to anybody, right?" says Jody Stone in *Smokejumper Magazine*. Ms. Stone is one of only 27 women smokejumpers in the United States. Until 1981, women left this dangerous job to men. This may seem like a wise decision to some, but not to Leslie Anderson. Ms. Anderson was one of the early women smokejumpers. She says she loved the adventure and challenge of fighting fire from the sky.

There are now 27 women smokejumpers in the U.S.

Summarizing Text

What's It Like?

> Oh, yeah!

> What did you do today?

> I went shopping. I tried on a lot of clothes and finally found some that were right for me.

You've spent all day shopping, looking for just the right clothes. Later, when you see your friend, you don't tell her everything you did every minute. You tell her only the most important information. You *summarize*. When you read, it's also important to summarize.

How Does Summarizing Work?

When you summarize, you ask yourself: *What did I just read? What are the most important ideas?* Summarizing keeps you focused on what's important and helps you remember what you read. To summarize:

- Start by identifying the topic, or what the selection is mostly about.

- As you read, identify the main idea, or what the author is mostly saying about the topic.

- Stay focused on what's important. Take notes or use a graphic organizer to gather the author's ideas.

- When you finish reading the entire selection, ask yourself: *What does the author think is most important to know? What do I want to remember?*

FOCUS POINT Read the passage and sample summaries on the next page. Which reader focused on what's important?

Life on Earth: A New View

WHAT DO ANIMALS NEED in order to survive? Sunlight and oxygen? Mild temperatures and moderate air pressure? For centuries scientists thought that all animals needed these basic things. Then in 1977 everything changed. That's when Alvin, a small submarine, traveled two miles below the surface of the Pacific Ocean.

The scientists inside the submarine were looking for an opening in an underwater volcano. They found one off the coast of the Galapagos Islands. But the scientists also found something much more startling. Life was thriving on the ocean floor!

Hundreds of strange creatures had adapted to the extreme environment. They were living in scalding water as hot as 400° C. Small organisms weren't getting energy from the sun. They were getting energy from toxic chemicals that poured out of the volcano! Large communities of animals were living in complete darkness under the crushing pressure of the deep ocean.

Some tubeworms grow in complete darkness.

These discoveries have changed some scientists' thinking. If life is possible in such a harsh environment on Earth, life might be possible in other parts of the solar system.

Sample Summaries

> In 1977, some scientists went to the bottom of the Pacific Ocean in Alvin, a submarine. They went two miles below the surface of the ocean.

> Scientists discovered that animals can live in very extreme environments without sunlight or oxygen. So some think that life can exist on other planets.

Summarize a Nonfiction Paragraph

When you **summarize** nonfiction, you figure out the most important ideas or events. Summarizing helps you check your understanding and focus on the things worth remembering. Read the paragraph on the next page.

1 **Identify the Topic**

Look for clues in the text such as the title, headings, pictures, and captions to see what the paragraph is mostly about. Then name the topic. For example, "Dangerous Jobs."

2 **Read to Get the Main Idea of the Paragraph**

The **main idea** is what the writer mostly has to say about the topic. You know you've found the main idea when you find that most of the details tell about it. Try it out:

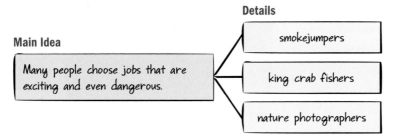

Details

Main Idea

Many people choose jobs that are exciting and even dangerous.

smokejumpers

king crab fishers

nature photographers

3 **Sum Up the Paragraph**

Pause at the end of the paragraph and put the topic, main idea, and important details in your own words. Look at the well-written sample summaries on the next page.

4 **Make the Ideas Your Own**

Move beyond the text and ask yourself: *What does this mean to me? Does it change my thinking in any way?*

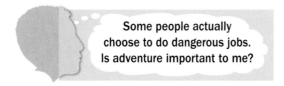

Some people actually choose to do dangerous jobs. Is adventure important to me?

Nonfiction Paragraph

THE WORLD'S MOST DANGEROUS JOBS

Smokejumpers risk their lives.

What's your idea of the perfect job? Would you like to work in a quiet office? Or would you like to have a daily adventure? Many people choose jobs that are exciting and even dangerous. They risk their lives every day when they go to work. Smokejumpers, for example, fight forest fires by parachuting from airplanes into the heart of the fire. Fishing for king crabs may sound relaxing, but it is actually one of the world's most dangerous jobs. Fishermen risk broken bones and falling into the freezing waters of the Bering Sea. Even nature photographers sometimes face danger. Imagine being sent to photograph erupting volcanoes or ferocious wild animals.

Find the topic

1. Read the **title** and the **first sentence**. Look at the **pictures and captions**.

2. Look for repeated **key words**, or words in bold type.

3. Then tell yourself the topic:

" This paragraph is mostly about dangerous jobs."

Sample Summaries

" Many people like to do dangerous work. Smokejumping, king crab fishing, and nature photography are dangerous jobs."

" Some jobs are really dangerous! Smokejumpers, king crab fishers, and nature photographers all risk their lives at work."

" Some people like the excitement of dangerous work. They do jobs like smokejumping, king crab fishing, and nature photography."

Summarize a Nonfiction Article

Once you're able to summarize a paragraph, you can summarize a long article that has several paragraphs. To summarize an article, follow these steps:

1 Identify the Topic

Read the **title** and **first sentence**. Look for repeated key words or words in bold type. Examine any headings and pictures. What's the topic? What is the selection mostly about?

2 Stay Focused As You Read

Try making a movie in your mind to picture what the writer is describing. Use self-stick notes or take notes in an organizer. Pause at the end of each paragraph. Reread any parts that weren't clear. Ask yourself: *What ideas or information did the writer emphasize?*

3 Sum Up the Article

When you have finished reading, summarize the entire selection. Start with a main idea statement. It sums up what the selection is mostly saying about the topic.

> **Main-Idea Statement**
>
> " **Aquarius is an underwater laboratory that helps astronauts prepare for trips to space.** "

Then add the ideas and information that the writer most wants readers to know. For example, **Astronauts practice wearing the same suits and using the same equipment they will use in space. They can live in the lab for months at a time.**

4 Make the Ideas Your Own

As a final step, move beyond the text. Ask yourself: *What do I want to take away from this? What have I learned? Does it change my thinking in any way?*

CAREER FOCUS

THE AQUARIUS LABORATORY: A WATERY WORKPLACE

> Title

> First Sentence

Most people drive cars or take buses to work; some ride bikes or walk. But in July 2004, four astronauts had a very strange and wet commute. They dove into the ocean, and after diving for two hours, they reached their deep-sea destination. What were the astronauts doing in the sea? They were going to **Aquarius**, an underwater laboratory that lies off the Florida coast.

TOPIC:
The Aquarius
Laboratory

Aquarius is the world's only underwater research laboratory. It helps astronauts prepare for trips to space because working on the bottom of the ocean is a lot like working on the Moon or Mars. Astronauts have a chance to practice wearing the same suits and using the same equipment they will use in space.

Aquarius helps astronauts prepare for trips to space.

The lab is both a home and a workplace. It is a little crowded inside—only 45 feet long and thirteen feet wide. One area has all the controls and equipment that keep the lab running. A second area is where people eat, sleep, and work.

The lab has everything people need to live and work.

People can live in the lab for months at a time. However, most lab missions last less than two weeks. Most astronauts believe that the time they spend as *aquanauts* is time well spent.

People can live in the lab for months.

The Aquarius Laboratory lies off the coast of Key Largo in the Florida Keys National Marine Sanctuary.

Summarize Poetry

When you summarize poetry, you unlock the meaning of the poet's words. You also respond to the poem's imagery.

1 **Focus on Meaning**

It's good to read a poem several times. First, read the poem on the next page once just for enjoyment. Then read it a second time very slowly, focusing on the meaning. What is the poet describing?

2 **Think About the Imagery**

Read the poem a third time. Focus on the poet's word choice and descriptions that appeal to your senses. Record your feelings. Try it out:

Lines from the Poem	How I Feel
singing inside creek music, heart music, smell of sun on gravel	These images create a peaceful, happy feeling. I feel the poet's happiness at being outdoors in a beautiful place.

3 **Sum Up the Main Idea**

Take a minute after you've read the poem and ask yourself: *What is the poet's message?* Poems often say or mean more than one thing. Whatever meaning you find, you should be able to connect it to lines in the poem.

WRITER'S WORDS	SAMPLE MAIN IDEA
I pledge allegiance to the soil . . . one ecosystem in diversity under the sun With joyful interpenetration for all.	The poet is devoted to the wonders and joys of nature.

For All

—GARY SNYDER

Focus on words that
appeal to your senses.
How do they make you feel?

Ah to be alive
on a mid-September morn
fording a stream
barefoot, pants rolled up,
holding boots, pack on,
sunshine, ice in the shallows,
northern rockies.

Rustle and shimmer of icy creek waters
stones turn underfoot, small and hard as toes
cold nose dripping
singing inside
creek music, heart music,
smell of sun on gravel

I pledge allegiance

I pledge allegiance to the soil
of Turtle Island,
and to the beings who thereon dwell
one ecosystem
in diversity
under the sun
With joyful interpenetration for all.

Summarize Fiction

When you read a good story, you want to follow its meaning as you're reading and later share what it's all about. To summarize fiction, focus on where the story takes place, who the characters are, and what happens in the story.

1 **Focus on the Characters and Setting**

Read the title and the first paragraph of the myth below. Identify the characters and setting. Who or what is the story about? When and where does the story take place?

Myth

Pele Finds Her Home

LONG AGO in the South Pacific seas lived Pele, the daughter of Earth's creator. Pele dug fire pits with her sacred stick and threw great streams of lava on the land. The lava destroyed many trees, but it made the soil rich. Pele protected her brothers who tended the fires. She also protected her sisters who danced the hula. But she lived apart from her sister Namaka, the sea goddess.

Namaka feared Pele, who was beautiful and strong. So the goddess sent a great tidal wave to destroy Pele and her household. Quickly, Pele's brother brought his canoe, and the family escaped. The family roamed the seas until they landed on the island of Kauai. Then Pele dug a fire pit and ordered the others to tend the fires. From the sea, Namaka saw the fire glowing in the sky. She knew Pele had survived. So Namaka flooded the island.

Pele fled to other Hawaiian islands, but Namaka always drove her away. Then, on Maui, Pele faced her powerful sister in a great battle. Pele perished and the family cried in sorrow.

Namaka returned to the sea, looked up, and shrieked. In the sky, she saw a beautiful woman in the red fire rising over Hawaii. Pele had become a goddess who would forever send lava from the Kilauea Volcano on Mauna Loa.

Identify the **setting** and the **characters**.

Conflict

Resolution

2 **Use a Map to Track What Happens**

As you read, pay attention to the **conflict**, or the struggle that the main characters face, the steps they take to overcome it, and the **resolution**, or the end of the struggle.

You can take notes in a story map to help you track the action. The story map will help you see how the conflict builds and how events bring the conflict to an end.

Story Map

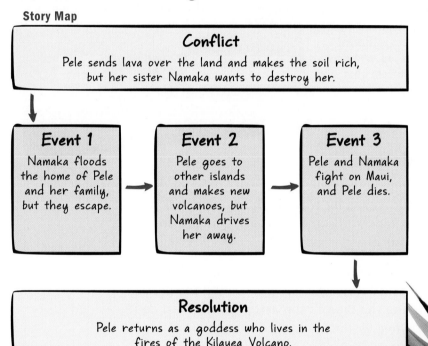

Conflict
Pele sends lava over the land and makes the soil rich, but her sister Namaka wants to destroy her.

Event 1
Namaka floods the home of Pele and her family, but they escape.

Event 2
Pele goes to other islands and makes new volcanoes, but Namaka drives her away.

Event 3
Pele and Namaka fight on Maui, and Pele dies.

Resolution
Pele returns as a goddess who lives in the fires of the Kilauea Volcano.

3 **Share the Story**

Review the key events using your story map. What would you tell your friends about the myth in just a few words?

4 **Connect It to Your Own Life**

Storytellers have told the Pele myth to explain how something in the natural world was created. What lessons might it teach about sibling rivalry and aggression?

What Matters Most to You?

What's It Like

People have different reasons for seeing a movie. You may want to check out the cars, and your best friend may want to hear the music. It's the same when you read. You connect with what matters most to you, and that may be different from what matters to someone else.

These cars are cooler than the cars in "Fast Fury."

The music is great!

Making It Matter

What matters most to you when you read? It depends on your purpose, or your reason for reading. It also depends on you—which of the writer's words and ideas are going to stand out and "speak to you"?

- If your purpose is to read for information, read to find what you want to learn. Start by previewing the passage and identifying the topic. Then ask yourself: *What do I want to learn from the text?*

- In addition to having a purpose for reading, every reader has different reactions to a piece of writing. What's important to you are your own personal reactions. As you read, ask yourself: *What stands out? What do I think is worth remembering?*

FOCUS POINT Read the article and the sample responses on the next page. What mattered most to each reader?

CHANGE OF SCENERY

EXTREME TRAVEL

When you wake up and look outside, do you see the same thing every day? For most of us, the answer is "yes." We see a street, some buildings, and maybe a few trees. But in two of the world's most unusual hotels, the answer is different.

Imagine waking up and looking through a sheet of clear ice. The Northern Lights of the Arctic winter fill the endless night sky with brilliant colors. Or, picture yourself looking out of your bedroom window into the face of a fish. People who have the time, interest, and money can have these travel experiences.

UNDERWATER HOTELS

Jules' Undersea Lodge is completely under water. The only way into the hotel is through a hole in its bottom. To get to the hole you have to dive 21 feet beneath the waves near Key Largo, Florida.

THE ICE HOTEL

Sweden's Ice Hotel, 200km north of the Arctic Circle

Every winter a new hotel is built in Jukkasjarvi, Sweden. Each room is made of carved ice. The bed is ice, the walls are ice, and the table and chairs are ice. Of course, the room's temperature is below freezing.

Most people spend just one night in an ice room. Then they spend the rest of their trip in warm, wooden cottages.

What Matters?

I had to be prepared to discuss this in class. So I focused on the facts—where people go for extreme travel.

What stands out for me is that some people are so bored they spend money to sleep on a bed of ice. Now that's really sick!

Focus on Your Purpose

Often when you sit down to read something, you've been asked to read it for a purpose. It might be to complete a homework assignment, study for a test, or get your driver's permit. Other times, you choose the purpose. Whether or not it's your choice, always keep your purpose in mind to make the most of your reading experience. Here's how:

1 **Identify the Topic**

The topic is what the book or article is mostly about. Read the title and look for repeated key words. Examine any pictures and captions. What is the topic? What do you already know about the topic?

2 **Develop a List of Questions**

What do you want to get out of reading the text? What new information do you want to learn? Develop a list of questions and answer them as you read.

3 **Record the Answers**

It's easy to get off track when you read. To help you stay focused, take notes or use a chart like the one below to record the answers to your questions. You may not always find the answers to all of your questions.

TOPIC: WOMEN DIVERS OF JAPAN

What I KNOW	What I WANT TO KNOW	What I LEARNED
Some people dive for money.	How tough is it to be an abalone diver?	cold water, dive 30 feet, hold breath for 80 seconds, darkness
Divers get paid for shellfish.	How much money do divers make?	(not answered)

WORLD

An *ama* dives for abalone.

Women Divers of Japan

By Makiko Oda

TOKYO, JAPAN – As the sun rises over Kuzaki, Japan, Shizuka steps into the ocean. She slips on her flippers. She wears a wet suit, because the water is cold. She hopes to find many abalone, a type of shellfish. Shizuka is an ama, or lady diver. She dives for abalone to supplement the money her family makes on their farm. The ama have done this for centuries.

As Shizuka prepares to dive 30 feet beneath the waves, she shakes her muscular arms. She will hold her breath for 80 seconds, barely pausing between dives. Down in the darkness, it is the strength of her lungs, arms, and legs that will keep her alive. With one last deep breath, Shizuka dives, a 73-year-old woman in fearless pursuit of a living.

Les
Bus

By A. Smith

Nowher
arrives fo
locally ha
decide fo
to suppor
transport
municiple
commute
is going t
have to fe
for intere
or depart
During th
recent bu
driver's
strike ma
people ha
use the tr
business
get to wo
Of course
the citize
were deli
sights of
assurance
Contrary
not have
been dire
affected,
thousand
people we
And for t
talking tr
organize
decided t

What Speaks to You?

Whenever you read, connect to what's personally important to you. Watch for words and ideas in the text that speak right to you. Here's how to connect:

1 Read with a Critical Eye

By now you've had a lot of experiences inside and outside school. Bring all that information up on your mental screen and read with a critical eye. Is the writing gripping or dull? Does the writer offer an opinion that you strongly agree with, or a description that catches your eye or ear?

2 Listen to Yourself

Sometimes unexpected ideas will spark your interest. Listen to what speaks to you as you read "Survival in the Frozen Andes."

> What stood out for me was how desperate the writer sounded. I wonder if I'd be driven to do what he did to survive.

Use these questions to keep the inner conversation going:

- *What do I want to remember about this passage?*
- *What parts are significant and worth sharing with someone?*
- *Are there any new ideas or interesting language?*

Survival
in the Frozen Andes

Sixteen people survived the crash for 70 days
before they were rescued.

We were flying from our homes in Uruguay to a rugby match in Chile, but our plane never arrived. Instead, on October 13, 1972, our plane crashed high in the Andes Mountains. Of the 45 people who were aboard when the plane went down, 13 died in the crash, and others were injured. We survivors desperately hoped for rescue. But who would be able to find us on the frozen peak? We huddled in the only shelter, the mangled fuselage of the plane.

Things grew worse. An avalanche fell. Now we were trapped inside the plane. We had little fuel for a fire and no food. There was no wildlife or vegetation near. We grew weaker. More people died as we struggled to dig out of the snow. After 70 days of torment, rescue arrived. I was one of only 16 people who survived.

I alone kept a diary of our ordeal. I kept it so people would understand, and so they might forgive us for what we did. Perhaps, if you experienced the mountain and the hunger, you might understand what we faced. Read these notes from my journal and decide for yourself.

We survivors are starving. Around us are the frozen bodies of our dead teammates, of the flight crew, and other passengers. We cannot bury them. They are preserved in the snow. We will use our fuel and do what we must do. We must eat. We must survive.

And I wonder now, who can blame us?

Strategy Summary

When you determine importance, you focus on the significant information. That way, you pay attention to what matters the most and take away what you want to remember.

- Figure out the **main idea**, or what the writer is mostly saying about the topic.

- **Summarize** by putting the main idea and important details in your own words.

- Look for words and ideas that **speak to you** as you read.

See how one good reader focuses on what is important when he reads fiction.

Fiction

FAMILY VISIT   3

    "Welcome to Volcano National Park!" I greet the latest group of tourists. "Here in Rwanda lives one of the world's most endangered species," I point out the mountain gorilla infants wrestling near their parents.

    "These gorilla families have narrowly escaped many dangers: poachers, a brutal civil war, and deforestation," I remind them.

> " The story is being told by someone who works at an African park that protects gorillas. I wonder what kinds of things would happen in that setting. "

> " If I was on the tour, I'd never forget it. It would convince me that saving the gorillas is important. "

Notice how this reader focuses on main ideas in nonfiction.
He also finds words that speak to him.

Magazine Article

Extreme Environments
Challenge Racers

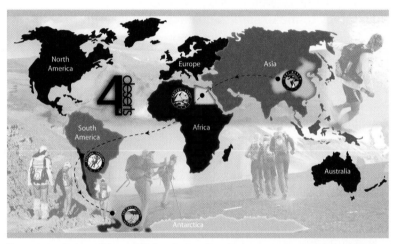

Runners race in four of the world's harshest environments.

Sandstorms. High-altitude mountain crossings. Temperature extremes, ranging from freezing to over 120 degrees. Carrying your own equipment as you race 150 grueling miles. Is your adrenaline pumping? Then you might want to test your endurance and enter the 4 Deserts race.

The ultra marathons will take you to four deserts on four continents: the Gobi Desert in China, the Atacama Desert in Chile, the Sahara Desert in Egypt, and the frozen desert of Antarctica. Few runners compete in all races. But those who do know they have conquered some of Earth's most extreme environments.

> Add up all the details = The 4 Deserts race is a 150-mile marathon through four deserts.

> "Adrenaline pumping" is my idea of excitement. Maybe I'll read more about this.

Ask Questions

When you go to a new place, your head fills with questions. You wonder: *Where do teens go to have fun? What's the best way to get around? Is there a place to get my favorite food?*

When you read, you also ask questions to find your way. Asking questions is a good strategy to make sure that you're actively thinking—before, during, and even after reading. Some questions may be simple to answer; others may take more thinking, or more reading. See the next page to see how some teens ask and answer questions about what they're reading.

What Do You Question When You Read?

" Sometimes I just stop reading and check if I'm getting it. I ask myself a question about what I just read. Then I answer it. This helps keep me on track. "

—Isabel

" What is the author trying to get at? That's what I'm asking when I read. It's like getting into the author's head when he or she was writing the book. "

—Cherise

" Do you ever realize that you are just reading words that don't make any sense? That's when I know I've got to stop and do something. So I stop and ask a question about a fact if it's an article, or about a character if it's a story. "

—Miguel

" When I read a story, I wonder what I would do if I were in the characters' shoes. Thinking about this helps me stay with the whole story better. "

—Owen

You can download more Readers Talk tips. 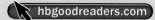 hbgoodreaders.com

Do You Get It?

You are at the foul line ready to shoot. Before the ball leaves your hands, you want to make sure you've got it right. You ask yourself questions: *Is my form correct? Am I holding the ball right?* When you read, it's also important to ask yourself questions.

How Do You Know If You Get It?

Before, during, and after reading, ask yourself questions to check your understanding. Here's how to use questions to make sure that you really get what you read:

- First, scan the text for the title and any headings and subheadings. You may want to turn them into questions.

- Use what you already know about the topic—what the reading is mostly about—to develop other questions.

- When you start reading, pause now and then and answer your questions. New questions will come up as you read. Answer these questions as you read, too.

- After you finish reading, ask and answer your own questions to firm up your understanding.

FOCUS POINT Read the passage and sample questions on the next page. Note the questions the readers use to make sure they get it. What other questions might a good reader ask?

Mission at Aktaj 7

When I signed up, I thought I'd be studying intergalactic aviation. Joe was daydreaming again. *I didn't realize that the Mars Colony Class of 2025 would have to study Earth languages.*

Joe's lava ring changed from orange to red. He blinked and his mind snapped back to reality. A new mission was about to begin. Ronit Haley's nasal voice echoed in Joe's earpiece. "Attention all Aktaj 7 students. Please report to your transonic rocket. Countdown is in sixteen minutes."

Joe dashed out of his Russian class. He jumped into the closest Cosmic Portal. It sucked him down a winding slide as though he were water flowing down a sink drain. Two robotic arms appeared and wrapped him in his space suit. When the doors opened, he was standing beside the rocket.

I don't know if I can face another mission, Joe thought, as he walked across the launch pad. He was still embarrassed by what had happened yesterday. He programmed his rocket to fly in the wrong direction. By the time he realized his mistake, Natalia Gortovoy had already completed her mission. She was just a sophomore! Would this mistake disqualify Joe from his goal—acceptance into the Intergalactic Academy?

Sample Questions

When I saw the title, I wondered: *What kind of mission is this? What kind of place is Aktaj 7?* I'm going to keep reading to find out more about them.

At first I asked myself: *What does the character mean by "Earth languages"?* Later the story mentioned that he was in Russian class. And the other student pilot has a name that sounds Russian. So it all fits together.

Fiction: Do You Get It?

When you read fiction, you can ask your own questions about the events and characters to make sure you are following them. When you can't come up with good answers to your questions, it's a sign that you're not understanding the story.

Questions for Reading Fiction

- **Ask Questions Before Reading**
  Before you read, ask yourself questions that you expect the story to answer. Read the title and chapter headings. Look at the illustrations. Then use them to create your own questions. Look for the answers as you read.

- **Ask Questions About Characters and Events While Reading**
  Use natural breaks in the reading to pause and review. Ask yourself questions such as: *What events were important? Why did that character do a particular action? Have I had experiences similar to the ones the story's characters had?*

  If you can't come up with an answer, reread to find an answer before reading on.

- **Ask Questions About What Words Mean**
  If a word seems important to the text, ask yourself if you get its meaning. If not, look for clues and use word parts to help you figure it out.

- **Ask Big Questions After Reading**
  After reading a portion of the text, or all of it, ask questions about the big ideas in the story. For example: *Does the story's main problem and solution make sense? What life lesson should I take away?*

World Wide *Spider* Web

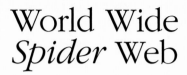

Once upon a time, there was an inventor who wanted instant access to all the information in the world. Professor Abelian tried astounding mathematical formulas, but he failed to invent a magic box that contained all the information in the world.

One day the professor remembered folk tales. "Science can't solve everything!" he declared. "I need a talking animal."

The professor poked the spider that was always weaving webs around the electronic gizmos in his not-so-magical box. "Please listen?" he begged, and explained his problem.

The spider rolled her eyes. "You know, Abelian, for a professor, you're a little dim. All that information can't FIT in this box! You need the help of this silver spider. It will weave a powerful net that will catch all information, including videos and downloadable audio files," she said. The spider was holding a tiny silver spider.

"*Catch* information?" The professor scratched his head.

The spider threw up two legs impatiently. "Think outside of the box, Ab. I'm talking about a HUGE net. A world wide web. Get it?"

Abelian agreed to take the silver spider. In return, the talking spider ordered the professor to find a formula that would turn her back into a princess. She planned to sign up with PrinceDates.com. Professor Abelian surfed the web from morning to night, and from that day on, they all e-mailed happily ever after.

How to Ask and Answer Questions

Before you read, you might ask about what to expect from the text:

" What kind of story will be about an inventor and a spider?"

While you read, you might ask about what's happening or what a word means:

" What is the spider describing?"

" What do *box*, *net*, and *web* mean here?"

After you read, you might ask about a big idea:

" How does the story make fun of folk tales?"

Nonfiction: Do You Get It?

When you read nonfiction, you can ask your own questions about the facts and ideas to make sure you're understanding them. Asking and answering your own questions will help you stay focused on what is important. When you just read words and the meaning does not come through, you know you're stuck.

Questions for Reading Nonfiction

- **Ask Questions Before Reading**
  Before you read nonfiction, scan the title, headings, and subheadings. Based on your preview, ask yourself questions that you think will be answered in the reading. Check for answers as you read.

- **Ask Questions About the Facts and Ideas While Reading**
  Pause at the end of paragraphs or sections. Ask yourself questions about the facts and ideas: *What are the key terms? What is the main idea?* If you can't come up with answers, reread and find them before reading on.

- **Ask Questions After Reading to Review**
  After you've read a longer section, ask questions to add up the facts and ideas. Think of questions that help you see if you get the main message. For example: *What are the most important ideas? What have I just learned? What is important to remember about this piece?*

Magazine Article

EYE ON THE FUTURE:
THE BIONIC EYE

A silicon chip may help people with damaged retinas see again.

Imagine that the retina of your eye is damaged, but you can see. A microchip in back of your eye does the retina's work. It changes light into visual signals sent to the brain.

Dr. Alan Chow and his brother, Vincent Chow, an electrical engineer, developed this amazing technology. They successfully tested the chip in blind animals. Later they implanted it in a few human patients. They wanted to learn if human bodies would accept or reject the chip.

After surgery, the Chows watched for signs that the chip was being rejected. Instead, the patients' vision improved. One patient saw the lights on a Christmas tree for the first time in fifty years!

A Tiny But Powerful Microchip

The powerful microchip is just millimeters wide. Yet it holds 4,000 to 5,000 solar cells that collect light. Those cells turn light into electrical impulses that stimulate the healthy cells in a patient's retina. The Chows predict that such stimulation could actually make the retina work again. They hope that in the future the chip will do more than help patients see objects. This invention will help them have some of their normal vision again.

How to Ask and Answer Questions

Before you read, you might ask:

" What is a bionic eye?"

While you read, you might ask about facts and ideas:

" How did the Chows test their invention?"

" Were the tests successful?"

" What is the microchip like?"

Use questions to review:

" How does the bionic eye work?"

Question-Answer Relationships

When you pick up a new CD, you have questions about it. Some of the answers you can find with the CD. For other answers, you might check the Internet or a newspaper. When you read other things, you also ask questions and find the answers in different places.

Questions and Answers: What's the Connection?

You ask different types of questions, so you have to find the answers in different ways. Once you understand the connection between questions and their answers, you'll find the answers more easily, and you'll understand what you're reading better.

- Some questions are connected to answers that are right there in the text.

- Some questions cover more than one part of the text. Then you have to think about the question as you search and gather information to answer it.

- Some questions ask about big ideas in the text. To find their answers, you have to bring in your own experience or check with others.

- Some questions are about how the text fits with what you already know, for example: *What made the author write this type of book?* You might not find answers right away, but keep these questions in mind.

FOCUS POINT Read the passage and sample questions on the next page. What types of questions did the readers ask?

http://hbgoodreaders.com

Isaac Asimov's VISION OF THE FUTURE

What will the universe be like thousands of years from now? Isaac Asimov spent the first part of his career imagining just that. He wrote the Foundation Series, which are stories and novels about galactic empires. Many believe the series was the author's best work.

Asimov grew up in Brooklyn, New York. While working at his parents' candy store, he read the science fiction magazines that were sold there. The magazines inspired him to write his own science fiction.

When Asimov was 21, he decided to pitch his newest story idea to John W. Campbell, Jr., the editor of Astounding Science Fiction. It was 1941 and Asimov had been writing professionally for three years.

But Asimov had no plot in mind. So he used a technique called free association. He opened a book and found a picture of a fairy queen with her arms wrapped around the feet of a soldier. This sparked his imagination. He envisioned soldiers . . . then empires . . . then empires of the galaxy.

Questions and Answers

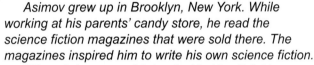

What was the *Foundation Series*? I see the answer in the same sentence. It was a group of stories Asimov wrote about the future.

I wonder—how did Asimov's father feel about his son becoming a writer? I'll check the Internet to see what I can find out about this.

Where Do Your Answers Come From?

Everything is going well. You're reading and paying attention to questions that come up in your mind. You stop from time to time to answer your questions. But where are the answers? That depends on the type of questions. Some answers are right in the text; but many others are in your head.

Right There Answers

Whether you're reading nonfiction or fiction, ask questions about what comes up in the text.

- **Ask Questions About Facts and Ideas**
  Nonfiction text presents facts and ideas. As you read, ask questions about the information the writer presents. You may find many of the answers right in the text.

- **Ask Questions About Details in a Story**
  Fictional texts have imaginary characters and events. Ask questions about who the main characters are, where the story takes place, and what happens. You'll find the answers to these questions right in the text.

A Perfect Techno World

Ask questions about details in the story.

H-K181 rolled over in her sleep flotation chamber. The cathodes attached to her temples detected that she was starting to dream. The tiny transponder in her bed clicked on to record those visions.

> Who is H-K181?

The girl awoke. *Another perfect day ahead*, thought H-K181 as she slid out of her sleep flotation chamber and stepped into the personal purifier. The germicidal ray had made the use of a bath or shower obsolete years ago. A conveyor moved her through the closet, which held several white garments.

"I want blue today," said H-K181, briefly touching her sleeve to the scanner. Nano particles imbedded in the fabric made the material change colors instantly. No sense worrying about someone wearing the same clothes. Now everyone could just scan a new color and have an original outfit on the spot.

> Why doesn't she worry about someone wearing the same clothes?

A teleporter was in the corner of the room. The girl stepped inside.

"I'm glad I don't live in the 21st century. This trip would take days in a jet," H-K181 mumbled as the door slid shut behind her. A nanosecond later, she arrived at the Cosmic Mall landing station on the other side of Earth. The door opened. She was ready for shopping.

At each store, H-K181 scanned her fingerprint to pay. No human store clerks were needed. She asked a robot where she could find a recharger for her flying shoes.

> Why don't they need human store clerks?

Where Do Your Answers Come From?, continued

Think & Search Questions

For some questions, you need to pull together different parts of the text to find the answer. The answer can be in a single paragraph, across paragraphs, or even across chapters of a book.

Ask Questions That Pull the Story Together

Ask questions that lead you to bring together information from different parts of the story:

- *What is the main problem and how do the characters solve it?*
- *What are the most important events?*
- *Does this character act the same way at the end as she acted at the beginning of the story?*

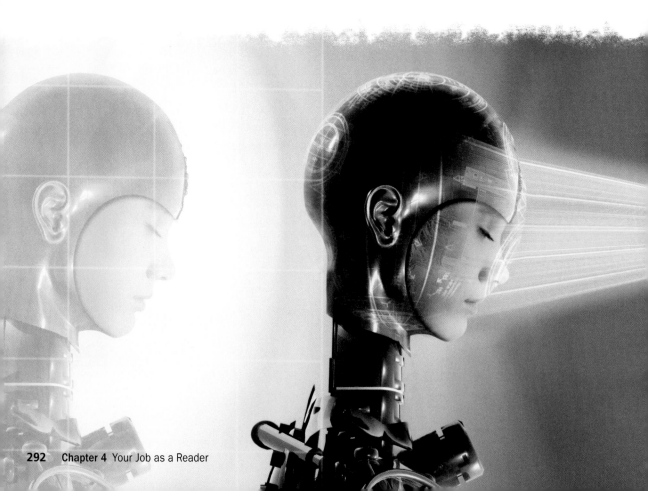

Ask questions that pull the story together.

That night, H-K181 crawled into her sleep flotation chamber for a short rest. Government scientists were trying to find a way for humans to go without sleep. But for now, rejuvenating her brain took at least two hours. Then another perfect day would start.

> What does "another perfect day" mean? Why does the author repeat this idea?

Suddenly H-K181 woke up shivering. She looked toward the corner of the room, but no transporter was ready to take her away as it did in her dream. The transponder was humming, reporting her location to Central Command at all times.

Now most humans followed the rules. They had to. Electronic sensors implanted under each person's skin sent waves to transponders to verify his or her location. A human on the run could be detected and apprehended in seconds.

> Does H-K181 want to run away? If she does, why?

H-K181 learned sign language to escape the vocal monitors that censored everyone's speech. She knew it was only a matter of time until technology controlled every word and thought.

H-K181 sighed as her older brother handed her some coffee. "Morning, Mattie," he motioned without words.

The transponder interrupted, "H-K181, you will soon be late for work. Tardiness will not be tolerated." She shuddered. She hated being called by her registration number.

She found some water and heated it in the atom scrambler. Then she splashed it on her face and relaxed for a few moments. Warm water was simple technology but right now it was the only technology she really enjoyed.

> How has the character changed from the beginning of the story? What is the author's main idea?

Where Do Your Answers Come From?, continued

On Your Own Answers

When you read, be open to any question that comes to mind.
The answers to some questions won't be in the text. You'll need
to use your own ideas and experiences to answer the questions.

- **Ask Questions That Draw On Your Experiences**
  Ask questions about how new information fits with what
  you already know: *How does this text compare with others
  on the same topic? Do I agree with the author's ideas and
  opinions? Is the writing convincing?*

- **Ask About the Big Ideas**
  After you finish reading, ask what the big ideas in the text
  are: *What is the significance of these ideas and information?
  How can I use this new information?*

A DARK FUTURE

HOW DO YOU IMAGINE the future? Will the world be peaceful and free of disease? Will governments use technology to control what people say and do? Three famous books paint a very dark future. The authors used frightening descriptions of the future to criticize what they saw happening in their own times.

The Time Machine

When H.G. Wells wrote *The Time Machine* in 1895, wealthy people spent their days playing games and buying expensive things. In contrast, the working class worked night and day to survive. *The Time Machine* criticizes society. It also sends a dark warning. If people do not treat each other with sympathy and dignity, society will break down.

In *The Time Machine*, the Time Traveler explores the future. The traveler first lands in the year 802,701 A.D. He finds a world of lazy, frail Eloi who live above ground. Below ground, the violent,

barely-human Morlocks work constantly to provide for the Eloi.

Will the inequality between the rich and poor become this drastic? Wells leaves the answer to the reader.

1984

George Orwell wrote the novel *1984* in 1949, shortly after the end of World War II. At that time, people around the world hoped that new technology would solve the world's problems. But Orwell feared that communist governments and corrupt leaders might use nuclear power and other technology to destroy and enslave humans.

Ask questions that draw on your experiences.

What science fiction books have I read? Did they also describe a "dark" future?

Do I agree with Wells' message in The Time Machine?

Did Orwell have good reasons to fear communist governments?

CONTINUED ON NEXT PAGE

Where Do Your Answers Come From?, continued

A DARK FUTURE, CONTINUED

In *1984*, Orwell creates a world where the government has complete control over its citizens. The government uses technology to monitor citizens' every move. Constant propaganda prevents people from thinking clearly as individuals. Telescreens monitor homes. The telescreens blare reminders that "BIG BROTHER IS WATCHING YOU." Anyone who tries to fight the government is tortured.

In *1984*, Orwell warns that the future could bring a world without privacy, individualism, and human rights.

Brave New World

Do citizens help the government strip away their rights? Aldous Huxley wrote *Brave New World* in 1931. It criticizes both the controlling government and its citizens.

Brave New World takes place in the 26th century. War and poverty no longer exist. The government works to keep everyone happy, including the working class. This happiness begins before birth.

George Orwell warned that technology could invade people's privacy.

Reproduction and childhood occur in a factory. While children sleep, they listen to recordings that teach them to be happy while working and buying expensive things. Family, relationships, and love are no longer important. But are people in this world happy? Or are they being controlled, like pet animals in a cage?

The three authors died long ago, but their warnings live on in their novels. Today, people still compare current events to the dark futures that Wells, Huxley, and Orwell invented. The issues they raised are still being debated—class struggles, privacy, and materialism.

Ask questions about big ideas.

How do I feel about the government watching what people do?

What would the world be like if this were true?

Have I learned anything new? Which of these issues is most important to me?

Author & You Answers

To enjoy what you're reading, it helps to get inside the writer's head. Ask questions that help you predict what the text will be like and connect with what you already know.

- **Ask Questions About the Author's Purpose**

  Every author has a purpose for writing—a reason for composing and presenting ideas. Get inside the writer's head by asking: *Did he or she write this mainly to give information, to entertain, or to persuade readers? Does the text include facts, opinions, or both?*

- **Ask Questions About the Author's Point of View**

  Like everyone else, authors have points of view about topics—they view the world from particular perspectives, with certain attitudes and opinions.

  Ask questions that help you reveal the author's attitude about the topic: *Does the writer have a personal connection to the topic? Is the writing friendly and humorous? Or is it analytical and concerned? Why does the author choose certain words?*

The texts on pages 298–299 are about the same topic: Classrooms of the Future. Read the texts and compare the two authors' purposes and points of view.

Where Do Your Answers Come From?, continued

Editorial

RICHMOND HIGH SCHOOL   **FEBRUARY ISSUE, VOL. IX**

Classrooms of the Future

By Hector Nguyen

Have you thought about what school will be like for kids in 2207? Will we still be sitting around tables with 29 other kids listening to a teacher's lecture? Okay. You probably haven't even thought much about what school is like for kids now. You're too busy having fun surfing the Internet, instant messaging, and downloading music. That's exactly my point!

I predict that the classrooms of the future are going to look very different from today's classrooms. In fact, there may not even be a need for classrooms at all. In the future, kids will learn at home using their personal computers. Isn't that what high school kids like to do most?

In the future human teachers will be replaced by electronic learning modules. Just download the lesson and you get point-by-point instruction. Have questions? Just talk into your voice-recognition device, wait sixty seconds, and hear the answer. In the worst case, you can always send a question the old-fashioned way—by e-mail.

And what about other students? You'll be able to set up a network so that you can share data with other kids. But who needs other kids anyway? In the future, you'll be setting your own pace and being your own person. No worries about peer pressure or other social stuff. Remote learning is already happening, and it's the wave of the future!

Number of...	
Students enrolled in U.S. high schools:	**16,400,000**
K–12 teachers expected to retire by 2010:	**331,440**
U.S. households with computers:	**70,000,000**
Hours teens spend on computers:	**3.5 per day**

Ask questions about the author's purpose.

Why did the writer choose this format and give statistical data?

Ask questions about the author's point of view.

How is the writer trying to influence what I believe?

Science Fiction

SPANISH 101 IN 2101 | J. Mahler   37

"*Hablo, hablas, habla*. Is that right?" I asked.

"*Co-rrec-to*," a metallic voice responded.

I was halfway through the first week of my learning module in Spanish 101. How many different verb endings can there be? Was I ever going to learn them all?

"*Página ocho. A continuar. ¿Listo?*" the audio was coming through loud and clear. But I had no idea what it was saying. I grabbed my printed instruction manual. I guessed how the words would be spelled, but couldn't find them anywhere.

"*No comprendo*," I muttered. The Help icon came up. So I pressed it. Nothing. *Nada*. Then I pressed it again. This time I got an avatar. She was a cute girl named Rosa, and she was smiling at me. Her English was better than my Spanish.

"Do you need some help?" Rosa asked.

"Uh, yeah. I mean, *Sí*," I said. "What do I do next?"

Rosa smiled. She blinked. Then she replied, "Do you need some help?"

This went on for a while. The more Rosa smiled, the more I frowned. Finally, I couldn't stand it anymore. I screamed, "I need help! I need a human! I need something!"

My mom stepped through the door and asked if I was all right. I told her what was happening. She smiled. She blinked. And then she asked, "Shall I call Mrs. Reyes at the high school? I think she's in charge of the Spanish program."

> **Ask questions about the author's purpose.**
>
> What happens to the character in the story?

> **Ask questions about the author's point of view.**
>
> Why does the author compare a real person to a computer avatar?

Strategy Summary

When you ask questions about what you are reading, you think along with the author. Asking and answering questions is a good way to make sure you're actively thinking about what you're reading.

- Ask and answer questions before, during, and after reading to **check your understanding**.

- Think about the connection between questions and their answers—**question-answer relationships**. The answers to some questions can be found in one or more parts of the text. Other questions ask about big ideas based on the entire text. You can get inside the writer's head by asking questions about the writer's purpose and point of view.

See how one good reader asks questions about details in a story and tries to get into the writer's head.

Science Fiction

A BARREN BACKYARD   51

Alina hated getting ready to go outdoors. It took her forty-five minutes of preparation. The Aero 720 suit and helmet were really uncomfortable.

Each morning, she tended her small bit of ground, fertilized the soil, and removed any acritoid particles that had fallen the night before.

"Would anything ever grow again?" She thought back to the ancient people: they simply opened a door and stepped out into a luscious garden. They had no idea what 2121 would be like.

> **Why does it take so long for her to go outside?**
> She needs lots of gear, so maybe outside is really polluted.

> **Why does the writer include these details?**
> They help me imagine what life without nature might be like. Maybe it's a warning.

Now see how another reader asks and answers questions to get the most out of his reading.

Nonfiction Article

making green space

Rooftop gardens are the wave of the future.

Cities of the future will be crowded. Planting a street-level garden will be out of the question. So, urban dwellers may choose a creative solution. They'll gather up their dirt, pots, flowers, and plants and head to their roofs. Amid the smog, concrete, glass, and steel, garden enthusiasts will create a haven from the busy, gray world below.

Some people are already heading to the rooftops. Rooftop gardens are not only beautiful, they're practical as well. They insulate against winter cold and summer heat. They reduce air pollution and dust, retain rainwater, and lower heating bills. Your city, maybe even your school, can be part of the rooftop revolution.

> **What are the benefits of rooftop gardens?**
> reduce pollution, retain rainwater, lower heating bills

> **Why is the writer telling me this?**
> Wants to convince me rooftop gardens are great in cities

Visualize

Firefighter. What do you picture when you hear this word? A brave person carrying heavy equipment? Flames, sirens, and smoke? People rushing in all directions? The word probably brings up vivid pictures that connect with all your senses, excite your imagination, and trigger feelings.

When you read you visualize, or use the writer's words to create pictures in your mind. You can "see" how a character in a novel looks, or you can "feel" a geometrical shape in your math text. Look at the next page to see how some teens form mental pictures to help them understand and experience what they read.

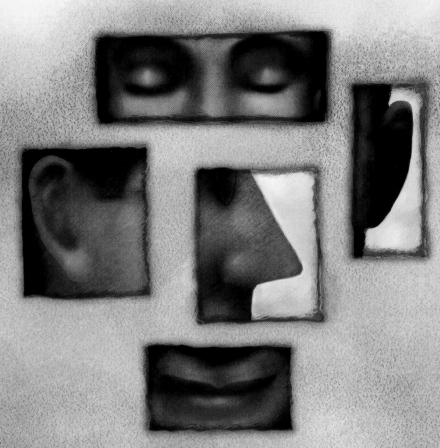

How Do You Visualize?

" When I read, I start creating separate images. Then I put them together and follow the action in my mind. It's kind of like watching a movie. "

—Randall

" I like to stop while I'm reading and picture what the writer is describing. If the author describes something that I've never seen, I use my imagination to see it. "

—Haley

" Sometimes when I read a story, I remember something that has happened in my life. I can remember how I felt. I even remember what the sights, smells, and sounds were. Then the characters in the book seem more real to me. "

—Aziz

" I write down words that describe important facts and ideas. Then as I read, I try to picture what those words are saying so that I can end up with one important picture that sticks with me. "

—Tuyen

You can download more Readers Talk tips. 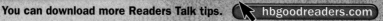 hbgoodreaders.com

Create Mental Images

You've never been to the Philippines, but your friend just got back from a trip there. To share his experience, you imagine the place he's describing. When you read, you form mental pictures to experience what the writer is describing.

My family spent a week at a fabulous beach.

How Do You Create Mental Images?

When you create mental images, you use the words that you read, along with experiences from your own life, to form pictures in your mind. It's like stepping into the text and experiencing what's happening there. Once you've got these mental images, you've got the writer's ideas.

Here's how to create mental images:

- Before reading, look at the illustrations or graphics. Use these as starting points to make your own mental pictures.

- As you read, pay attention to descriptive details that help you imagine events, places, and people. Add what you know from your life to form mental pictures of what you're reading. Ask yourself: *What do the words make me see, hear, touch, taste, and smell?*

- Combine these images into a photo album with pages you can mentally flip through or into a movie that plays in your mind.

FOCUS POINT Read the passage on the next page. How did the readers create mental images? Which words helped make these images?

César Chávez
MAN OF IRON PRINCIPLES

WHAT CAN PEOPLE ENDURE FOR A CAUSE THEY BELIEVE IN? Could they walk for hundreds of miles, or go without food for 25 days? Dedicated to improving the lives of migrant farm workers, César Chávez endured these things willingly.

Chávez was born in Yuma, Arizona in 1927. During the Great Depression, his family was forced to become migrant farm workers. They moved from place to place following the harvest. By the time he was in seventh grade, he had gone to more than thirty different schools.

Picking grapes and cotton was back-breaking work. Families worked long hours for little pay. The lucky ones rented shacks in fields; others had to sleep in their cars. Some farm owners even made the workers pay for the water they drank.

Chávez was determined to win rights for farm workers by helping them organize a labor union. In March 1966, he led a group of striking workers on a 340-mile march to Sacramento, the California state capital. Then in 1968, he began a 25-day hunger strike to draw attention to a national boycott of grapes. Through his efforts, farm workers received higher pay and better working conditions.

In the 1960s, migrant farm workers had very few rights.

> Use the photo as a starting point for the pictures you form in your mind.

Mental Images

> The march to Sacramento reminds me of the civil rights marches Dr. Martin Luther King led in the 1960s that I've seen on TV.

> I can imagine how awful it was for the farm workers to work all day in hot, dusty fields and then have to sleep in a shack or car.

Create Images for Nonfiction

Creating mental pictures when you read factual text helps you understand the material. It helps you keep the ideas from science or history texts in your head—just like a photo album keeps photos in place.

Store Mental Photos

Here's how to make a mental photo album for nonfiction:

1 Preview Before You Read

Look at the photographs and graphics. Use these as a starting point to create your own mental images as you read.

2 Look at the Language

As you read, look for words that describe and explain things. Use these words to form mental pictures. Ask yourself: *Can I picture this? What would this look like?*

3 Add Your Experience

Add in what you know from your own life. If you're reading about a tornado in science, you can picture a storm you've been through or one you've seen on TV.

4 Sharpen Your Focus

As you read on, look for more facts to make your pictures richer and clearer. Change the images, if needed, to fit with any new information.

Read the article and make a mental photo album.

TO THE
OCEAN'S DEPTHS

People have always wondered what the ocean depths were like. However, deep sea exploration was very dangerous. The deeper the water, the greater the water pressure. If divers went far down into the sea and came up too quickly, they would become ill and even die. Then, in 1947, Auguste Piccard invented a deep-sea vessel called a *bathyscaphe*.

The bathyscaphe descends into the sea when water is pumped into two tanks. It rises to the surface when iron pellets are released. The bathyscaphe set a world record in 1960. Two divers took it 35,000 feet down to the deepest known spot on Earth. The divers surfaced in good health.

Create Images for Nonfiction

Use the diagram and the writer's descriptions.

Imagine the bathyscaphe descending.

Then picture it coming up to the surface.

A bathyscaphe is made of many different parts to help it descend and ascend.

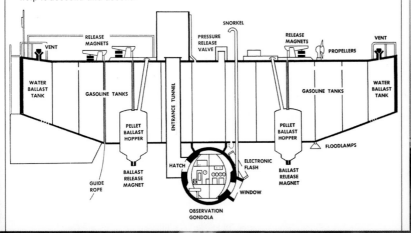

SNORKEL

RELEASE MAGNETS

VENT

PRESSURE RELEASE VALVE

RELEASE MAGNETS

VENT

PROPELLERS

WATER BALLAST TANK

GASOLINE TANKS

ENTRANCE TUNNEL

GASOLINE TANKS

WATER BALLAST TANK

PELLET BALLAST HOPPER

PELLET BALLAST HOPPER

FLOODLAMPS

GUIDE ROPE

BALLAST RELEASE MAGNET

HATCH

ELECTRONIC FLASH

BALLAST RELEASE MAGNET

WINDOW

OBSERVATION GONDOLA

Create Images for Fiction

When you read novels, short stories, or other fiction, the events usually unfold in a sequence—from beginning to end. You can combine the pictures you form to make a mental movie in which you see characters and events in action.

Make a Movie in Your Mind

Here's how to make a mental movie when you read fiction:

1 Preview Before You Read

Look at any illustrations or other visuals. Use these as a starting point to create pictures in your mind as you read.

2 Look at the Language

While reading, look for words that describe the setting, characters, and events. Use the words to form mental pictures. Ask: *What would this character (or scene) look like?*

3 Add Your Experience

Add in what you know from your own life. You can imagine characters looking like people you know or a setting looking like a place you've visited or seen in a movie.

4 Put the Pictures Together and Sharpen the Focus

Put the pictures into a sequence to make your movie. As you read on, look for more information that will make your movie clearer. Edit your movie, as needed, to fit with any new details or information.

Realistic Fiction

ALL THE RIGHT STUFF | Lisa Gómez   65

No one knew what would happen when the X-1 fighter plane breached the speed of sound, not even Captain Yeager. But it was too late for the pilot to back down now. He folded his long, lean body into the pilot's seat of the bullet-shaped plane and pulled the cockpit door shut.

A B-29 plane carried the X-1 up into the clouds. Yeager took deep breaths through his oxygen mask. His thick gloves and aviation gear protected him against the freezing air.

Reaching an altitude of 28,000 feet, the X-1 detached from the underside of the B-29. Now it was up to Yeager. He fired the rocket engine filled with exactly two minutes worth of fuel. The X-1 roared and shuddered. Faster and faster, it streaked through the sky—600 miles per hour, then 700.

Yeager struggled to hold the plane steady as the waves of air pounded it like a jackhammer. "It's breaking up!" Yeager yelled into the headset. The plane would surely explode under such pressure. Then, total silence. Unimaginable beauty. Absolute peace.

He'd done it—he'd flown supersonic, past the speed of sound. And it was better than anyone could have imagined.

Make a Mental Movie

Use the writer's descriptions:

- **What does the X-1 look and sound like during the flight?**
- **What does Yeager see and feel?**

Left Page: Charles Yeager with the X-1 "Glamorous Glennis." This Page: A B-29 with the X-1 attached. The X-1 in flight, October 1947.

Use All Your Senses

Before your family reunion, you hadn't seen your cousin for two years. When you look back on the party, you use all your senses. You picture how your cousin looked and hear her voice. You remember how the food smelled and tasted. When you read, you use your senses like this to experience the text.

How to Use Your Senses

When you use all your senses, you use the writer's words, along with your own experience, to really get into the text. Here's how:

- As you read, look for words that tell how things look, sound, smell, taste, and feel.

- Think about your own experiences and add them to the information in the text.

- Use your imagination to fill in the gaps when the text only gives you some information.

- Keep track of your reactions and feelings.

FOCUS POINT Read "Who Am I?" and the readers' responses on the next page. How did each reader tap into his or her senses?

Who Am I?

—Mawi Asgedom

MY NAME IS Selamawi Haileab Asgedom—Mawi, for short—and I shouldn't even be around to write this book. I should have died a long time ago—eaten by a hyena, killed by black fever, or blown up by a rebel group. But I wasn't killed. I've made it to age twenty-six and feel blessed to be here now.

I was born half a world away in Ethiopia, in a small town called Adi Wahla. I would have grown up in Adi Wahla, except for one problem: Ethiopia was in the midst of a thirty-year civil war with its northern region, Eritrea. Unfortunately for my family, our village was located right on the Ethiopian-Eritrean border.

Men from our village fled the brutal armies, and one day, my father fled as well. He walked hundreds of miles to Sudan, leaving the rest of us in Ethiopia. Six months later, my mother took my five-year-old brother Tewolde, my baby sister Mehret, and me on the long trek to meet up with my dad. I was three years old.

www.mawispeaks.com

As a child, Mawi Asgedom walked hundreds of miles to flee war-torn Ethiopia.

Readers Use Their Senses

I picture the family walking for days and days. I see them hunched over. They are exhausted and hungry. It's amazing they made it.

I can hear soldiers yelling to each other and guns firing bullets. Just imagining this scares me. Mawi's family must have been very frightened.

Have a Virtual Experience

When you tap into all of your senses as you read, you experience what the author is writing about. Using your senses helps the text come alive.

How Can You Experience What You Read?

Follow these steps to experience a text:

1 Look at the Language

Pay attention to words that appeal to your senses.

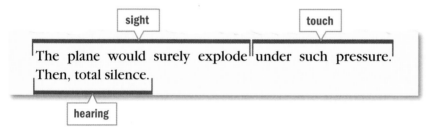

2 Add What You Already Know

Use your five senses to create mental pictures from those words. Add your own experience to imagine the people, places, and events being described. When the writer describes the speeding jet, think about one that you saw in a movie or on TV. How did it sound, look, and feel?

3 Fill in the Images

Use your imagination to fill in pictures when the author only gives you some information related to the senses. A chart like this can help you really get into your reading.

Visualization Chart

Words in the Text	My Own Experience	What I Imagine
The plane would surely explode under such pressure. Then, total silence. Unimaginable beauty. Absolute peace.	I saw a movie where a jet was shaking until it reached a certain speed. Then it became really quiet and the pilot relaxed.	I picture the pilot being scared and excited. Then I imagine him feeling happy and enjoying the view.

TOO HOT
TO HANDLE

Ever wonder what your personal limits are? I test mine every time I go to work. I light a torch, dramatically wave it around in the air, and then put the burning flame into my mouth. It's natural to wonder why anyone would want to swallow fire. So let me say from the start: It's a living.

People really enjoy my fire-eating stunts, and I'm paid to do them. There are easier ways to make money, but I love the drama. I enter a darkened tent, holding the flaming torches above my head. I can feel the audience watching every move and sense the tension palpably mounting. They know what's coming and can't believe it. Smoke wafts around them. They

hear the fires hiss. Then when I swallow the flames, some people gasp. Many applaud. That's what keeps me playing with fire. But remember—DON'T TRY THIS AT HOME. I'm a professional and know all the trade secrets. Every move is choreographed and rehearsed, with many safety precautions in place.

continued on next page

Have a Virtual Experience

1. Look for words and phrases that **appeal to your senses.**

2. Add what you already know.

" **I know what it's like to be in an audience watching someone doing something scary or brave.**"

3. Fill in images when the text doesn't give enough information.

Read and Respond

Do you ever laugh while reading a story? Do you ever feel nervous or worried when you read an exciting historical account? You're reacting to the text, and that's good! As you read, be aware of how certain words and phrases make you feel.

Track How You Feel

Here's how to really get involved with what you're reading:

1. Pay attention to words that describe people, places, and events. Use these words to create mental pictures.

2. Ask yourself: *How do the words and pictures make me feel?* Think about how your experiences and imagination help create those feelings.

3. Go back and figure out the specific words and phrases that led to those feelings.

As you read the essay on the next page, note words that make a picture in your mind. Then ask yourself: *How does this mental picture make me feel?*

Response Journal

	Words and Phrases	My Response
○	I do tumbling stunts with fire.	When I read this, I felt a little bit nervous for her.
	This creates patterns of light in the dark tent.	This sounds kind of fun— like making art with fire.

TOO HOT TO HANDLE, *continued*

    To make my performance more dramatic, I do tumbling stunts with fire. I hang upside down from a giant iron ring that's surrounded in fire. The ring turns as I slowly descend from the top of the tent. Everyone watches in hushed silence.

    On the ground, I feverishly dance across the sand in an iron skirt. All around the hem are large candles burning brightly. This creates patterns of light throughout the dark tent. Then I deftly juggle torches—first three, then six at a time. It's all part of a carefully planned ballet. We rehearse for weeks. Then it's finally show time. We're ready, and so are all the fire blankets and extinguishers!

Strategy Summary

When you visualize, you use the writer's words to create pictures in your mind. This helps you understand and more fully experience what you read.

- **Create mental images** by noticing descriptions and adding what you know from your life. Flip through the pages of your mental photo album or let the images play like a movie in your mind.

- **Use all your senses** by looking for words that tell how things look, sound, smell, taste, and feel. Add your own experiences to what you read.

See how one good reader uses her senses to create mental pictures and get into the story.

Fiction

HITTING THE LIMIT   145

Jack carved across the halfpipe, picking up speed. Wind-blown snowflakes stung his face and blurred his vision.

"I'm going for a front 10 like Shaun White! Rock n' Roll!"

The wind picked up as he hit the lip, throwing him higher than he thought possible.

"Oh, no!"

Jack flew up at an angle. For a second, he thought he might not be able to land his board.

Somehow, mid-air, he managed to shift his weight. Boom! He nailed the landing perfectly. He cut a path through the fresh snow. He took a deep breath and smelled the pine trees. "It doesn't get much better than this!" he thought.

> " **I picture Jack snowboarding. I can feel the cold wind and see a blurry landscape.**"

> " **I feel his excitement when he does a trick.**"

Now see how another good reader creates mental pictures and uses his senses to keep the ideas in his head when he reads nonfiction.

Nonfiction

DANCING FOR A CAUSE

Students dance to raise money for charity.

STROBE LIGHTS PULSE THROUGHOUT A DARKENED GYM. Bodies turn, bend, and dip to the beat of the music. Can they keep this up for twenty-four grueling hours? In spite of aching muscles and bleary eyes, these volunteers are determined to try. They are testing their endurance for a cause.

Students from colleges across the country are participating in dance marathons. They are raising funds for the Children's Miracle Network. The funds help children who are treated in the network's 170 children's hospitals. Each day, those kids experience personal tests of endurance. They are fighting the effects of disease and injury.

" I can picture the lights, music, and people dancing."

" The photo makes it look like fun. But if I were dancing for 24 hours, I'd be really tired."

" Now I picture the kids in the hospitals. They must be happy that the dancers are helping them."

Make Connections

Suppose the brakes on your car need repair. When you start working on them, you remember what you learned last year when you helped your friend fix the brakes on her car. In this way, you bring what you already know to the job at hand. This helps you understand what needs to be done and makes the job a whole lot easier to do.

When you read, you connect to things you already know from your past experiences, the world around you, and other texts you've read. This helps you control your reading and increase your understanding. Look at the next page to see how some teens make conections while they're reading.

How Do You Make Connections?

"As I'm reading, I look for things that I can connect to in my life. I add my own experiences to what I'm reading to understand the passage better. "

—Jasmine

"When I read a story, I try to put myself in the characters' shoes. I understand the story much better when I relate to what the characters are going through. "

—Fernando

"The other day I was reading about earthquakes in science. Right away I remembered hearing about an earthquake on the news last night. When I connect my reading with things like this that I already know, then what I'm reading has more meaning for me. "

—Abdalla

"I look for things that are familiar when I read. So, if I'm reading science fiction, I look for stuff that I've read in other science fiction stories—like cool technology that doesn't exist yet. When I know what to expect, the story makes more sense and is more fun to read. "

—Eva

You can download more Readers Talk tips.  hbgoodreaders.com

Connections Are Everywhere!

What's It Like ?

When you go to a new movie theater, you use what you already know about movie theaters to get a ticket, buy snacks, and choose your seat. When you read, you use what you already know to make sense out of what you're reading.

How to Make Connections

When you make connections, you put together information from the text with information you know from outside the text. This helps you understand what you're reading and makes you think about ideas in new ways. To make connections:

- Figure out what the **topic** is before you start to read. The topic is what the writing is mostly about. Ask yourself: *What do I already know about this topic?*

- While you're reading, pay attention to what the selection reminds you of—experiences you've had, things you know about the world from TV, songs, school, and so on, and other texts you've read.

- Stop now and then to think about how the things you're reminded of tie in to what you're reading.

FOCUS POINT Read the passage and the sample connections on the next page. How do the readers connect to the text?

Alone in a CROWD

It was another typical April morning in Kansas. It was only 6 AM, but I could feel the sun and the heat. I buried my head under the covers, already dreading the day. As always, Tía Amelia knocked on my door and whispered. *"Buenos días, Carmen. ¿No quieres comer?"*

"I'm not hungry," I grumbled to myself. At breakfast I told my grandmother that I didn't want beans and tortillas every morning. I knew this hurt her feelings. I sat and ate, thinking about how much my family embarrassed me. I hated eating Mexican food all the time. I hated that my parents didn't speak English when we were at home. But how could I expect my family to stop being who they were?

I've had a lot of bad days lately. I am the only student from Mexico in my class, and I'm lonely. When I go back home, my family asks me how the day went, but I don't want to talk about it. At home I want to be alone, but that never happens in a close family like ours.

Last week my math teacher said that being alone in a crowd is fine as long as you don't chase the crowd away. I wonder what advice she'd give for finding one friend in a crowd.

Readers Connect

This reminds me of the year my cousins came to live with us. Sometimes I wanted more privacy. So, I can understand how the writer feels.

There are a lot of news stories about families coming to the U.S. from Mexico looking for better jobs. The writer's family may have gone to Kansas for the same reason.

Link to Your Experience

Bring what you know from your experience to what you read. Your experience includes events in your life, your feelings, and what you have learned from other people. When you make connections, you add your experience to what you're reading. Here's how:

1 Identify the Topic

Before reading, identify the topic, or what the reading is mostly about. For example, "Anywhere But Here" is about embarrassing moments at school. Think about what you know about the topic based on your own experience.

2 Look for Links

As you read about ideas and events, think about what they remind you of in your own life.

WHAT THE TEXT SAYS	MY CONNECTION
Then you trip. Suddenly you're "wearing" your lunch. When the cafeteria explodes with laughter, you want to disappear.	I remember my first year on the football team. During an important game, I dropped the ball and everyone booed. I can understand how awful the writer must have felt.

3 Use Your Connections

While reading, stop to think about the connections you're making. Ask yourself: *How does my own experience help me understand this text?*

ANYWHERE BUT HERE   15

Have you ever done something so embarrassing that you just wanted to crawl into a hole? If so, you're not alone. Of course, there are different degrees of embarrassment.

For example, suppose you're walking through the school cafeteria with a tray of food. You take a second look at the roast beef and wonder if it is finally going to kill you. Then you trip. Suddenly you're "wearing" your lunch. When the cafeteria explodes with laughter, you want to disappear.

An even more humiliating situation is when you want to impress someone and your plan goes wrong. For instance, you walk into school and spot the girl you've been dying to ask out. She's standing at her locker. You smile and begin to talk to her, but there's something strange about the way she looks at you.

As she walks away she says, "You better watch out for those pigeons." You're confused. You go to the bathroom and look in the mirror. Then you nearly fall over with embarrassment when you see what's in your hair!

continued on next page

Link to Your Own Experience

1. Use the title and repeated words to figure out the topic.

2. Ask yourself what **specific events** remind you of in your own life.

3. Think about how these links to your experience can help you understand what the writer is getting at.

323

Link to Your Experience, continued

16   ANYWHERE BUT HERE, CONTINUED

My personal disaster came in the second month at my new high school. I really wanted to be part of a group, but I didn't know anyone and wasn't sure how to fit in.

Then someone tossed me a flyer about a party on October 29. "It must be a Halloween party," I thought, "and here's my chance to meet some kids."

I spent days working on my robot costume. I found some sheet metal and foil for my head and arms. Then I rigged some sound effects with a battery and speaker.

The night of the party, I walked in, ready for a big entrance. Then I froze. Everyone was wearing jeans. I was the only one in a costume!

Someone knocked on my metal head and said, "Hey. How did you make those sound effects?" Slowly I unfroze. The guy talking to me was Omar, and he and I discovered we had a lot in common. After that, I felt like I was beginning to fit in.

As you read, you can use a graphic organizer to help you make connections to your experience.

Ask Yourself	Links to Your Own Life
What do I know about the topic?	No one likes being embarrassed, but it happens to almost everyone at some point.
What do events and ideas in the text remind me of?	When I moved, I didn't know any of the kids in my neighborhood. I really felt left out, just like the writer.
How does my experience help me understand the text?	I understand the way the writer feels because I went through a similar experience.

Link to the World of Ideas

You may not realize it, but you have tons of knowledge about the world beyond what you've personally experienced. For example, you may know a lot about a sport that you've never played or a place you've never visited. When you link what you know about the world with what you're reading, you really get a handle on what the writer is saying.

When you upload this new understanding to your brain, you have even more knowledge to call on the next time you read about the topic.

Where Does Knowledge Come From?

Every day you take in information from the world around you. All the songs, conversations, movies, family stories, TV shows, and books become bits of data that you can use and re-use over and over again.

News
Weather
Sports
Music
Datebook
e-mail

nting of astronomer and
lorer Amerigo Vespucci using
astrolabe to make a star map

re stars and planets were.
laus was thrilled. He would
how to make star maps,
Ptolemy's. The main
ument he would use was an
abe. He would line up a
f the astrolabe with

Link to the World of Ideas, continued

Connect to What You Already Know

When you connect what you know from the world around you to your reading, you get a much clearer picture of what the writer is saying. Often you can see how an idea or belief works in real life. Here's how to connect to what you know:

1 **Identify the Topic**

Before reading, figure out the topic, or what the reading is mostly about. Ask yourself: *What do I already know about this topic from TV, music, other people, and so on?* For example, "On the Mat" is about a girl who competes on a wrestling team. What have you read, seen, or heard about this topic?

2 **Look for Links**

As you read the story, pay attention to what you already know from news stories, TV shows, school, movies, and so on. Ask: *What does this text remind me of from the world around me?*

3 **Build Your Understanding**

While reading, stop from time to time to use what you know. Ask yourself: *How does what I already know from the world around me add to my understanding of this text?*

Fiction

Aleesha Wilson walked into the girls' locker room to change into her sweats. "I'm finally doing what I want," she thought proudly. Aleesha had won a spot on an all-male wrestling team, and she had fought hard for the chance.

At the end of 9th grade she had wondered, "Why should wrestling be a boys-only sport?" She decided to ask the Board of Education to allow her to join the team. A federal law was on her side.

Title IX stated that no one could stop Aleesha from participating in a federally-funded program just because she was female. Her school did not have a girls' wrestling team, and the sports program received money from the government. So, the board had to allow Aleesha to try out for the team. She was judged the same way the boys were, and she made the cut.

Now Aleesha opened the door to the gym and all eyes focused on her as she took her place on the mats. She was proud of being the first girl in her school to wrestle. This was her chance to prove that she could be a true competitor.

Connect to What You Already Know

" I saw a wrestling match on TV once. You have to be pretty strong to wrestle."

" I've heard of Title IX. A woman in my state went to court to play on her high school varsity soccer team."

Link to the World of Ideas, continued

Form New Knowledge

When you read, you combine what you are learning from the text with what you already know to form new knowledge. The new information, ideas, or insights add to your brain power. Then in the future, you can call up this new knowledge to help you understand material that you're reading for the first time.

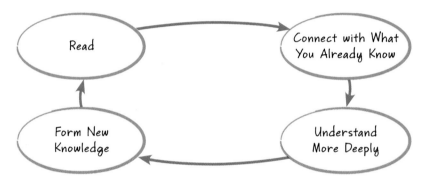

Follow these steps to form new knowledge:

1 **Identify the Topic**

Before reading, figure out the topic of the selection—what it is mostly about. Then think about what you already know about the topic.

2 **Notice Unfamiliar Content**

As you read, take note of the ideas and information that are unfamiliar. Ask yourself: *What is new to me?*

3 **Think About How New Ideas Fit**

While reading, stop briefly from time to time to grab hold of the new ideas and information. Ask yourself: *How does this new knowledge fit with what I already know?* Sometimes the new ideas match what you already know. When they don't, you have to think about them and read on to get more information.

TEENS Find THEIR CALLING

Getting Others Connected

Thirteen-year-old Anders Jones hopped into a cab. He was with his father on vacation in Jamaica. The cab ride opened Anders's eyes. He learned that the taxi driver's children went to a school with 850 students, but the school had only one computer.

Jones thought about his own junior high school back home in the U.S. It had as many students, but about 200 computers! Jones knew that in the future, jobs would require computer skills. It seemed unfair that students in Jamaica would not have the opportunity to learn these important skills.

So he made a life-changing decision. He created Teens for Technology to help the Jamaican students. Thanks to Jones and his organization, by the end of 2006 there were more than 2,200 computers in schools throughout Jamaica. Today Teens for Technology has expanded to Thailand, Vietnam, Pakistan, Indonesia, and Haiti. Who knew that a simple cab ride would be the start of a new life for Jones and for hundreds of thousands of students around the world?

Anders Jones started Teens for Technology to help students in Jamaica.

continued on next page

Form New Knowledge

1. Ask yourself:

" What do I know about the topic?"

2. Take note of **new ideas and information.**

3. Think about how the new information fits with what you already know:

" I had heard that some teens try to help kids in other countries. Now I know about Anders and Teens for Technology."

Link to the World of Ideas, continued

Teens Find Their Calling, *continued*

Some Teens Focus on Local Problems

Some teens in Gibson City, Illinois, were moved to action when their friend Greg Arends died. Greg was killed in a car accident, but his twin brother Steve survived the crash thanks to a seat belt.

Concerned teens have helped save lives by reminding teens to buckle up.

A group of teens decided to make more people aware of the need for safety on the roads. Some sewed the words *Buckle Up* on towels. The school band wrote a safety awareness song.

Students made road signs reminding drivers to slow down and wear seat belts. The signs were a lifesaver for one driver. Brandon Hoke saw one of the signs and buckled his seat belt. He later crashed into a truck and survived because he had buckled up.

Teens Make a Difference

According to one survey, 73% of young people in the U.S. believe they can make a difference in their communities. Seventy percent have participated in activities that improved their neighborhoods. Anders Jones and the teens of Gibson City are examples of teens who help others, and along the way find out just who they are.

New information may not always fit with what you've heard:

" I thought I heard on TV that only a small percent of teens believe they can make a difference. I'll have to do some checking to see which number is correct."

Connect with Other Texts

When you read, the text often reminds you of something you've read before. For example, a character in a novel may make you remember a similar character in another story. You gain a deeper understanding of what you're reading by thinking about how texts you've read in the past are similar to or different from what you're reading now.

How Can You Connect Texts?

There are three ways you can link texts:

- **By the Ideas**
  Different authors often write about the same topic. They may present similar or different information. For example, "experts" may disagree about some health issues:

  Topic: Drinking Soda

  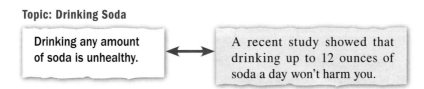

- **By the Author's Writing Style**
  Writers of fiction and nonfiction have their own style, or way, of writing. Their style shows their personality. Often you can tell who has written something by the writer's choice of words, type of sentences, and the tone, or attitude, that comes across.

- **By the Genre**
  A genre is a kind of writing; for example, biography, essay, or short story. Suppose last year you read a biography of the female aviator Amelia Earhart. When you start to read a biography of Bessie Coleman, another aviation pioneer, you can expect similar information.

Connect with Other Texts, continued

Link Texts by the Ideas

Ideas can be funny, shocking, boring, or unbelievable. But no matter what, reading selections are built around them. When you connect ideas from other texts with what your current text says, you get a deeper understanding of what you're reading.

Here's how to link texts by the ideas:

1 Identify the Topic

Before reading, identify the topic, or what the text is mostly about. Then start thinking of other texts you've read on the same topic.

2 Look for Links

As you read, connect what other texts have said with what the text you are reading says.

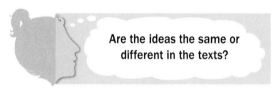

Are the ideas the same or different in the texts?

3 Increase Your Understanding

While reading, pause from time to time to use the ideas from other texts. Ask yourself: *How does what I know about the ideas from other texts add to my understanding of this text?*

Essay

RICHMOND HIGH SCHOOL   SEPTEMBER ISSUE, VOL. III

A Big Decision

By James Clifton, Class of 2008

Do you know where you're going after high school?
I wish I had more time to decide. Actually, I wish I didn't have to decide at all. I'm not ready to make any big decisions. But, by the time I finish my senior year next year, I *have* to make a choice: school or job? My future is up to me, but guess what? I'm stuck right here in the present.

I've never been afraid of making decisions before, but this one scares me more than any basketball game or final exam. I lay down at night and the wheels keep spinning in my brain. I can't sleep. Do you have the same problem?

My friend Ramón isn't sitting around, wondering what to do with his life. He's going to a trade school to become an electrician and start his own business. My pal K.C. knows what she wants to do, too— she's headed to college to become a doctor. K.C. is always sure about everything.

I'm not sure what will make me decide, but one thing I know—time is running out.

Links to Ideas

" I read a magazine article that said you can make a lot more money with a college degree. So I think the writer should choose to go to school. "

" I read a novel about a teen who had to work to help support her family. Things turned out okay for her, so maybe the writer shouldn't worry so much. "

Connect with Other Texts, continued

Link Texts by the Author's Style

Like singers who have a cool, recognizable musical style, authors have an individual writing style, or way of writing. Whether they write fiction or nonfiction, authors use language in ways that set them apart from other authors. When you recognize an author's style, you know what to expect as you read.

Here's how to connect texts by author's style:

1 Identify the Writing Style

Before reading, think about the style the author used in other texts you've read. Ask yourself questions that will help you know what to expect in the text you're reading:

> **Questions About the Author's Style**
>
> " Did the author use informal or formal language?"
>
> " Were the sentences short or long?"
>
> " What was the author's attitude like?"
>
> " Was the writing serious, or did it make fun of things?"

2 Look for Links

As you read, notice whether the author uses the style you were expecting. Note ways it is the same or different.

3 Guide Your Reading

Use your knowledge of how the author usually writes to guide your reading. For example, if you know the writer does not always say things directly, you may have to read between the lines to make sense of the text.

THE FACE OF DOUBT | Tamara Greene   29

"What were you just talking about?"

My parents were whispering in the kitchen. "Oh, nothing," they replied. They looked tense and I could tell they were hiding something from me.

There was a dark, disturbing shadow hanging over our house. My parents spent a lot of time talking on the phone behind closed doors. They stopped talking when they heard me walk by.

My father had always been pretty open about things. One night I had seen him lock an envelope inside a desk drawer. I wondered if it was good news or bad, business or personal.

Usually I was glad to be an only child. Now I wished I had a sister or brother to talk to. I kept telling myself, "It's nothing. Stop being so neurotic."

Then one Friday night, I came home early from soccer practice. My parents were in the kitchen looking intently at a letter. I startled them and my dad quickly put the letter inside an envelope. My mom looked at him and said, "It's time, Rodolfo. It's time."

She handed me the envelope. "We've been wanting to tell you something. Now is a good time."

Inside the envelope I found a letter written in blue pen and a photograph. I looked at the picture and said, "She looks exactly like me." Then I understood.

"Yes. You have a sister. A twin sister," my dad said softly.

My mind raced, and I felt faint. "I guess I'm not who I think I am," I barely whispered.

Link by Author's Style

Suppose you have read other stories by Tamara Greene, so you know her writing style.

You know to expect short paragraphs and informal language.

You expect the story to be told in first-person.

You know to pay attention to details that will help you solve a mystery.

Connect with Other Texts, continued

Magazine Article

MAKING DATING SIMPLER

By Owen Conte

Aren't first dates awful? Well, I have a great solution to the problem—technology. Since technology always makes life easier, why not just have computer-controlled dating? That way we don't have to deal with all those annoying choices.

Imagine this. You meet your first techno-date at a low-priced restaurant. (*Techno-date* is what you'll be calling your special him/her in the future.) A portable computer has picked the place and ordered your meals. Did you know that soy burgers and sprouts were good for you?

As usual you're worried about saying something dumb on the first date. But not tonight. When you start to bring up a topic that your techno-date might disagree with, a small microchip buzzes in your ear and tells you exactly what to talk about—the weather or last night's TV lineup. Your date talks about the weather a lot, too. Those microchips sure are working overtime.

By the end of dinner, you feel like you've known each other for mega-eons. (*Mega-eons* is another word you'll be using in the future.) Your date knows you love soy burgers. You're impressed by her lengthy descriptions of "clouds with a chance of precipitation." Now isn't that a future-perfect date?

Link by Author's Style

What is this author's style?

Does he use informal language and ask questions?

Is his writing sarcastic, so you know he means the opposite of what he says?

How will you use your knowledge of Owen Conte's writing style to guide your future reading?

Link Texts by the Genre

Do you like hip-hop, rock, or jazz? These types of music can be called *genres*. Like music, writing can be categorized into genres, or types, too. Fiction and nonfiction are the two major genres. These can be broken down into other genres.

Examples of Genres

Fiction	Nonfiction
Mystery	Web Site
Science Fiction	Biography
Folk Tale	Letter
Short Story	Magazine Article
Myth	Diary

Connecting the genre of what you're reading to another text will help you figure out the author's purpose for writing and recognize the features the texts have in common. For example, when you read a folk tale you can expect to find the features you've come across in other folk tales you've read.

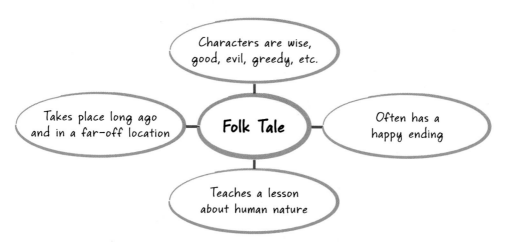

Use the Reader's File on pages 344–357 to find features of other specific genres. Just as road signs help you know what's ahead, making connections to the genre will help you know what's ahead in your reading.

Link Texts by the Genre, continued

How Do You Link By Genre?

Here's how to use genre to get the most out of your reading:

1 **Identify the Genre**

Preview the text to decide whether it is like the fiction or nonfiction texts you've read before. You can download the genre checklist at hbgoodreaders.com to help you decide.

Then, start thinking about the specific genre. For example, if it's fiction, is it a mystery or science fiction? Once you have a hunch about the genre, begin thinking about what you can expect to find as you read. See the Reader's File pages 344-357 for lists of what to expect when you read different genres.

2 **Look for Links**

While you're reading, take note of how closely the text follows the genre you expected. Pay attention to how the author's purpose and special features of similar texts show up in the selection you are reading.

Use an organizer like this to note what you discover about the genre.

Link by Genre

Major genre: Fiction

Genre: folk tale

Author's Purpose: to entertain and teach a lesson about human nature

Special features I expect: a story that takes place long ago, characters with obvious traits

3 **Direct Your Reading**

To help you stay focused while reading, use what you know about why authors write that genre. As you move along, use the special features to help you figure out what the author is saying.

The Foul-Tempered ~*Princess*~

Once upon a time, a grand Sultan had a beautiful daughter named Salma. But Salma had a very high opinion of herself and a foul temper. When the charming Prince Balbir expressed his desire to marry her, Salma rejected him. He had not sufficiently praised her beauty.

As Salma's seventeenth birthday approached, a painter with long hair and beard offered to paint the princess's portrait. Salma agreed, but she said, "You must paint me exactly as I am."

"Fine," the painter said, "but you may not see the painting until your birthday." Salma reluctantly agreed.

The morning of her birthday, Salma ran to greet the artist with his painting. Her excitement turned to anger when she saw a scowling face on the portrait staring back at her. "Who is that awful woman?" she yelled out. "That's not me!"

Hearing her complaints, the Sultan rushed in. After one look at the portrait, he said lovingly, "Dear daughter, I'm sorry to say that often, that *is* you."

Hearing his words, Salma saw the truth about herself and vowed to change. The artist then revealed his true identity as Prince Balbir. Now that Salma promised to control her temper, she would become his bride and the two would live happily ever after.

Link by the Genre

Preview the text:

" From the title and first sentence this seems like a folk tale. So it will take place long ago and may teach a lesson."

How closely does this follow other folk tales?

" Like other folk tales, the story characters represent human traits. The princess is vain and has a bad temper."

What lesson do you think the writer wants to teach?

" I think the lesson is that no one likes people who are always mad, no matter how rich or beautiful they are."

Link Texts by the Genre, continued

Read the poem below. Make connections to other poetry you've read to help you understand it.

Poem

What Is This?

—STEEVEN A. SMITH

What is a picture?

Is it a moment

frozen in time to be relived and cherished

or a paralyzing insight as to who we were then?

How much have we changed?

The past held so many paths.

Each decision made

for better for worse

likened into those things which formed your identity

Were the times happy?

Maybe.

Are you afraid of the future?

The beauty of a picture lies not within its material form

but the sight it gives into a human mind

and the soul which thrives behind it.

Link by Genre

What type of writing is this? What do you expect?

" Unlike other poems, this one is not divided into stanzas. When you read it out loud, it has a rhythm but the words don't rhyme. "

Make connections to help you understand the poet's message:

" Like other poems, this one uses a metaphor. A picture is the person you were at a certain time in the past. "

Make All the Connections

Now try putting it all together. As you read the article that begins below, make connections to ideas, author's style, and genre.

Nonfiction Article

Ruben Rivers:
SOLIDER, CITIZEN, AND HERO

THE WORLD WAS AT WAR— this time with Nazi Germany. Ruben Rivers, a young farmer from Oklahoma, wanted to do his part. So, along with two of his brothers, he immediately enlisted in the Army. It was 1942.

Ruben was assigned to the 761st Tank Battalion in Louisiana. The nineteen-year-old was ready to do whatever his country asked of him. He would even give his life, the ultimate sacrifice. But, would he ever see combat?

Black soldiers, like black citizens all over the United States, were facing discrimination and segregation. Soldiers like Rivers were assigned to separate units. They often dealt with poorer living conditions than their white comrades, and they faced prejudice daily. But perhaps the hardest thing to bear was not being allowed to fight.

Ruben Rivers

continued on next page

What other texts have you read that present historical events in the form of a story?

What do you notice about the writer's style?

What other texts have you read with ideas about racial segregation in U.S. history?

Make All the Connections, continued

Ruben Rivers, *continued*

That changed for Ruben Rivers when his battalion was called into combat. In 1944, the 761st, or the Panthers, as they called themselves, shipped off to Europe to face the enemy. During the battalion's first battle in France, Ruben Rivers showed his heroism.

Rivers's unit was directed to capture a town in German territory. Rivers drove the lead tank. He put his life in danger when he got out of his tank. In broad daylight, he removed a fallen tree that the enemy had put on the road. Rivers received a Silver Star for his bravery.

Rivers was awarded a medal for his bravery.

One week later, Staff Sergeant Rivers again would lead his unit into battle. As his tank rumbled along, he hit a mine. He suffered a serious leg injury. When his officer ordered him to be sent home, Rivers replied, "This is one order, the only order, I will ever disobey."

In spite of great pain from his injury, Rivers stayed in battle three more days. Then a direct hit on his tank killed him instantly. Rivers earned a Medal of Honor, the highest honor a soldier can receive.

Unfortunately, it was not given to him, or to any other African American, for almost 50 years. Discrimination was once again at work. Finally, in 1997, President Clinton gave the medals to six African Americans for their bravery in World War II. One medal was accepted by Ruben Rivers's sister, while his captain stood by. Surely, Ruben would have been proud, but medals are not what made the man.

Guide your reading by making connections:

" I know that the author is writing about real events as though they're a story. I also know the author sticks to the facts and tells about the events in time order. "

Genre Smarts

Get the goods on genre. The Reader's Files on the following pages give you a snapshot of many different genres, or types of writing, along with the authors' purposes. The pages also give you checklists of the features you can expect to find when you read the particular genre. Use these pages and the checklists to help you make connections by genre when you read.

Fiction
Short Story
Myth
Fable
Mystery
Science Fiction
Historical Fiction
Parody

Nonfiction
Narrative
    Biography
    Memoir
Expository
    Content-Area
        Article
Procedural
    How-to Article
Persuasive
    Letter to
        the Editor
    Essay

Drama

Poetry

DR. JEKYLL and Mr. Hyde
by Robert Louis Stevenson
adapted by Kate McMullan

THINGS FALL APART
CHINUA ACHEBE

AYN RAND
ANTHEM

Genre Features

Fiction

Everyone likes a good story. Fiction is a major genre, or type of text, that tells a story. In general, fiction writers want to entertain their readers, but they also want to share their ideas about people and life.

Fiction has several different forms, or subgenres. Each subgenre has its own features. When you recognize these features, you know what to expect as you read.

Short Story

Do you want a quick read? Try a short story, one type of fiction. The **author's purpose** is to entertain you by presenting exciting characters who solve a problem in a few pages.

> **WHAT TO EXPECT IN A SHORT STORY**
>
> ☐ A few characters, who are introduced quickly
> ☐ A setting and powerful conflict
> ☐ Problems, plot events, or issues that are revealed quickly
> ☐ A plot that focuses on a single event

---

48   **EXPECT THE UNEXPECTED | Gavin Liu**

"Dead?" she gasped. Ella had run to the phone expecting her husband's voice, not news of his death. Her heart was racing and she felt faint. As she looked around the room, she felt small and invisible. It was filled with signs of him. Someone looking at the room wouldn't even know that Ella existed. That's what her entire life had been like. She took a deep breath. Ella intended to change all that. She would make herself known.

Here, you meet the **main character** right away.

This is the **conflict**, or problem, the character must deal with.

Myth

Ever wonder what causes a volcano to explode or why the Big Dipper has seven bright stars? For thousands of years people have been telling myths to answer questions like these. The **purpose** is to explain things about the natural world.

WHAT TO EXPECT IN A MYTH

☐ An imaginative explanation of nature or natural events

☐ A setting and conflict

☐ Gods and goddesses, and sometimes animal or human characters

☐ Plot, or events, that focus on how things in nature came to be

---

ARACHNE THE WEAVER   3

Arachne was a talented weaver. But her pride got her into trouble. She thought she was a better weaver than the goddess Athena. This made Athena very angry.

"You consider yourself a superior spinner, Arachne," Athena told her coldly, "but you are small in mind and spirit. Go live your life as a tiny creature that spins the day and night away!" From that day on, Arachne lived as a spider, spinning webs.

This myth attempts to explain where spiders come from.

Fable

Storytellers tell fables for the **purpose** of teaching a moral, or lesson about life.

WHAT TO EXPECT IN A FABLE

☐ A moral, or lesson about life, sometimes directly stated at the end

☐ A setting, plot, and conflict

☐ Imaginary characters that often are animals

The Wolf in Sheep's Clothing
—Aesop

A wolf disguised himself as a sheep and joined a flock that was grazing in a field. He soon led a small lamb astray and made a meal out of her.

Moral: Appearances can be deceiving.

This fable features animal characters.

Genre Features

Fiction, continued

Mystery

Would you like to be a detective? Read a mystery and follow the clues to figure out who did what and how they did it. In some mysteries a detective is one of the main characters. The **author's purpose** is to have readers enjoy piecing together clues to figure out unexplained events.

> **WHAT TO EXPECT IN A MYSTERY**
> ☐ A plot that focuses on a crime or mysterious event
> ☐ A number of different settings and clues
> ☐ A main character who is trying to explain what happened
> ☐ Characters who may or may not be responsible for what happened

---

74   THE FULLERTON CASE | Rashon Miller

    Detective Saepharn had seen many crime scenes, but she had never seen a kitchen quite like this. The floor was covered with smashed plates, splattered food, and large paw prints. The thief had entered through a side window and gone into the hallway. He had found the safe behind a painting and stole $10,000 in cash and twice that amount in jewels.

    Detective Saepharn searched for clues. She took some samples. Maybe they contained evidence that would lead her to the intruder and the stolen cash and jewels.

What mystery is the detective trying to solve?

What are some clues that the writer gives you?

Science Fiction

Would you like to travel to the distant future? Science fiction will take you there. It's a type of fantasy story an author creates by combining real science with fiction. The **author's purpose** is to transport the reader to a world where things that seem fantastic are possible.

WHAT TO EXPECT IN SCIENCE FICTION

☐ Human and fantasy characters
☐ Scientific facts and technology mixed with imaginary things
☐ Descriptions of life in the future or in a make-believe world
☐ Descriptions of how real or imagined science affects people

The Paper Caper

by J. Sánchez

Minutes before my report was due, I held my wrist to the scanner to log onto the teaching portal. I quickly uploaded the data and headed for the transporter beacon.

Suddenly an alarm went off. Then a voice said, "Student Thalia M-54368, report to the disciplinary portal." Why would they want me? I looked down at my identification wristband, and realized it wasn't *my* wristband!

The writer combines real and imagined technology.

Genre Features

Fiction, continued

Historical Fiction

Are you a history buff? In historical fiction the author weaves a believable story that takes place in a specific time in history. The **author's purpose** is to have the reader enjoy an exciting story while learning about a time period long ago.

WHAT TO EXPECT IN HISTORICAL FICTION

- ☐ A time and place from the past
- ☐ Factual information researched by the author
- ☐ Made-up characters and/or real people who lived in the past
- ☐ Invented dialogue
- ☐ Plot that may combine made-up and real events

122   A REBEL IN THE RANKS | F. Caldwell

The time had come for him to tell her. It was a cold Thursday mornng, September 18, 1862.

"Ma, I've joined the Army," Jim said with a defiant tone.

Lila Pierce looked up from her gardening and wiped her hands on her apron. She was trying to get all the bulbs planted before the first freeze came to New Haven.

"I just hope you don't die in that uniform like your uncle." Jim had expected an argument. Enlisting was his rebellion—his way out of New Haven and his family's house. Even if he had known that more than a quarter of all Union soldiers were dying or getting wounded, he would not have changed his mind.

> The story takes place in a time period in the past.
>
> The **characters and dialogue** come from the writer's imagination.
>
> The writer also includes **factual information.**

Parody

Do you like to poke fun at ideas? If so, read a parody. In this genre, the writer imitates the style of a piece of writing in a humorous way. The **author's purpose** is to make fun of another piece of writing.

In his parody, Lewis Carroll followed the language and style of the original poem. He changed the focus from how a bee makes honey to how crocodiles eat small fish.

WHAT TO EXPECT IN A PARODY

☐ Language similar to the language in the original work
☐ Changes to words and ideas to make the original look silly

The Original

Carroll's Version

Against Idleness and Mischief
by Isaac Watts

How doth the little busy bee
Improve each shining hour,
And gather honey all the day
From every opening flower!

How skillfully she builds her cell!
How neat she spreads the wax!
And labours hard to store it well
With the sweet food she makes.

How Doth the Little Crocodile
by Lewis Carroll

How doth the little crocodile
Improve his shining tail,
And pour the waters of the Nile
On every golden scale!

How cheerfully he seems to grin,
How neatly spreads his claws,
And welcomes little fishes in,
With gently smiling jaws!

Genre Features

Narrative Nonfiction

Nonfiction is a major genre, or type of text. Nonfiction writers tell about real people, places, and events. In narrative nonfiction the author writes about events as though he or she were telling a story.

Biography

A biography is one type of nonfiction. The biographer's **purpose** is to tell the true account of the life of a real person, called a *subject*. Sometimes a person writes his or her own life story. That type of writing is called an *autobiography*.

WHAT TO EXPECT IN A BIOGRAPHY
☐ A true story about the life of a famous or important person
☐ Events told in time order, often beginning with the person's birth and ending with the person's death
☐ Careful research by the writer about the person's life and the historical period in which the person lived

SOJOURNER TRUTH
AMERICAN FREEDOM FIGHTER

Sojourner Truth was an outspoken black American freedom fighter and a passionate defender of women's rights. She was born in New York in 1797. For the first forty-five years of her life, she was known as Isabella Baumfree.

The Sojourner Truth U.S. postage stamp was issued in 1986.

The narrator describes events using the third-person point of view and pronouns such as *she, he,* and *they*.

Memoir

A memoir is a type of autobiography. In a memoir, a person writes about his or her own life. The **author's purpose** is to record an important time in his or her life and share it with readers.

WHAT TO EXPECT IN A MEMOIR

☐ An account of someone's past experiences

☐ Descriptions of important or challenging times in the person's life

☐ Events told in first-person signaled by the words *I, me,* and *my*

WHEN I WAS PUERTO RICAN | Esmeralda Santiago   205

"Next week you will be a *teeneyer*," Papi said as we sat on the porch smelling the night air.

"What's that?"

"In the United States, when children reach the age of thirteen, they're called *teeneyers*. It comes from the ending of the number in English. *Thir-teen. Teen-ager.*"

I counted in English to myself. "So I will be a *teeneyer* until I'm twenty?"

"That's right. Soon you'll be wanting to rock and roll." He laughed as if he had told a very funny joke.

"I don't like rock and roll," I protested. "Too noisy. And it's all in English. I don't understand the songs."

"Mark my words," he said. "When you're a *teeneyer* it's like something comes over you. Rock and roll sounds good. Believe me." He laughed as if he knew what he was talking about. I hadn't seen him this happy in a long time

"Well it's not going to happen to me." I pouted and ignored his chuckles at my expense.

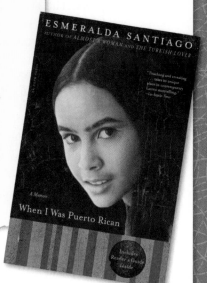

Expository Nonfiction

In expository nonfiction, the author presents information about real events, real people, or the real world. Most of what you read in textbooks is expository nonfiction. The **author's purpose** is to give readers information about a subject.

Content-Area Article

Content-area articles present factual information, along with photographs, diagrams, and other graphics.

WHAT TO EXPECT IN A CONTENT-AREA ARTICLE
☐ Information about real events, ideas, and/or people
☐ Facts and sometimes the author's opinions
☐ Titles, main headings, and subheadings that organize information
☐ Photos, charts, and other visuals with important information

Sports Title IX

What Is Title IX?

Title IX is a federal law that prevents sex discrimination in sports. The law applies to students in all schools that receive funds from the U.S. government.

How Does Title IX Protect Student Athletes?

If a student wants to play on a team, the law says that the school has to give both male and female students a fair chance to play that sport.

Content-area articles organize information into sections with headings and subheadings.

Most people support women's access to sports programs.

PUBLIC OPINION
Do You Approve of Title IX?

Yes
█████████████████████ 79%

No
███ 14%

Do not know enough
█ 4%

Not sure
█ 3%

2000 Wall Street Journal/NBC News Poll

Procedural Nonfiction

How do you set up a computer or use a digital camera? You probably check the user's manual. That is an example of procedural nonfiction. The **author's purpose** is to give a step-by-step explanation of how to do something.

How-to Article

How-to writing includes recipes and directions. Writers use this type of writing to expain how to do something in a certain order.

WHAT TO EXPECT IN HOW-TO WRITING

- ☐ Numbered step-by-step directions, written as commands such as *think about* and *make*
- ☐ Possibly diagrams or pictures to help explain the steps
- ☐ Additional explanation in paragraph form, if needed
- ☐ Lists of materials, when needed

Richmond High School | Couseling Office

How to Apply for College

Applying for college takes preparation. Follow these steps:

1. Think about your goals, experience, and interests.

2. Talk with your family or caregivers about costs, location, and your goals.

3. Make an appointment with your school counselor to discuss your grades, financial needs, and so on.

The writer recommends that you follow certain steps in order.

STATE UNIVERSITY
Application For Admission

PLEASE NOTE: All items on both sides of this form MUST be completed. ☐ Fall 20__ ☐ Winter 20__ ☐ Spring 20__ ☐ Summer 20__

1 SOCIAL SECURITY/ ID NUMBER
___ - ___ - ___

2 BIRTH DATE
__ / __ / __
Month/Date/Year

PLACE OF BIRTH
State (if U.S.A.) or Country

3 GENDER
☐ Male   ☐ Female

4 LAST NAME
PREVIOUS NAME (if applicable)
FIRST NAME
MAILING ADDRESS OR P.O. BOX
MIDDLE INITIAL
EMAIL
Street   City   State   Zip Code
TELEPHONE (___)___

5 CITIZENSHIP STATUS
U.S. CITIZEN ☐ Yes ☐ No
If not a U.S. citizen, indicate status below:
☐ (2) Permanent Resident /

6 ENROLLMENT STATUS
(Enter approp

Persuasion

What would the world be like if everyone thought exactly the same way? Pretty boring. In persuasive nonfiction, writers present their personal opinions about a topic and give reasons and evidence to support their opinions. Their **purpose** is to persuade readers to think a certain way or to take certain action.

Letter to the Editor

Many people have strong opinions about what they read in print and digital newspapers and in magazines. So, they write letters to the editor to persuade other people to think the way they do. Newspapers and magazines publish these letters.

WHAT TO EXPECT IN A LETTER TO THE EDITOR

- ☐ A strong position that agrees or disagrees with a published article
- ☐ Facts, personal experience, and sometimes emotional language to convince the reader
- ☐ May present both sides of the issue

READERS SPEAK

Editor—I am writing in response to Sandra Gee ("Outlaw Dangerous Animals," Jan. 28). I own a purebred Rottweiler. According to the American Kennel Club, Rottweilers are calm, intelligent, and make good companions for their owners.

Ms. Gee misidentifies Rottweilers as aggressive and unpredictable. It's time to put an end to these stereotypes that have plagued the breed for generations.

DEVON KING
Brooklyn

The writer includes **facts** to support his argument.

Here he gives his opinion on the topic.

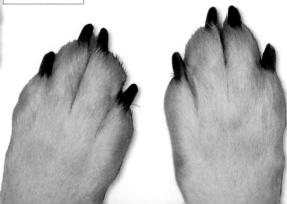

READER'S FILE

Persuasive Essay

An essay is a short piece of nonfiction about a specific topic. In a persuasive essay, writers present their opinions, along with facts, examples, statistics, and sometimes visuals. Their **purpose** is to convince you to think or act the way they do.

WHAT TO EXPECT IN AN ESSAY

☐ A statement that clearly tells the author's opinion

☐ Details that support the author's argument, including facts, statistics, quotations, and experts' opinions

RICHMOND HIGH SCHOOL September Issue, Vol. III

Let Teens Decide

By Chantrea Sok, grade 9

Schools should get rid of their dress codes. Being a teen is all about figuring out who and what you are. Tattoos, earrings, and orange hair aren't dangerous. They're just expressions of your identity. Thousands of kids who dress like this have gone to college. They are good students and good people. Don't judge them by what they wear. Let's get rid of bad rules now and let teens decide for themselves.

In this essay, the writer **states her opinion** in the first sentence.

She **uses a fact** to support her opinion.

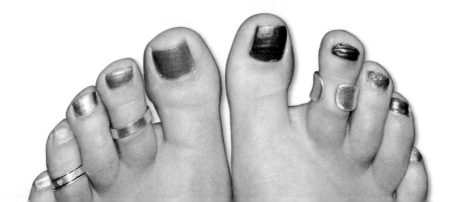

Genre Features

Drama

Drama is a major genre that includes plays. Most plays are written to be performed in front of an audience. So, the play is made up of dialogue, or conversation between actors. The playwright's **purpose** is to entertain and tell a good story. Some playwrights also want to get people to think about a social or political issue.

WHAT TO EXPECT IN A PLAY

☐ Acts and scenes that divide the play into sections

☐ Lines of dialogue

☐ Stage directions that describe the setting, character's thoughts or actions, and movements on stage

---

16   JUST IN TIME

ACT ONE

Scene One

TONYA and AL, *dressed in hip clothing, are* sitting on the front steps of an inner city high school and talking *before class starts.* MAI LINH, *wearing conservative, old-fashioned clothes, sits far away from them on the steps, staring into space. They all have backpacks at their feet.*

AL: I just got my pictures back from my trip to Chicago.

TONYA: Ooh, let's see them before the bell rings.

AL (*quietly*): Do you think Mai Linh wants to see them, too?

TONYA: Yeah. She'd probably like that. Hardly anybody's been talking to her since she moved here.

AL (*to* MAI LINH): Hey, Mai Linh, do you want to see my pictures?

MAI LINH (*looking embarrassed*): Okay. But my English isn't so good.

> Plays are divided into acts and scenes.

> **Stage directions** explain where the characters are and what they do.

> Lines of **dialogue** are the words a character says.

Poetry

Is a poem a poem if it doesn't rhyme? Yes! Poetry is a form of literature. Usually, poems are arranged in lines, or verse form, with words that create a rhythm. A poet's **purpose** is to express an idea or feeling by using language that forms pictures in readers' minds and brings out strong feelings.

WHAT TO EXPECT IN POETRY

☐ Lines divided into verses or stanzas
☐ Language devices such as rhythm, repetition, and sometimes rhyme
☐ Language that appeals to your senses and creates vivid mental pictures
☐ Words that express emotions

Good Hours

—ROBERT FROST

I had for my winter evening walk—
No one at all with whom to talk,
But I had the cottages in a row
Up to their shining eyes in snow.

And I thought I had the folk within:
I had the sound of a violin;
I had a glimpse through curtain laces
Of youthful forms and youthful faces.

This poem is divided into stanzas. Each one has four lines.

The poet used **repetition** to emphasize his point.

To appreciate the rhythm, read the poem aloud.

Strategy Summary

When you make connections, you add what you already know to what you are reading. This increases your understanding and helps you think about ideas in new ways.

- First, figure out the topic and tap into what you know. As you're reading, pay attention to what the selection **reminds** you of.

- To **make connections**, link what you're reading to your own experiences, things you know about the world, and to other texts you've read.

Notice how this good reader makes connections when she reads nonfiction.

Nonfiction Article

SCHOOL SPIRIT

The motto of the Indiana School for the Deaf is "Through Unity, Identity; Through Identity, Pride." At many schools, being deaf or hard of hearing would be considered a disability. Here, the students see it as a source of pride. Their annual talent show includes mime and American Sign Language (ASL) poetry.

" We show school pride for winning teams. These kids have pride in their skills, like all winners do."

" I've seen mimes perform in street theater. It's cool. I'd like to see actors use ASL."

Hearing-impaired teens use sign language to communicate.

Notice how this reader connects to his experiences when he reads an essay.

Lake County Daily | Weekend Edition

EDITORIAL

OPINION

The Right to Be Me

by Zeenat Telhami

When you look at me, what do you see—the clothes or the person? Every day I wear hijab, a headscarf that covers my hair and shoulders. I'm one of many Muslim women who wear clothes like the hijab, burka, or abaya. We're students, mothers, and working professionals. We're your neighbors, your teachers, and your classmates.

When we wear hijab, some people look at us with pity. They assume we're covered up because we're mourning, miserable, or oppressed. Don't worry. You may think I'm repressed, but I'm freely exposing my faith and identity to everyone who sees me. The truth is, I'm just being me.

" **I know what it's like to be judged by the clothes you wear.**"

" **I know there have been a lot of stories in the news about Muslim women's clothing. I think people shouldn't judge you if they don't know you.**"

" **This writer reminds me of an author I like. They both use short sentences and casual language. It's like they're talking to me.**"

Make Inferences

Suppose you plan to hang out with a friend. When you go to his house, he seems grouchy. He looks like he hasn't slept in days. There are books and papers stacked up all over his room. Even though he hasn't told you, you're able to figure out that he stayed up late finishing a report. You just made an inference—you put together clues with what you know to figure out what has been left unsaid.

When you read, you figure out things the author hasn't told you directly. Look at the next page to see how some teens make inferences when they read.

How Do You Make Inferences?

" When I read, I pick up on what the characters do and say. Then I put that together with what I know about people in real life to figure out the kind of person each character is. "

—George

" I watch for clues about the author's message. Sometimes it's descriptions that give me clues. Sometimes it's what a character says. Then I fill in with my own experience to figure out what the author is saying about life. "

—Stella

" I read like I'm a detective. I pay close attention to the facts and ideas in the text to see where they lead me. I add in stuff I know to figure things out. "

—Victor

" *What is the meaning of all this?* That's what I always ask myself. I add what I know to what the author says to get the author's meaning. "

—Elena

You can download more Readers Talk tips.  hbgoodreaders.com

I Read, I Know, and So

What is she doing? You've seen people making movies before, so you figure out that she's making a film for a school project. When you read, you can also put information together to figure out what the writer doesn't tell you.

What's the Author Really Saying?

Authors directly tell you some facts and ideas, but they leave other things unsaid. You have to make inferences, or combine what you know with what authors say, to figure out what they have not told you directly. Here's how:

- **You Read** Look for ideas and information that the author emphasizes.

- **You Know** Think of what you already know about the ideas or facts. Ask yourself: *What does my experience tell me about how the information fits together?*

- **And So . . .** Combine what you read with what you know to figure out what the author has not told you directly. Ask: *What does the author lead me to think?* That's the "And so . . . ."

FOCUS POINT Read the passage on the next page and the sample inferences. What facts and background knowledge did the readers put together to come up with their inferences?

Hayao Miyazaki:
Anime Director

FLOATING CASTLES. Enchanted forests. Pirates, princesses, and foreign agents. You've stepped into the world of Hayao Miyazaki, director and animator of Japanese *anime* movies. Among his most popular films are *Princess Mononoke* and *Spirited Away.*

Miyazaki was born in Tokyo, Japan, in 1941. He began drawing at a young age. He recalls, "I had the presumptuousness, around age 12-13, to think I was the best drawer in the world!"

His career as an animator began in 1963. He soon gained high praise for his incredible drawing ability. Miyazaki takes anywhere from one year to

Hayao Miyazaki and an image from his movie *Spirited Away*

one and one-half years to produce an animated film. He insists on personally drawing most of the 140,000 frames for his movies—by hand!

As both a writer and a director, Miyazaki uses art as an outlet. "I run away from reality," he says. "Animation is my only mode of expression."

duced
efore
U.S.
r bus
ilter
d can

Sample Inferences

This reader made an inference about how the director works.

> I think he's a perfectionist and maybe a little bit old-fashioned in the way he makes movies.

This reader made an inference about the director's personality.

> Miyazaki's words and actions make me think he must be an extremely confident person.

Making Inferences in Fiction

What's a novel or mystery without great characters? Fiction writers tell you a lot about their characters, but not everything. You often have to make inferences to figure out what characters are thinking and feeling, and why they act in certain ways.

Inferences About Characters

Here's how to figure out what makes characters tick:

- **You Read** Pay attention to what the characters say and do. Take note of what they seem most concerned about. Notice what other characters say about them and how they're treated.

- **You Know** Think about people you know and situations you've been in that are similar to the ones in the story.

- **And So . . .** Combine what you've read and what you know to figure out what the author leaves unsaid about the characters. Use a diagram like this one to help you.

Character Diagram

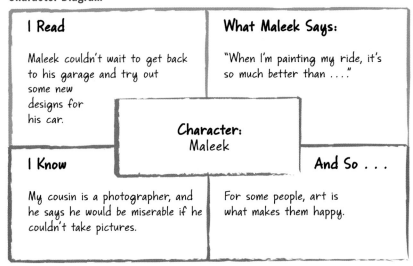

I Read

Maleek couldn't wait to get back to his garage and try out some new designs for his car.

What Maleek Says:

"When I'm painting my ride, it's so much better than . . . ."

Character:
Maleek

I Know

My cousin is a photographer, and he says he would be miserable if he couldn't take pictures.

And So . . .

For some people, art is what makes them happy.

MALEEK MAKES THE TEAM | Will Simon   137

Maleek launched the shot from center court. It swished in the hoop, bagging another win for West Troy High School. In the locker room, Maleek shoved the uniform into his bag and hurried out. He couldn't wait to get back to his garage and try out some new designs for his car. Then Coach Suzuki waved him into his office.

"What is it, Coach?" Maleek asked.

Coach Suzuki looked up at Maleek. His expression was serious. "Soccer is starting soon and I know the coaches have been trying to contact you. What's going on?"

Maleek shrugged slightly. "I've been working on my car," he spoke quietly looking down at the floor.

"Something wrong with your car?" asked the coach.

"No," said Maleek, "I've just been working on it for the big Art Car Festival." Coach Suzuki raised an eyebrow.

"Can't you play soccer and work on your car?" The coach leaned forward. "You know, playing soccer could lead to a college scholarship and a whole future for you."

Maleek returned the coach's gaze, and the words came fast. "Designing art cars is something special. Playing basketball or soccer are great, but when I'm painting my ride, it's so much better than . . . ." His voice trailed off, and he dropped his eyes again. He wanted to end the conversation as quickly as he possibly could.

> Based on this information, what can you tell about Maleek?

> How do you think Maleek feels? How can you tell?

> What problem does Maleek have? When have you been in a similar situation?

Making Inferences in Fiction, continued

Fictional stories have **themes**, or messages about life. For example, one theme might be "Artists should never give up, even when they don't feel successful." Authors do not typically state the theme directly. You have to combine story details with what you already know about life to infer, or figure out, the theme.

Inferences About the Theme

Here's how to figure out a story's theme:

- **You Read** Pay attention to what the author emphasizes in the story. Look for things the characters say and do and events that relate to big ideas and lessons about life.

- **You Know** Think about experiences you have had that have taught you things about life. Ask yourself: *What do I know that can help me understand the author's message?*

- **And So . . .** Put together details from the story and what you know to figure out the unstated theme. Ask yourself: *What is the author saying about important issues in life?*

Read the page from "Sad But Really True" to see how one reader combined what she knew about people with the details the author presented.

SAD BUT REALLY TRUE | Armin Gupta   33

"I said no, and that's the end of the story."

"Please, Mom," Sophie begged, "Just a small tattoo—a butterfly on my ankle. What's the harm?"

Sophie saw the stern "No Is No" look come over her mother's face and realized that she wasn't going to convince her. She grabbed her backpack and headed out the door. When she got to J.Z.'s house, she was furious.

"I don't care what she says. I don't care if I'm grounded. I'm going to get that tattoo."

This tattoo must be really important to her.

J.Z. listened quietly. Finally Sophie stopped to come up for air. J.Z looked at her and said, "Why? What's the big deal? You don't need to have a tattoo. Besides, you've already tried blue hair and piercing your nose, and your life hasn't changed. You're still Sophie Méndez—boyfriendless 4.0 G.P.A. student at eternally boring Richmond High."

Her friend doesn't support her idea.

Sophie bristled angrily, "Well I may still be me, but I don't want to be. Everybody loved my blue hair. It was really great while it lasted. Wasn't it?"

Theme: Good friends are helpful.

J.Z. smiled and shrugged. "Let's go shopping and get some really killer earrings. That'll make you feel better."

Making Inferences in Nonfiction

When you read nonfiction, such as an article about modern art, the author doesn't spell out everything about that topic. You have to figure out some things from the information that the writer gives you and from what you already know. When you read between the lines, you get the author's full meaning.

Inferences About Factual Information

Here's how to make inferences when reading nonfiction:

- **You Read** Pay attention to what the author emphasizes about the topic and how it is presented. Nonfiction authors usually give lots of facts and examples. Sometimes they compare things, list important features, or explain steps.

- **You Know** Think about what you already know about the topic. Ask: *What facts and ideas do I already have about this topic? What examples can I think of?*

- **And So . . .** Combine what the author says with what you know to get the unstated meanings. Ask yourself: *What does the author leave unsaid about this topic?*

Use an inference chart like this to make inferences when you read nonfiction.

Inference Chart

I Read	I Know	And So . . .
"Some people who create art have never gone to art school. Does this mean they are not true artists?"	I've seen paintings in art shows that were done by people who never went to art school.	So, I think the author is saying you don't have to go to art school to create good art.

TREASURED Trash

Pastel Thong Totem, 2000. John Dahlsen. Stainless steel and found objects.

Look around. Do you see any trash? It's everywhere. Fast food bags, candy wrappers, paper cups, and plastic bags are strewn along fences and tangled in tree limbs. Most people would consider this trash ugly and unsightly. But to artists like John Dahlsen, it's a source of inspiration.

Art from Debris

While attending art school in Australia, Dahlsen used to gather driftwood to make furniture. Twenty years later, he decided to go back to the same spots in Australia. But this time, he noticed the trash: plastic debris in every shape and color.

Since then, Dahlsen scours beaches to collect trash. Then he transforms the objects he finds into art. He arranges colored plastic bags into modern wall art. He sculpts plastic debris into freestanding works. Dahlsen stacks up driftwood, buoys, bottles, and flip-flops. They rise up like modern totem poles. His small sculptures and paintings sell for nearly $2,000. Larger pieces sell for upwards of $15,000.

What information confirms each of these inferences?

Dahlsen finds artistic inspiration outdoors.

Dahlsen's art makes trash look different.

People value Dahlsen's unusual art.

Making Inferences in Poetry

Poets choose their words carefully and often arrange them in lines of verse. They usually use language to create strong feelings in readers. When reading poetry, combine the words in the poem with your feelings and experience.

Inferences About the Poet's Message

Here's how to figure out what the poet is trying to say:

- **You Read** Read the title and the verses aloud a few times to focus on the descriptions. Pay attention to words that appeal to your senses. Also, look for any words that repeat.

- **You Know** Connect things in the poem to your own experience. Have you ever felt the way the poet is feeling? Have you had a similar experience?

- **And So . . .** Combine what the poet tells you with your past experience and feelings to understand the poem. Try using an organizer like this one to make inferences.

Inference Diagram

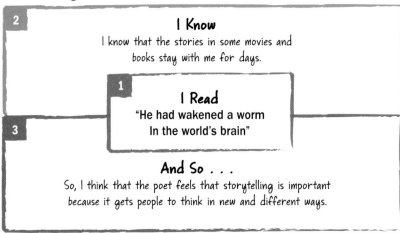

2
I Know
I know that the stories in some movies and books stay with me for days.

1
I Read
"He had wakened a worm
In the world's brain"

3
And So . . .
So, I think that the poet feels that storytelling is important because it gets people to think in new and different ways.

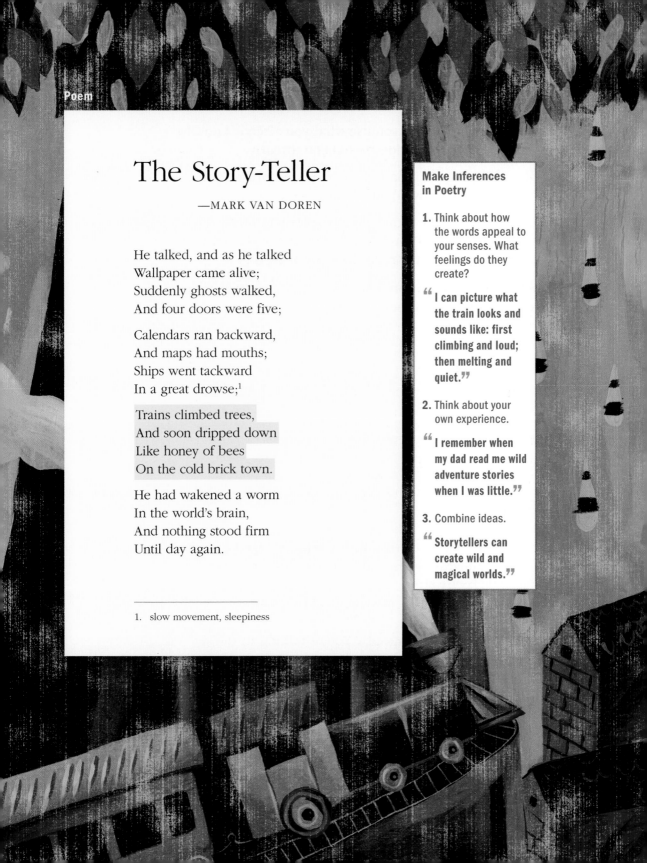

The Story-Teller

—MARK VAN DOREN

He talked, and as he talked
Wallpaper came alive;
Suddenly ghosts walked,
And four doors were five;

Calendars ran backward,
And maps had mouths;
Ships went tackward
In a great drowse;[1]

Trains climbed trees,
And soon dripped down
Like honey of bees
On the cold brick town.

He had wakened a worm
In the world's brain,
And nothing stood firm
Until day again.

---

1. slow movement, sleepiness

Make Inferences in Poetry

1. Think about how the words appeal to your senses. What feelings do they create?

" I can picture what the train looks and sounds like: first climbing and loud; then melting and quiet. "

2. Think about your own experience.

" I remember when my dad read me wild adventure stories when I was little. "

3. Combine ideas.

" Storytellers can create wild and magical worlds. "

Strategy Summary

When you make inferences, you use what you already know to figure out what the author doesn't tell you directly.

- Look for ideas and information in the text. Think about **what you already know** about them.

- Then, combine what you read with what you know to figure out what the author means but does not exactly say. Think of it this way: **I read. I know. And so . . . .**

See how one good reader combines what she reads with what she knows to make an inference.

Fiction

WORDS ON WING   36

The subway roared through the tunnel approaching Waverly Square. Tired commuters poured into the cars. All the seats were taken by mothers with crying babies, waitresses coming off their shifts, and children holding backpacks and brown bag lunches.

The businesswoman and the teen didn't have a choice. The subway was so crowded they had to stand cramped in a corner facing an advertisement. It announced the Second Annual Citywide Poetry Slam.

"'Words are my wings. . . .' read the businesswoman out loud. Not bad."

"Glad you like it," Marcus said. "You're talking to the author."

> " I read the highlighted text."

> " I know that many subways have the same ads."

> " And so . . . I bet a lot of people will show up for the poetry slam, and Marcus will be proud."

See how another good reader makes inferences when reading a nonfiction article.

Art Brightens NORTH PHILADELPHIA

Vacant lots now hold striking mosaics and glittering sculptures.

In 1986, artist Lily Yeh sparked life back into a run-down Philadelphia neighborhood. After painting a mural on the side of her friend's building, she decided to clean up the adjacent lot. Community members joined in. They filled the abandoned lot with sparkling benches, adobe walls, and a mosaic in the shape of trees.

Soon, the entire neighborhood was inspired. Yeh helped establish the Village of Arts and Humanities. This community improvement program has transformed over 150 lots. The lots are now gardens, green spaces, and a two-acre farm. These improvements have helped bring the neighborhood back to life.

" I read the highlighted text."

" I know it takes good ideas, money, and a lot of hard work to change a neighborhood."

" And so . . . , I understand that Lily Yeh is both an artist and a successful community activist."

Synthesize

What's your favorite pasta dish? It's probably a combination of different things you've tried and liked. You take different ingredients and create something new that's all your own.

Reading can be a lot like cooking. You synthesize, or combine information to come up with ideas that you never thought of before. Sometimes you combine information in a single text; other times you combine information from different texts. Look at the next page to see how some teens synthesize text information when they read.

How Do You Put It All Together?

" I compare what different authors say about a topic. I pay attention to what each one presents—what one says that the other doesn't. Then I form my own idea. "

—Rita

" I like to figure out how to get all the important information from one book. Each section of the book usually has different facts and ideas. So I check out what each section says, and then I combine those ideas. I get the overall meaning that way. "

—David

" How is the information similar or different from what is in other texts? That's what I think about when I read. Then I fit it into a big picture. "

—Marcia

" I have a lot of opinions, and I like to take a stand. So when I read, I look for different facts. This helps me form opinions and support them. Then I can argue with the authors in my mind, and with other people in person! "

—Leon

You can download more Readers Talk tips. hbgoodreaders.com

Put It All Together

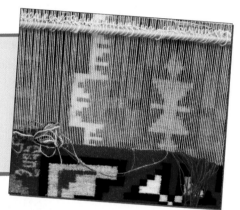

How Does Synthesizing Work?

When you synthesize, you bring together ideas from what you are reading and blend them into new understandings.

To synthesize:

- Pay attention to the important ideas. Think about how they fit together and what they have in common. How do the writer's ideas compare with other things you are reading and learning?

- Then decide how the ideas go together in a way that is new to you. Figure out how what you are reading and learning fits together in a way you hadn't thought of before.

- Read with a critical eye. Do you agree with the writer's ideas and opinions? Take a position.

FOCUS POINT Read the blog entries on the next page. Pay attention to the important ideas that are highlighted, and see how the reader puts them together.

RAY SPEAKS OUT

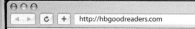

SCHOOL SECURITY

October 15, 2006

The metal detector beeped at me today, and it didn't even faze me. I just emptied my pockets and walked through the machine again. I don't even notice the security guards anymore. Now we have to use clear plastic bags instead of backpacks. School authorities want to be able to easily detect who has dangerous objects like guns. When will we be safe enough?

September 6, 2006

The metal detectors, security guards, and cameras at school are meant to keep us safe, right? But I don't appreciate feeling like a prisoner in my own school. Some of these rules don't make sense to me. We can't even use our cell phones. Even at lunch, we can't leave the cafeteria. Tell me, when am I supposed to use the bathroom?

New Understanding

> I used to think that I would want security cameras, officers, and metal detectors to keep my school safe. After reading the entries in Ray's blog, now I understand that there is a limit to the freedoms students are willing to sacrifice to be safer.

Form Generalizations

When you **form generalizations**, you take ideas from the text, together with your personal knowledge, and form an idea that applies to many situations. Generalizations often use the words *many, most, all,* or *some.* For example: *All people have rights and responsibilities* and *Most young people in the U.S. attend school until they are 18.*

You make such a generalization to help organize your knowledge and so you know what to expect when you encounter new information in the future. For example, when you read "Working for a Living: Child Labor," you'll probably find new ideas to add to your understanding of this topic. To form generalizations:

1 Identify the Important Ideas

Focus on what the writer emphasizes and what you find noteworthy.

2 Determine What the Ideas Have in Common

Think about how the important ideas fit with one another. Draw on your own experience or knowledge.

3 Decide What to Think

Form a broad statement that covers many of the examples presented in your reading.

The passages on pages 379–382 all deal with one aspect of the theme Rights and Responsibilities: Child Labor. As you read, focus on the important ideas and think about how they fit together. What can you learn about child labor?

Working for a Living: Child Labor

Do you have a job after school or on the weekends? Currently, 5.5 million teens are employed. Many work to earn extra spending money, save for college, or help support families. Although teens don't earn top dollar in these jobs, they must be paid a minimum amount. This minimum wage is just one of many regulations that protect you at your job. Employers must follow other rules, too. Yet it was not always this way.

Children had always been part of the labor force. On farms, they were expected to help plow, plant, and harvest the crops. Without adults and children working together, families could not survive. Starting in the mid-1800s, the Industrial Revolution offered workers new opportunities. Families moved from farms to cities where new factories needed workers. And children still worked to help the family survive.

Boys and girls of all ages worked at different kinds of jobs. They shucked oysters and cut fish. They sold newspapers on street corners. They blew glass, assembled boxes, and rolled cigars. Children worked from dawn to dusk. Some began their jobs after dinner and worked through the night. All were paid less than $1.00 a day.

Young boys working in a coal mine, South Pittston, Pennsylvania, 1911.

By the late 1800s, many states passed child labor laws to help protect children from excessive work. But federal laws were slow to follow. In 1904, the National Child Labor Committee succeeded in passing only one law. Two years later the Supreme Court struck it down. In 1924, Congress tried to pass a national child labor law. The law did not pass.

> **Identify the important ideas.**
>
> " Laws did not always protect young workers."
>
> " Children had to work as hard as adults."

> **Think about how the ideas fit together.**
>
> " Child labor was a problem in the U.S. for many years, and child workers needed protection."

continued on next page

Working for a Living, continued

Then the stock market crashed in 1929, and the Great Depression followed. Unemployment and homelessness soared in the U.S. People were desperate for jobs just to put food on the table. Because of the country's unstable economy, adults were willing to work for the low pay that children earned.

Identify more important ideas.

" FLSA protected children in the U.S. from working long hours and hazardous jobs."

To help solve this problem, in 1938 President Franklin D. Roosevelt signed the Fair Labor Standards Act (FLSA) into law. Part of this federal law limited child labor practices. The law established the number of working hours allowed per day and per week. Children could no longer work in hazardous jobs. The law also guaranteed that children would earn a minimum wage for their work.

Through the years, the FLSA has changed to increase protection for young workers in the United States. But 246 million children in other countries are not so fortunate. The United Nations Convention on the Rights of the Child (UNCRC) has recognized basic rights of all children. One hundred ninety-five countries have agreed with the UN's mandates. But many poor countries have few resources. They cannot enforce their own child labor laws. Without enforcement, children end up working in unsafe and abusive conditions. Some children are even sold into slavery for life.

Think about how the ideas fit together.

" Children in poor countries work in unsafe conditions."

Decide what to think.

" Although the U.S. has laws that protect child workers, child labor is still a big problem in many countries."

Many activists, leaders, and ordinary people continue to fight for children's rights. But a solution has yet to be found. Around the world there are young people working in unsafe environments. They are not as fortunate as working students in the United States.

In many poor countries, children are still forced to work.

Magazine Article

OUR SECRET SHAME:
CHILD LABOR AND SLAVERY

Many children around the world do **hazardous work**. Hazardous work exposes children to abuse. It forces children to work underground, underwater, at dangerous heights, or in confined spaces. Sometimes children have to work with dangerous machinery, equipment, and tools. They might handle or move heavy loads. Employers also force children to work in unhealthy environments.

Children in New Delhi, India protesting against child labor.

The worst forms of child labor include:

Trafficking A child is moved from one country to another to work in forced labor or illicit activities.

Forced and bonded labor Children are sold or "rented" to an employer.

Armed conflicts Some nations use 15 to 17-year-old boys to fight in the front lines.

Illicit activities Children are involved in illegal work, including producing and distributing drugs.

Global Estimates
Child Labor and Slavery*

Trafficked children	1,200,000
Children in forced & bonded labor	5,700,000
Children in armed conflict	300,000
Children in illicit activities	600,000
Children in hazardous work	170,500,000
*Source International Labour Organization 2002	

Identify the **important ideas.**

" Child slavery and forced labor are global problems."

" Millions of children do illegal or hazardous work."

Think about how the ideas fit together.

" Dangerous work ruins the lives of millions of children worldwide."

Form Generalizations, continued

Consumer Report

FAIR TRADE FOR ALL

Every day many people in the United States enjoy cups of coffee and bars of chocolate, but they may not realize how these items are produced. A lot of products like coffee and cacao beans are **hand-picked by children**.

Modern Sweatshops

In 2001, several reports showed that more than **284,000 children** were working in hazardous conditions on West African cocoa farms. About 12,000 of them were taken from their families and sold into the trade.

Around the world, **70% of working children** are forced to perform farm labor. The children plant and pick crops such as bananas, tea, vegetables, and fruits.

It's not just the agricultural industry that uses child labor. The clothing, sporting equipment, and jewelry industries also use child labor.

What Should I Buy?

In 1999, an organization called Global Exchange, which promotes social, economic and environmental justice around the world, started a **Fair Trade campaign.** One of the organization's main goals is to make sure products are not made by children. It also helps poor countries by guaranteeing a minimum price for products, supporting community development, and promoting sustainable farming.

Today, Fair Trade certified products are more common on store shelves. But they are still only a small part of what people buy. Ultimately, you decide what to buy. You can get educated about where products come from and help prevent the use of child labor. You can also look for products that promote fair labor practices.

For more information, see the following Web sites:
www.fairtradefederation.org
www.fairtradeaction.org
www.coopamerica.org

Identify the important ideas.

" People may not know that many products they buy come from child labor."

" Most working children perform farm labor."

Think about how the ideas fit together.

" Children make many products that people buy. Fair Trade products don't use child labor."

Decide what to think.

" When people decide to buy products, they also decide whether or not to support child labor."

Pause and Reflect

Now that you've read three different texts on the same topic, you've pulled together a lot of information. You've thought about what the important ideas are and how they go together. Pause and reflect on this new information. Decide what you're going to take away from all the reading you've done.

To help you synthesize the information:

- Use a synthesis chart like the one below.

Synthesis Chart

"Working for a Living"
Since 1938, FLSA has protected children in the U.S. from working long hours or hazardous jobs.
Child labor is still a big problem in many countries.

"Our Secret Shame"
Child slavery and forced labor are global problems.
Millions of children do illegal or hazardous work.

"Fair Trade for All"
People may not realize it, but many products they buy are produced by child labor.
Most working children perform farm labor.
Fair Trade products don't use child labor.

What new information did you learn about child labor?

- Then make a statement that covers what you read and helps you remember and use it later.

Sample Generalizations

" Many children in poor countries are made to work in dangerous conditions because their families need the money."

" Children who work in underdeveloped countries face many types of hazardous conditions."

Draw Conclusions

When you **draw a conclusion**, you pay attention to everything you learn about a topic. Then you make up your mind about the topic.

From a Single Text

When you draw a conclusion from a single text, you pay attention to the ideas from all parts of it.

1 **Identify the Important Ideas**

Focus on what the writer emphasizes and what you find noteworthy. When you read the article about Francesca Karle, pay attention to the writer's description of her actions and words, and what other people say about her work.

2 **Determine What the Ideas Have in Common**

Think about how the ideas and information go with one another. For instance, what does Francesca's filmmaking have to do with her work feeding homeless people?

3 **Decide What to Think**

Form an opinion of what you are reading. What do you think of Francesca's work and the attention it has received? What conclusions can you draw?

Synthesis Map

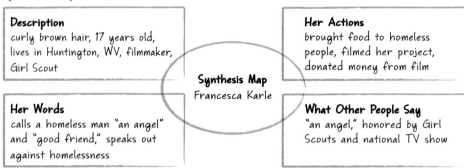

Description
curly brown hair, 17 years old, lives in Huntington, WV, filmmaker, Girl Scout

Her Actions
brought food to homeless people, filmed her project, donated money from film

Synthesis Map
Francesca Karle

Her Words
calls a homeless man "an angel" and "good friend," speaks out against homelessness

What Other People Say
"an angel," honored by Girl Scouts and national TV show

From what you read about her, do you agree that Francesca is a kind person? Does her work deserve praise? Based on what she has done so far, do you think she will do more to help homeless people?

Francesca Karle: On the River's Edge

Noelia Rivera, Global Press International, Los Angeles

She is a filmmaker. She is a Girl Scout. And to many people she is an angel, says Larry Roberts. Seventeen-year-old Francesca Karle tosses her curly brown hair, and laughs as she touches the thin, white-haired gentleman's hand. "He's an angel, too," said Karle. "And a good friend."

Francesca's compassionate nature led her to volunteer at a local shelter. Serving meals to those in need motivated Francesca to do more. She wanted the community to know that the homeless had names, dreams, and families. Like Larry Roberts. Larry used to live on the riverbank in Huntington, West Virginia. Then Francesca came along with hot meals, a smile, and her camera. She listened and filmed for days.

Francesca worked tirelessly editing her film, *On the River's Edge*, for more than six months. The film earned her the Gold Award, the

Girl Scouts' highest honor. Francesca's film also premiered on the main screen of the historic Keith Albee Theater. Soon after, *On the River's Edge* gained national recognition when Francesca appeared on *CBS's The Early Show* and was honored before a national audience as "An American Hero."

Francesca donated all the film proceeds to the Cabell-Huntington Coalition for the Homeless and Huntington City Mission. Today, Francesca continues to speak out against homelessness across the country. And when she's home, she still visits her friends at the riverbank.

Francesca Karle made a difference in Larry Roberts's life.

" The writer describes Francesca as a compassionate person."

" Her actions fit with her being a kind person."

" She made a film about the challenges that homeless people face."

This information gives a more complete picture of Francesca. Decide what to think.

" Francesca seems to deserve being called an angel and hero."

Draw Conclusions, continued

From Multiple Texts

When you draw conclusions from multiple texts, you use several sources to examine the same topic. Multiple texts give you different viewpoints and different kinds of information for thinking about the topic.

1 **Gather Materials on a Common Topic**

Bring together reading materials that deal with the same topic, then start thinking about how the materials are the same and how they differ.

2 **Identify the Important Ideas**

As you read, take note of what each writer emphasizes as well as what you want to remember later.

3 **Keep Track of the Important Ideas**

To hold your thinking, record important ideas in a graphic organizer. See page 391 for an example.

4 **Decide What You Think**

Use the graphic organizer to compare the reading selections' important ideas and make up your mind about the topic. Ask yourself: *Given all this information, what do I now think about this topic?*

The passages on pages 387–390 all deal with another aspect of the theme Rights and Responsibilities: Public Security and Safety in Schools. As you read, focus on the important ideas and decide what you want to think about the topic.

Who Is Watching You? THE NEW AGE OF SECURITY

You're at a train station and hear a voice over the speaker, "Please step onto the platform." You step up, backpack in hand, and push the red button. In seconds, the iris of your eye is scanned, your backpack and body are x-rayed, and you are cleared to board the train. No waiting. No lines. No hassle. And the entire scene has been videotaped.

Sound like science fiction? It's not. Many countries including the United States are using video surveillance, scanners, and biometrics for security. What exactly are these technologies and how do they affect you? Read on to learn more.

> " The writer is saying that many countries are already using high-tech security devices. "

Video Surveillance

In many places, security cameras monitor people and the surrounding area. To alert people to their presence, there are signs with cute phrases like "Smile! You're on Video" or "Wave to the Camera." These cameras discourage criminals from committing crimes. But video systems are not just used for crime prevention. They are also used as evidence in court after a crime is committed.

> " How do video cameras contribute to public safety and security? "

Many schools now use video cameras to monitor hallways.

Many public places and private companies use video cameras to document everyday events and activities. Some security cameras record all the time; others record only at certain hours. With passive monitoring, security workers review the tapes at a later time looking for any suspicious or criminal activity.

Other video systems actively monitor people and surroundings while the action is occurring. Security personnel watch screens with live images of airports, courthouses, schools, stores, and streets. With active monitoring, security workers can stop crimes in progress. They can also send law enforcement to the correct location when accidents or crimes first happen.

> " Security personnel use two types of monitoring: passive and active. "

Most monitored areas use both passive and active methods of security. Security personnel observe activity while it is occurring and also record it. This provides the most effective video surveillance.

continued on next page

" How do scanners contribute to public safety and security?"

Scanners

Scanners are another type of device used by security personnel. Some examples are metal detectors, x-rays, and infrared beams. These scanners help screen for dangerous items like guns or explosives.

Metal detectors are either hand-held or walk-through devices. They beep when metal is present. But the detectors cannot tell what the metal is. So security personnel must investigate each time the scanner goes off.

X-ray scanners, on the other hand, are typically used to scan

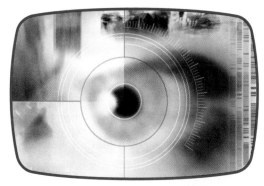

An iris scan is one way to check a person's identity.

luggage before passengers board planes. Today x-ray scanners are also being used in schools, government buildings, bus depots, and train stations.

Many companies and public facilities plan to take security one step further. Two new scanners are currently being developed. One uses radio frequency signals to scan shoes for explosives. Another uses wide band sensors to see movement through walls. Other new scanners are sure to follow.

" The writer is saying that interest in new types of scanners will continue."

Biometrics

Biometric devices monitor people's entry into buildings or public transportation. These devices identify people by their unique features. They scan fingerprints, palms, and irises. They also scan faces and analyze voices. Then the data is sent to a computer. The data is matched with information in the database. Passive facial recognition even allows a hidden camera to scan large crowds of people. This helps pinpoint suspects in less than a second. New technologies are emerging everyday. Soon biometric security devices will be found almost everywhere.

" How do biometrics contribute to public safety and security?"

How do you feel about this statement? Is it a good thing or a bad thing? Why?

THE **RIGHT THING**

Suppose a friend tells you about a plan to attack your school. He even goes so far as to tell you that you should get out if you hear shooting. What would you do in this situation? Would you take him seriously and alert authorities? Or would you think he's just frustrated and not really serious?

In September, 2006, in Green Bay, Wisconsin, seventeen-year-old Matt Atkinson found himself in this exact situation. During his fifth-hour class, long-time friend Shawn Sturtz confided in Matt. Shawn was full of rage. He was depressed and suicidal because of a breakup with his girlfriend and constant

Students walk to East High School in Green Bay, Wisconsin.

teasing by students. Shawn told Matt how he planned to attack students the next day with the help of his two friends, William Cornell and Bradley Netwal. Matt sat in shocked silence. What could he possibly say? Matt left school that day with a heavy burden.

He knew Shawn, William, and Brad had personal problems. He also knew they needed help dealing with them. But he still wasn't completely convinced Shawn was serious about the plan. What if Matt was wrong and it was all a big joke? Would the police think he was somehow involved? What would the other students at East High think about him if he sold out his friends?

Matt wrestled with these thoughts. Then he talked with his mom, Nancy Dury, who told him he had to make his own decision to do the right thing.

continued on next page

Identify the **important ideas.**

" A student tells his friend that he plans to attack his school. "

What is the important idea about crime prevention?

" In this case, it depended on a person taking action, not on technology. "

Draw Conclusions, continued

THE RIGHT THING, continued

And he did.

On September 14, 2006, Matt Atkinson decided that saving lives was more important than keeping a secret. Before school, he spoke with Associate Principal Matt Mineau, who then alerted Green Bay authorities. The police took Shawn Sturtz and William Cornell in for questioning. Bradley Netwal was taken into custody shortly after.

Green Bay police found that the plan was not just talk. They found explosives, guns, and suicide notes in the students' homes. Fortunately, no weapons were found at school.

Soon everyone learned that Matt Atkinson had

Matt Atkinson, his mother, and Associate Principal Matt Mineau talk with reporters.

exposed the plot. At the press conference, Matt talked about living with the guilt if his friends actually went through with the plan. Matt also stated he knew that if the plot wasn't true, his friends would finally get help. Matt's decision to speak out likely saved many lives. Clearly, people like Matt Atkinson care about their communities.

How did Matt Atkinson prevent a serious crime from taking place?

When you find important information, record it in a synthesis chart like the one on the next page.

How did Matt decide what to do?

What do you think of his decision-making process?

TAKE THREATS SERIOUSLY

The National Crime Prevention Council recommends that you follow these tips if you hear of threats to safety.

- Consider any threat or risk that puts lives in danger an emergency.
- Don't wait. Tell someone in authority about the potential incident.
- Call 9-1-1 to report the threat.

Pause and Reflect

Now that you've read three different texts on the same topic, you've pulled together a lot of information. Use a synthesis chart like the one below to pause and reflect on this new information.

Topic: Public Safety

Selection	What promotes public safety?	How does it work?
"Who Is Watching You?"	cameras	• passive: people review what cameras record • active: people watch what cameras are showing live
	scanners	• metal detectors beep at all metal • x-rays scan what people carry • radio waves check shoes for explosives • wideband sensors see movement through walls
	biometrics	devices scan people's fingerprints, palms, irises, voices, and faces to identify them quickly and accurately
"The Right Thing"	a friend who hears plans for an attack	a person notifies authorities, who notify police, who investigate
"Take Threats Seriously"	people following tips from others	• take threats seriously • don't wait, tell someone • call 9-1-1

Sample Conclusions

" After reading these selections, I think alert and responsible people contribute to public safety as much as modern technology."

" Nowadays you can't go anywhere without being watched or recorded. Technology devices help stop crime, but we have to make sure that we're not giving up too much personal freedom."

" Although technology is getting more and more sophisticated, I believe professionals are more important for public security because they are the ones to follow up and take action."

Compare and Contrast Ideas

When you read more than one text on a topic, **compare and contrast** the writers' key ideas. Then you can combine the ideas to come up with your own conclusions.

- **Focus on Important Ideas** As you read each text, jot down the ideas the writer emphasizes or that you can use later.

- **Focus on Similarities** After you read different texts, review your notes. Ask yourself: *What do these writers or sources agree on?* Note the answer.

- **Spot Important Differences** Also note specific examples of how the sources disagree or have different information.

- **Put the Ideas Together** Organize your notes in a diagram like this one:

Venn Diagram

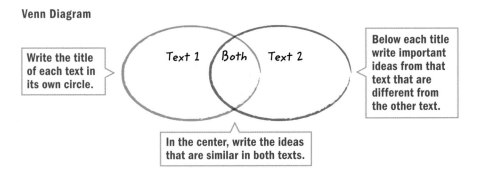

Write the title of each text in its own circle.

Text 1 / Both / Text 2

Below each title write important ideas from that text that are different from the other text.

In the center, write the ideas that are similar in both texts.

- **Sum It Up** Use the completed diagram to weigh the ideas. What conclusions can you draw? What new opinions do you have?

The passages on pages 393–394 deal with another aspect of the theme Rights and Responsibilities: The Struggle for Civil Rights. Read the passages to compare and contrast the writers' ideas. Then draw your own conclusions about the topic.

If We Must Die

—CLAUDE MCKAY

*This poem was written in response to
lynchings and race riots in Harlem in 1919.*

If we must die, let it not be like hogs

Hunted and penned in an inglorious spot,

While round us bark the mad and hungry dogs,

Making their mock at our accursed lot.

If we must die, O let us nobly die,

So that our precious blood may not be shed

In vain; then even the monsters we defy

Shall be constrained to honor us though dead!

O kinsmen! we must meet the common foe!

Though far outnumbered let us show us brave,

And for their thousand blows deal one deathblow!

What though before us lies the open grave?

Like men we'll face the murderous, cowardly pack,

Pressed to the wall, dying, but fighting back!

▼ *The Return of
the Soldier*,
1946, Charles
White. Pen and
ink. Library of
Congress.

Idea: Death should come honorably.

Idea: Someday everyone will realize that the people who died for civil rights were honorable.

Idea: Even though people were being killed by crowds, they should fight back courageously.

Compare and Contrast Ideas, continued

Historical Account

Our March for Voting Rights

Teens marched for civil rights in the 1960s.

BLACK TEENAGERS IN the 1960s did not have the freedoms that young people have today. Back then, African Americans had to fight for their civil rights. Can you imagine what it was like to try to change the world?

Amelia Boynton participated in one of the most important events of the Civil Rights Movement, the fight for African American voting rights. On March 7, Boynton helped lead about 525 people on a 54-mile march to Montgomery, Alabama.

In 1965, black citizens made up over half of the population of Alabama. But only two percent were registered voters. Unfair rules prevented blacks from registering and voting. African Americans wanted laws that guaranteed their rights.

The protesters marched despite violent opposition from citizens and police. They only walked a short distance before police stopped them. Boynton was gassed and beaten. Many marchers were injured.

On March 17, Federal Judge Frank Johnson Jr. ruled that the demonstrators had the right to march. On March 21, they set out for Montgomery again. By the time the demonstrators reached Montgomery, the number of marchers and supporters had grown to 25,000. Partly because of this march, the U.S. Congress passed the Voting Rights Act of 1965. Boynton traveled to Washington D.C. to meet with President Lyndon Johnson after he signed it into law.

> **Idea:** In the 1960s, black teens courageously fought for civil rights.

> **Idea:** Protestors faced violent opposition, just like in 1919.

> **Idea:** The march in Alabama influenced the government to pass a new law protecting voting rights.

Pause and Reflect

Now that you've read two texts on a similar topic, you can draw your own conclusions. Complete a Venn diagram with the important ideas from each text. Using the diagram helps you see what the writers agree on and if they disagree. Then you can put the important ideas together to come to your own conclusion.

Venn Diagram

"If We Must Die"

People must stand up and fight for their freedom.

Someday, everyone will honor them.

When confronted with violence, people should fight back.

People fought for civil rights.

Protestors faced violent opposition and even death.

They continued protesting despite the risks.

"Our March for Voting Rights"

In the 1960s, black teens courageously fought for civil rights.

African Americans fought for the right to vote.

Sample Conclusions

" The struggle for human rights has gone on for a long time. Different people fight for their rights in different times. "

" People are willing to fight, and sometimes die for, what they believe in. That's their right and responsibility. "

" While civil rights have improved, we should continue to be inspired by people from the past and speak out against racial discrimination. "

Take a Position

When you **take a position**, you decide what you think. You are on one or another side of an argument. You use reasons or evidence that you found in the texts. That way, the new ideas that you gained from your reading help you form your own opinion.

1 Identify Your Issue

Ask yourself a question about the texts you will read. Then think about facts, opinions, and arguments you already know that connect to the question.

2 Find Evidence

Read several texts for information on the question or issue. Take notes to trap the information you find.

3 Weigh the Evidence

After you have gathered information from several texts, organize the information in a Pro/Con chart. Think about how much evidence there is for or against each position.

Pro/Con Chart

ISSUE: Should Volunteering Be a Requirement for Graduation?

Pro	Con
Many people could use some help.	Teens already have a lot going on in their lives.

4 State Your Position

Review the information in your chart. Think about what information is important to you. Use the information to take a position.

The passages on pages 397–398 deal with another aspect of the theme Rights and Responsibilities: Volunteering. As you read, look for information that can help you take a position on the question: *Should volunteering be a requirement for graduation?*

Helping Others in Need

This teen received help from volunteers at Locks of Love.

Madonna Coffman established Locks of Love to help people who lose their hair due to disease. Some diseases such as alopecia often cause complete baldness. The organization collects hair from volunteers to create custom-fit wigs.

Coffman learned that when underprivileged children lose their hair due to medical conditions, many cannot afford wigs. Real human hair wigs can cost as much as $5,000. This act of volunteering seems simple. One person grows her own hair and donates it to help someone else. In addition to the donor, many people volunteer in the Locks of Love organization to help people in need.

Another organization, the American Red Cross, uses volunteers across the country. The organization provides relief to victims of disasters. Those volunteers willingly do unpaid work for the good of others.

Some people doubt the value of volunteering. They wonder if people who take free help might come to rely on others instead of helping themselves. Some volunteer organizations have been criticized. There are people who believe they misused funds given as donations.

But most people seem to believe in volunteering. According to the *Volunteer Growth in America Report*, volunteering has reached a 30-year high in the United States. Today, over 27 percent of adults and teens volunteer.

Growing hair is a simple way to volunteer and help other people.

This information argues against volunteering.

Some teens think it's important to volunteer. Do I?

Take a Position, continued

Volunteer—It's Your Responsibility

Editor—Some people avoid volunteering, and we teens are among them. Teens live busy lives playing sports, socializing, pursuing hobbies, and working at jobs for pay. It's easy to think that money or personal satisfaction is the only reason to work hard. But in all communities, people rely on volunteers. Volunteers act as safety nets for others who are falling on hard times.

Though we may not have extra money to donate to an organization or cause, some teens have succeeded in solving problems or helping others in our communities. A good example is Juan Reyes. He visits the children's ward at Northside Hospital. Dressed like a clown, Juan appears at 4 P.M. twice a month. He entertains the kids with his singing and guitar playing. By dinnertime, the kids are singing along, having forgotten their troubles for a while. Juan reports that those days make him feel pretty good, too.

You don't have to have musical talent to volunteer. Just help an organization that interests you. You can be a volunteer for UNICEF, which works to help protect children's rights. Volunteer opportunities exist in every community. And people discover talents they never knew they had while they take responsibility. Do you like to work with your hands? Volunteer to build and renovate playgrounds through the KaBOOM! program. It's as easy as going online to www.helping.org and finding an organization that interests you!

LASHON THOMAS
Union City

Con—
Teens are busy with sports, hobbies, and jobs that pay.

Pro—
All communities rely on volunteers.

Pro—
Volunteers feel good about helping.

Pro—
Volunteers discover talents and take responsibility.

Pause and Reflect

As you're reading different texts on the same issue, take notes to trap the information. Then weigh all the evidence by organizing the information in a Pro/Con chart. What's your position on the issue? You can use the information in the chart as talking points in a class debate.

Pro/Con Chart

ISSUE: Should Volunteering Be a Requirement for Graduation?

Pro	Con
Many people could use some help.	Teens already have a lot going on in their lives.
Some volunteering is pretty simple like growing your hair or singing for sick kids.	Some people may start to depend on free help, instead of helping themselves.
Volunteers help victims of disasters.	Some charities have wasted money.
All communities rely on volunteers.	Teens are busy with sports, hobbies, and jobs that pay.
Volunteers feel good about helping.	Many teens already have responsibilities outside of school—like babysitting and cooking.
When you volunteer, you discover talents you didn't know you had.	

Add facts and opinions based on your own experience.

Sample Positions

" Volunteering has a lot of benefits. It gives teens a chance to take responsibility and help their communities. It should be a part of everyone's education. "

" I don't think it's fair to expect every student to volunteer. Some teens need to work after school to make money or to help their families. That should come first. "

" Requiring students to do a few hours of volunteer work seems reasonable. There are a lot of people who could use some help. "

Strategy Summary

When you synthesize, you combine information from different parts of a single text or from different texts. You come up with big ideas that you've never thought of before.

- Pay attention to important ideas and what they have in common. Figure out **how the ideas fit together** in a way that you haven't thought of before.

- You might **take a position** on the writer's ideas and opinions about the topic.

See how one good reader combines important ideas to synthesize when he reads an essay.

Essay

SCHOOLING FOR DOLLARS

The Educational Improvement Now™ Corporation has taken over Grant High School. For students like me, it's been a nightmare. We now have the corporate logo printed on everything, including the bass drum in the marching band. Every classroom has a banner with the EIN logo, too.

I suppose I could live with that, but it's affecting us in other ways. First, we can't participate in school sports or clubs until all our grades get up to EIN's Top-Level.

" I've read other articles about schools run by private companies. People hope it will improve students' performance. I think it's better to keep local control of a school."

LET US PLAY!

See how another reader synthesizes information and uses the information to form an opinion.

Essay

RICHMOND **Headlines**

RICHMOND HIGH SCHOOL   SEPTEMBER ISSUE, VOL. III

Public Noise and Private Choice

By Jill Watson, grade 11

I was listening to the radio in my car waiting for a green light when noise from another car invaded my life. The driver chose to blast his music. The bass was so loud my teeth ached. The music drowned out my radio and a siren from an ambulance. When I pulled into the next lane, I nearly collided with the ambulance speeding by!

People argue they have the right to play music loudly. What about my right to hear what I want? What about my right to protect my hearing? Our community must take a stand on public noise.

" Teens get in a lot of accidents because they're distracted. It makes sense to control the noise. But I already feel like I'm losing my freedom in public places thanks to security cameras. So I disagree with this writer. "

Put Your Strategies to Work

Get in the Driver's Seat

As you worked through this chapter, you've tried out a lot of different tools and learned which ones work best for you. The first step is always to figure out what type of text you'll be reading and tap into what you know. Then you can use your predictions as a road map to your reading.

Magazine Article

Sniffing Out Disease

THE WORK of cancer researchers may prove that dogs are a medical marvel for cancer patients. Dogs have a keen sense of smell. Because of this, researchers believe dogs may be able to detect cancer more quickly than even modern technology.

Stories from the Field

Over the years, stories have surfaced about dogs' abilities to sense when someone had cancer. In 1989, a medical journal in England brought this phenomenon to the attention of medical professionals. It reported that a woman's dog was fixated on a mark in her skin. According to the journal, the dog was very persistent. The woman finally went to her doctor. The spot turned out to be skin cancer.

Research Begins: Breast and Lung Cancer

Similar stories led researchers to investigate dogs' sensitivities to the disease. In one study, five ordinary dogs were trained to find signs of breast and lung cancer. They were taught to detect it on the breath of the cancer patients. Researchers first taught dogs to sit or lie down when they detected cancer in a breath sample. The dogs were trained for three weeks. Then researchers conducted a study. The study included 86 cancer patients and 83 healthy people. Of the sick patients, 55 had lung cancer and 31 had breast cancer.

continued on next page

Plan Your Reading

Preview and Tap Into What You Know

" Cancer is a big problem in the U.S. And I know dogs can really help people."

Preview and Predict

" I can tell this is nonfiction. The headings tell me the type of information the writer will give."

Preview and Set a Purpose

" I want to find out if dogs can help find cancer."

Stay in Control

You've seen that you can control your reading by checking in with yourself from time to time. As you read, you keep your purpose in mind and make sure that you're understanding what you're reading.

Sniffing Out Disease, continued

Computer illustration of a cancer cell

Researchers put tubes containing breath samples in front of the dogs to smell. The dogs found breast and lung cancers as often as 97 percent of the time. The animals could even detect lung cancer and breast cancer in very early stages.

Another Type of Cancer

Another study used dogs to detect bladder cancer. Researchers trained six dogs for over seven months. The dogs learned to recognize different odors. They sniffed urine samples from healthy people. They also sniffed urine samples from people with cancer. After training, the dogs detected bladder cancer 22 out of 54 times. Statistics say that most people have only a 14 percent chance of discovering bladder cancer on their own. In comparison, researchers believe the dogs' 41 percent success rate is a good start.

An Electronic Snout?

Early detection of cancer increases a patient's survival rate. Researchers hope dogs will play a role in early screening one day. But some doctors are not so sure. Are dogs in busy doctor's offices a practical solution? Once again, researchers are turning to technology. This time they hope to develop an electronic nose. Researchers hope the device would work as well as the snouts of trained dogs. Then ordinary pets will deserve credit for inspiring this amazing medical advancement.

Monitor Your Reading

Make Comments and Keep Your Purpose in Mind

" The results are pretty amazing, but they're based on only two studies. I'm not sure dogs can find cancer. "

Check In With Yourself

" Did I really understand what an electronic snout is? "

Put Your Strategies to Work, continued

Choose the Right Strategy

When you read, you usually use a variety of strategies. Choose the ones that work best for you. See how Ahote changes strategies as he reads fiction.

Memoir

<table>
<tr><td>10</td><td style="text-align:right">LAB NOTES</td></tr>
</table>

Mr. Shaw, my high school biology teacher, was unforgettable. Every day he'd greet us with "Biology! It just grows on you!" as we groaned and got to work.

He wore bright blue-framed glasses. The lenses were always smudged with greasy fingerprints and stuff we used in class. He looked like a moving lab experiment.

On alternate Wednesdays, Mr. Shaw performed for us. He sang songs like "The Mitochondria Blues." He'd strum his guitar, wearing a vest, lime green pants, and snakeskin boots. Topping it off was his headband: I ♥ life.

At that time, I thought he was a bit weird, but fun. Certainly more interesting than my other teachers. They all seemed to stand in front of the classroom and talk at us, not with us. But Mr. Shaw was different. He cared about what we thought. He wanted to know how we felt and what got us excited about enzymes and cell division.

He asks himself questions.

Why was Mr. Shaw unforgettable?
He joked around and dressed in crazy clothes.

He uses his senses to imagine the scene.

I can picture his glasses and his clothes.
What a goofy guy!

He questions the author.

Why does the writer include this scene?
Mr. Shaw was different from most teachers.

It was 1970 and life for us was pretty good. We were sophomores and busy with our friends and school and maybe trying to save the world in our spare time. We had no idea what Mr. Shaw had been through, or the pain that he was covering up.

Then I saw him in the parking lot one day before school. He was reading a letter and looked very upset. I think he may have been crying. I tapped on the window and waved. When he got out of the car, I asked him, "Are you okay?"

He shrugged. Then he quietly said, "I was reading a letter from my kid brother Danny. He went to Vietnam last year. He was only nineteen."

He makes inferences.

Something bad must have happened to Mr. Shaw.

He makes connections.

I've read other things about the war. A lot of young soldiers were drafted. Many died there.

Choose the Right Strategy

See how Danielle uses a flexible set of strategies for reading this nonfiction selection.

Magazine Article

WARTS AND ALL

And then she said she had no idea WHAT I was talking about!

2002

IMAGINE READING AN OLD diary or journal from 6th grade. Do you remember your secret crush, or the fights with your brother? How about all the reasons you deserved to marry the hottest singer?

Now imagine reading all those top-secret thoughts on stage in front of a crowd! People around the country are doing it as part of a live-comedy show. They think it can both <u>heal and entertain</u>.

Originally, the diaries were meant to be secret. Now they have audiences rolling with laughter. It's like stumbling upon an old love letter from Junior High.

. . . *By now you may be wondering who I am, why I'm writing you, and how you could possibly turn down a date with someone as cool, smart, and handsome as me.*

This writing is a window into a given time in your life, and it's <u>the kind of thing that audiences love</u>.

She relates the text to her own life.

> You'd have to be pretty confident to read your diary out loud to a bunch of strangers. I'd be pretty nervous.

She synthesizes information.

> Everybody has pitiful, embarrassing moments. So we can all relate to what people wrote in their diaries.

continued on next page

Reading personal confessions may not seem like entertainment, but the shows have been enormously successful. Think back. What were your most embarassing moments in sixth grade? What would make your Top Ten list?

She asks and answers questions.

Why would people want to do this?

I once read about "catharsis." It's when you feel better after you open up.

1. Falling or tripping
2. Wearing your clothes inside out
3. Pimples
4. Braces
5. Dropping something
6. Breaking something
7. Being called to the office
8. Not being invited to a party
9. Getting sick in class
10. Getting sick in the cafeteria

She decides what she wants to remember.

The main idea is that we all have embarassing things happen. They're part of growing up and being human.

Feel better now? Everyone suffers through junior high school. And survives. Some of us have permanent records of the suffering. Thanks to these old journals and diaries, we don't have to suffer, or laugh, alone. ■

Skills in Action

> **"G**ood books don't give up all their secrets at once.**"**
>
> —STEPHEN KING

IN THIS CHAPTER

Skills in Action

Categorize

To **categorize** is to put things that are alike into groups, or categories. When you talk about movies as "action films" or "comedies," you are talking about movie categories. When you read nonfiction texts, it's good to group new ideas and information into categories.

What Are Some Examples?

Writers often present information organized by category.

- Many science and social studies texts, like the one on page 411, contain headings that are clues to categories of information. In an article about weather systems a heading, such as "Tornadoes," tells you that the information about tornadoes is grouped together in that section.

- Newspaper editorials usually try to present both sides of an issue such as a city's plan to expand a parking lot. To help you form your own opinion, categorize the arguments presented into "Pros" and "Cons."

Words Related to Categorizing

Classify is a synonym for *categorize*. Both words have to do with putting things into a group based on what they have in common. Study the chart to learn more words related to categorizing.

Academic Vocabulary

Word History	Word and Definition	Example
From the French *catégorie* meaning "group"	**category** (ka'-tə-gôr-ē) *n.,* a group of things that have something in common	Crocodiles fall under the **category** of predatory animals.
Part of the word family *class*, meaning "group"	**classify** (kla'-sə-fī) *v.,* to put into groups	Zoologists **classify** crocodiles and dinosaurs in the same group.
	classification (kla'-sə-fə-kā-shən) *n.,* a system for putting things in groups	According to their biological **classification**, dinosaurs and crocodiles are both reptiles.

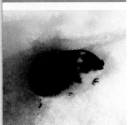

Animals must adapt to the harsh conditions of the tundra.

Life in the Tundra

The tundra is one of Earth's coldest places. The average winter temperature is 30°F below zero. Some amazing plants and animals have adapted to these extreme conditions.

Plants in the Tundra

Summers are short in the tundra, but the days are long. To get as much sun as possible, the flowers of some plants turn toward the sun to take in more light. These include Arctic dryads and Arctic poppies. Other plants, like wooly louse worts and rock willows, grow small hairs to keep them warm and protected in the winter.

Animals in the Tundra

Animals in the tundra have ways of coping with the bitter cold winters. The Arctic ground squirrel, for example, avoids the cold by going into a deep sleep. This is called **hibernation**. It slows both breathing and heart rate. Other animals, like grizzly bears, can go in and out of a light hibernation. Some smaller animals like lemmings and shrews dig tunnels in the snow. The hard-packed snow keeps cold air out of their winter homes.

How to Categorize

1. Use the **headings** as clues to a category of information

2. Look for **examples** that belong in the category.

3. Record **important information** about the examples.

Idea Diagram

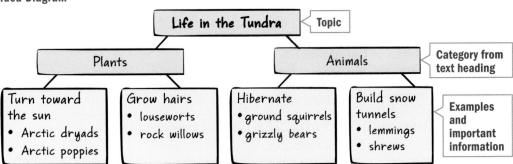

Categorize, continued

Sometimes the writer doesn't include headings that cue categories. Then you have to look a little harder to see how information fits together. Here's how:

1 **Focus on the Descriptions**

Look for the characteristics, or features, of the things the writer is describing. For example, a travel writer may describe Austin as having *"a great music scene"* and San Antonio as having *"good restaurants."* You can group other cities described in the article according to these features.

2 **Look for Details That Explain How Things Are Alike**

As you continue reading you discover that Aspen, Colorado is *"a terrific place for snow skiing"* and the Grand Canyon *"has fabulous river rafting."* What do these places have in common? They fit a category: Places with great outdoor activities. Continue reading and look for more places that fit in this group.

3 **Look for Names of Categories**

As you read, look for category names. Sometimes they are signaled by the phrases *types of* or *examples of.*

Read the passage on the next page. Then look at how the graphic organizer categorizes the information.

STARS—NOT WHAT THEY SEEM

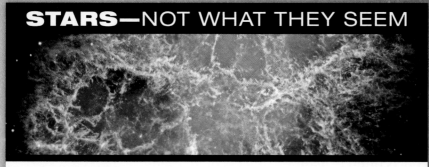

The amazing Crab Nebula

From Earth, most stars look like tiny points of white light. However, stars can be very different. Scientists have classified stars based on certain characteristics, such as their size and the rate at which they burn their gases.

Proxima Centauri is the closest star to the Sun. It is smaller than the Sun and nearly 18,000 times dimmer. Another small star, Wolf 359, is the fifth closest star to the Sun. For many years Wolf 359 was known as the dimmest star in the night sky. Because both of these small, dim stars burn slowly, they look red. So, scientists call them red dwarfs.

Larger stars, like the Sun and its neighbor Alpha Centauri A, burn fuel differently than a red dwarf. This difference explains why we can usually see these yellow dwarf stars in the night sky.

Two of the brightest stars in the sky are Betelgeuse (pronounced *beetle juice*) and Rigel. Both burn about 50,000 times brighter than the Sun. Called supergiants, they are also the biggest stars in the sky.

Look for Categories

In this article, stars are classified according to their size and burn rate.

Idea Diagram

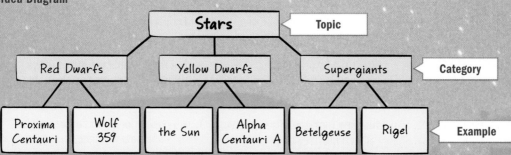

Stars — Topic

Red Dwarfs   Yellow Dwarfs   Supergiants — Category

Proxima Centauri   Wolf 359   the Sun   Alpha Centauri A   Betelgeuse   Rigel — Example

Cause and Effect

Since your doctor knows about medicine, she saved someone's life. Prescribing the right medicine is a **cause** that led to an **effect**: saving a life. When you read, understanding causes and effects will help you see how events are connected.

What Are Some Examples?

You can find cause and effect in both nonfiction and fiction texts.

- Newspaper reports often explain the effects of an event. If some bands gave a concert to raise money for a charity, a report would include what happened as a result of the fund raising.

- In history texts, writers often discuss the reasons that events such as wars or migrations happened. You will also read about the results, or effects, of these events.

- Characters in fiction make choices that have effects, too. The results can change both their lives and the lives of other characters.

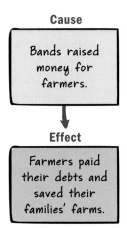

Cause

Bands raised money for farmers.

Effect

Farmers paid their debts and saved their families' farms.

Words Related to Cause and Effect

Many people confuse the noun *effect* with the verb *affect*, which has a related meaning. Study the chart to learn more about words related to cause and effect.

Academic Vocabulary

Word History	Word and Definition	Example
From the Latin *afficere*, meaning "to influence"	**affect** (ə-fekt') *v.*, to do something that changes someone or something	The death of a friend **affected** Rudy's outlook.
From the Latin *efficere*, meaning "to bring about"	**effect** (i-fekt' or ē-fekt') *n.*, something that happens because of something else	The most significant **effect** of the scholarship was that she was able to study medicine.
Compound word: *out + come*	**outcome** (out'-kəm) *n.*, something that happens as a result	I'm hoping for a good **outcome** after the candidate's debate.

Cause and Effect in Nonfiction

When you read nonfiction, ask yourself what makes events happen and what are the results, or effects, of these events. Words such as *since*, *because*, and *reason* signal a cause. *As a result, so*, and *therefore* signal an effect.

Magazine Article

Music on the go is now part of daily life.

GIVING LIFE A
SOUNDTRACK

Andreas Pavel wanted to take music with him everywhere he went. As a result, in 1972, he invented the stereobelt. This invention was the world's first personal music player with earphones.

Pavel tested his stereobelt for the first time during a hiking trip in Switzerland. As he watched the snow falling and listened to music, he realized how important his invention was. He had built a machine that would let people set the events of their everyday lives to music.

The stereobelt was the first machine that allowed people to take their own music out of their homes and into the world. Today we can take music just about anywhere.

How to Identify Causes and Effects

Use **signal words** to help you find **causes** and **effects**.

- A cause is the reason that something happens.
- An effect is the result.

Here the writer presents an effect without using a signal word.

Sometimes the effect of one event can become the cause of another. This is called a chain of events.

Chain of Events

Cause	Effect/New Cause	Effect
Andreas Pavel wanted to take music with him everywhere.	He invented the stereobelt.	People can listen to music anywhere.

Cause and Effect in Fiction

Ever wonder *why* a story event happens? That's a cause. Ever wonder *what happens* as a result of a character's action? That's an effect.

Finding Multiple Causes

Just like you, characters often have more than one reason for doing something. And events in a story can happen for several reasons, too. You can make an organizer to help you map all the causes that lead to one result, or effect.

Multiple Causes

Jenna wanted to buy her own car.	
She didn't have enough saved from her allowance.	**Effect** → Jenna got a job at a department store.
No one could loan her the money.	

Finding Multiple Effects

A single action may have two or more effects. As you read, use a graphic organizer to map the different effects of a character's action or a story event.

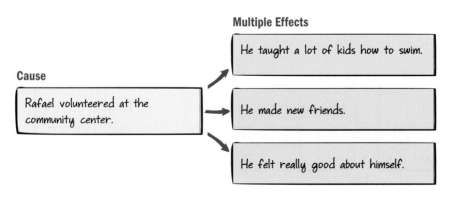

Multiple Effects

He taught a lot of kids how to swim.

Cause

Rafael volunteered at the community center.

He made new friends.

He felt really good about himself.

As you read the story, think about how the events are connected. Look for the reasons that an event happens. Look for the effects of each event.

Fiction

THE CIRCLES IN THE FIELD | 143

The summer night seemed just like any other on the quiet Iowa farm. Then, out of nowhere, eerie whirring sounds pierced the silence. Colored lights flashed above the house like long strings of confetti. Thick smoke began to fill the cloudless sky. A wolf's cry echoed in the distance.

Disturbed by the noise, Chaco began to bark furiously. His barking woke the whole Lindstrom family. Mrs. Lindstrom, Rachel, and Paul went outside to investigate. They couldn't believe what they saw—elaborate crop circles! The field that was once filled with flowing wheat was now flattened and cut in a perfect pattern of circles. They were stunned, and though no one would admit it, a little scared. Still, Rachel could hardly wait to get to school to tell her friends.

The news spread quickly. By noon that day, the farm was transformed again—this time into what looked like a movie set. Whirling helicopters hovered overhead. People with microphones and TV cameras rushed everywhere. Everyone had questions, but no one seemed to have any answers.

How to Identify Multiple Causes and Effects

As you read, ask yourself: *What happened*, and *Why*?

Look for a chain of **causes** and **effects.**

▲ Aerial view of crop circle

You can use a graphic organizer to track the causes and effects.

Multiple Effects

Cause

| The Lindstrom family discovered crop circles on their farm. |

→ They were stunned and scared.

→ Rachel told her friends about the circles.

→ TV reporters arrived at the farm.

Characters

Do you know John Henry, La Llorona, and Frankenstein? Are they famous? Well, sort of. They are well-known **characters**, or made-up people in stories. Fiction writers create characters—people or animals—that seem so real you think they may have really lived.

Why Are Characters Important?

You can find characters in novels, plays, and even poetry.

- Most fiction revolves around characters, the reasons they do things, and their feelings and actions. *Main characters* are key to the story. *Minor characters* play less important roles.

- Once you know the characters, you get really involved in the story. You can even guess what they're going to do next.

- Being aware of the characters' *traits*, or qualities such as courage or envy, helps you understand their feelings and the message the author wants to convey about human nature. Sometimes you can put yourself in the characters' shoes. Identifying with them may help you understand people in your own life, too.

Words Related to Characters in Fiction

The main character in a story is called a *protagonist*. The reason that a character does something is called a *motive*. Study the chart to learn more about words related to characters in fiction.

Academic Vocabulary		
Word History	**Word and Definition**	**Example**
From the Latin movēre, meaning "to move"	**motive** (mō'-tiv) *n.*, the reason that someone does or says something	Her **motive** for leaving the party early was to get home before her curfew.
Borrowed from French rôle, meaning "roll"	**role** (rōl) *n.*, the part a person plays in a play or movie	I wanted to play the **role** of Atticus in *To Kill a Mockingbird*.
From the Greek prōtagōnistēs, meaning "competitor at games; actor"	**protagonist** (prō-ta'-gə-nist) *n.*, the main character in a novel or other work of fiction	In some novels, the story is told from the viewpoint of the **protagonist**.

How Do You Get to Know Characters?

There are many ways to get to know the characters in a story or novel. As you read the story below, look for information that helps you understand that Jamila is ambitious. Based on what you know about Jamila, what do you predict she will do?

Short Story

JAMILA'S WAY TO THE TOP   37

Jamila sat in the Monday morning meeting, listening to the Editor-in-Chief, Ms. Hyde: "I can't believe it. Twelfth Street is hit by a major fire, and *Lake County Daily* doesn't get a picture."

Jamila's heart raced, "I have some photos." Everyone stared at the young intern. "Of the fire," she explained. "I passed it on my way here, and I knew I had to get some shots."

"If you have a good front-page photo, we'll run it," said Ms. Hyde. "Mr. Goodman told me you're an up-coming star."

Now Jamila's heart raced even more. Everyone at the paper was counting on her. She went back to her computer and looked over the digital photos on her desktop. She searched and searched, but none of her photos was very good. The towering flames she remembered looked small and tame. No drama, no front page.

"I can adjust the photos to make the fire more dramatic," she thought, "but that's against the paper's rules. And it would be dishonest." Jamila had never done anything like this before, but now she saw a great opportunity. "What should I do?" she asked herself.

How to Know What a Character Is Like

Look at:

- the character's **words,** thoughts, and actions.

- **what other characters say.**

- **what the author tells you.**

Characters in Drama

In short stories and novels, writers describe characters' thoughts and actions. However, in drama—or plays—you learn about characters through lines of dialogue and stage directions.

What a Play Looks Like

JUST IN TIME   3

ACT ONE

Scene One

TONYA and AL, *dressed in hip clothing, are* sitting on the front steps of an inner city high school and talking *before class starts.* MAI LINH, *wearing conservative, old-fashioned clothes, sits far away from them on the steps, staring into space. They all have backpacks at their feet.*

AL: I just got my pictures back from my trip to Chicago.

TONYA: Ooh, let's see them before the bell rings.

AL (*quietly*): Do you think Mai Linh wants to see them, too?

TONYA: Yeah. She'd probably like that. Hardly anybody's been talking to her since she moved here.

AL (*to* MAI LINH): Hey, Mai Linh, do you want to see my pictures?

MAI LINH (*looking embarrassed*): Okay. But my English isn't so good.

> **Stage directions** explain where the characters are and what they do.

> **Lines of dialogue** are the words a character says.

> Playwrights also tell you *how* the character says the lines.

When you read a play, read the stage directions to find out what the characters do and how they move or speak. Try reading the lines of dialogue out loud to help you get into the characters' heads and personalities. See how the stage directions and dialogue help you know that José has a high opinion of himself.

JUST IN TIME   17

ACT ONE

Scene Two

KANEESHA, *dressed in jeans, is in her living room, where there is one comfortable-looking chair and a table with a birthday cake and paper plates on it. A knock is heard at the door, and KANEESHA opens it to find TONYA and AL, also in jeans.*

TONYA: Happy birthday, Kaneesha! (*They hand her small gifts.*)

KANEESHA: Thanks, Tonya, Al. Didn't José come with you?

AL (*sarcastically*): The great José? Arrive with the public?

KANEESHA (*laughs*): Come on, guys, have some birthday cake.

(*They cut small pieces of cake and sit on the floor to eat it. A loud knock is heard at the door, and KANEESHA answers it to find JOSÉ, wearing a dressy shirt and khakis. He hands her a wrapped CD.*)

JOSÉ (*looking around the room and strutting in*): This just came out yesterday. Am I good, or what? (*He takes a big piece of cake and pushes past the others to plop down in the comfortable chair.*) I'm sure Tonya and Al brought you very nice little presents, though.

KANEESHA: Thanks, José. What have you been doing?

JOSÉ: I showed my older brother and his friends how to really play basketball yesterday. And I had a hot date with someone you don't know.

TONYA (*trying to be polite*): Oh, that's nice, José.

How to Understand a Character

Think about what

- the character **does** and **says**

- the **other characters say** about him

Characters   **421**

Comparison

Writers often make **comparisons**, or tell how two or more things are the same and/or different.

What Are Some Examples?

You can find comparisons in both nonfiction and fiction texts.

- Many magazine and newspaper articles include comparisons. A sports article about basketball might compare two teams by describing their different coaching styles and players' skills.

- Science and history texts are full of comparisons. A history writer might compare two types of governments, for example, a democracy and one ruled by kings. Showing the similarities and differences helps you think about the pros and cons of each form of government.

- Novels and short stories reveal how characters are alike and different. If a writer compares two sisters, for example, readers can see how their personalities affect their actions, decisions, and relationships with other characters.

Words That Signal Comparisons

Writers use words such as *alike, likewise,* and *also* to clue you in to similarities. To announce differences, they use *unlike, however, in contrast,* and *whereas.* Study the chart to learn more.

Academic Vocabulary

Word History	Word and Definition	Example
Compound word: *like + wise*	**likewise** (līk'-wīz) *adv.*, in the same way	Using mass transportation cuts down on pollution. **Likewise**, riding bikes helps the environment.
Compound word: *how + ever*	**however** (hou-e'-vər) *adv.*, on the other hand, but	Most old cars use a lot of gasoline; **however**, many new cars are fuel efficient.
From the Latin *contra + stare*	**in contrast** (in kon'-trast) *prep. phrase*, on the other hand	Most cars run only on gasoline. **In contrast**, hybrid cars use both gas and electricity.

Comparison in Nonfiction

As you read factual information, pay attention to the ways that things are similar and different.

EDITORIAL

Dump the Truck!

These days too many city people are using trucks as pleasure cars. Those monsters are just too big for narrow streets. And they guzzle gas, too.

Driving a car is a better option. Cars are smaller and get better gas mileage. Trucks are just too big for most city parking spots. In contrast, cars fit easily into parking places on streets and in parking garages. If you want to be able to haul heavy loads, then a truck makes sense. Unlike cars, they are designed to hold cargo. So if you really need a truck, you can always rent one for a day or two. After all, how often do you move or haul tons of bricks or firewood? Think about it. There's really no reason for most people in our city to keep on truckin'!

A monster truck

How to Understand Comparisons

1. Use the title and first few sentences to figure out the topic.

2. Identify **what the writer is comparing.**

3. Look for **adjectives ending in -er** and phrases that signal comparisons.

You can use a diagram to show how things are alike and different.

Y Diagram

Cars
- smaller
- get better gas mileage
- fit in parking spaces

Trucks
- big for city streets
- use more gas
- can haul a lot of cargo

At the top of the Y, record how the things are different.

Both
- vehicles—ways to get around
- used for pleasure
- run on gasoline

Here you write how the two things are alike.

Compare Texts on the Same Topic

Two texts written about the same topic can be very different. To compare two texts, ask yourself:

- **Did the authors write for the same purpose?**
  Authors usually write to **inform**, **entertain**, or **persuade**. Of course, an author may write for more than one purpose. Since authors don't usually tell you their purpose directly, you have to figure it out from how they organize their writing and what they say.

- **Do the authors have the same viewpoint?**
  The **author's viewpoint** is the way the author feels about the topic he or she is writing about. It affects the author's choice of words and descriptions—positive, negative, or neutral. When an author presents two sides of an issue, the author gives a **balanced** view. An author who presents only one side gives a **biased** viewpoint.

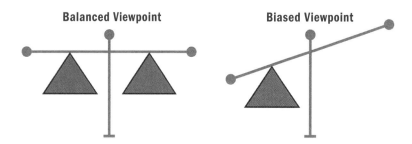

Balanced Viewpoint   Biased Viewpoint

Read the blog below. Does the blogger give a biased or balanced viewpoint?

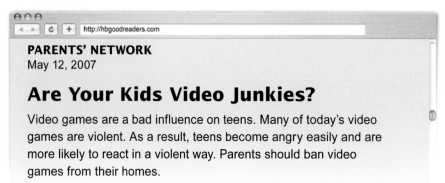

http://hbgoodreaders.com

PARENTS' NETWORK
May 12, 2007

Are Your Kids Video Junkies?

Video games are a bad influence on teens. Many of today's video games are violent. As a result, teens become angry easily and are more likely to react in a violent way. Parents should ban video games from their homes.

Topic:
Video Games

Viewpoint:
They are a bad influence on teens.

Purpose:
to persuade parents to ban video games

Compare the two essays below. What does each writer say about the topic: Teens and Computers?

READERS SPEAK

Plugged In

By Tony Ramirez, teacher

A new report suggests a trend in how American children are using their time. In 2005, almost 86% of youth between 8 and 18 have a computer at home, and 74% have Internet access at home.

Spending time online has some parents and teachers concerned. Parent Nancy Stewart says, "I worry about my children's health. Sitting at the computer doesn't give them any exercise."

Some see benefits in Internet use. "I wouldn't want my students to get *all* their information from the Internet," says Michelle Jones, a ninth-grade English teacher. "But I'm glad something so popular has them reading and writing."

> This writer presents both sides of the issue: **pro** and **con.**

> This writer presents only one side of the issue. She uses the words *educational* and *reliable* to suggest the Internet's positive features.

READERS SPEAK

Give Kids a Break

By Thuy Ng, 10th grade student

As a teenager, I want to respond to "Plugged In." Many teens do spend a lot of time in front of computers. But that does not mean it is bad for society. The Internet can actually be educational. I might not read a newspaper every day, but I check the news online. I just surf the Web sites of newspapers and TV stations. When I have a big research project, I still go to the library. But when I have to look up information quickly, I use the reliable sites online. I'm so glad to have this technology.

You can use a chart like this one to compare texts.

Comparison Chart

	Author's Purpose	Author's Viewpoint	Facts and Information
"Plugged In"	to inform	BALANCED: Some people worry about kids spending too much time on computers, but others see the benefits.	Kids don't exercise; may not use the library Gets kids reading and writing
"Give Kids a Break"	to persuade	BIASED: Spending time on computers is educational.	Good way to get the news; helps with research

Comparison, continued

Compare Fiction and Nonfiction

Nonfiction and fiction authors may write about the same topic, such as the sinking of *Titanic*, but approach it very differently.

▲ Newspaper account reporting the real event

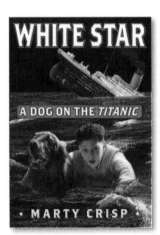

▲ Book cover of a fictional account

What Are Some Differences?

- **Purpose** Usually, fiction writers' main purpose is to entertain you. Nonfiction authors write to persuade or inform you although they sometimes throw in some drama or humor to entertain you, too.

- **Organization** Fiction texts involve a plot, with a beginning, middle, and ending. Nonfiction texts are organized around key ideas or events.

- **Information** Fiction writers don't have to stick to the facts. They make things up to tell a good story. Authors of nonfiction state the facts and may include opinions.

- **Viewpoint** When fiction writers tell a story through a character's eyes, the viewpoint may or may not be what the writers themselves think. In nonfiction texts, you can tell what the author thinks about the topic from the information and words the author chooses.

Compare the two passages on the next page.

Rockin' Rock Climbing

Rock climbing is gaining popularity.

At this very moment, someone in the world is probably dangling from the side of a cliff. More and more people are becoming interested in the exciting sport of rock climbing. Many learn the sport at indoor rock gyms. Then, they move to real cliffs. That's when the thrills begin.

STAYING SAFE

Climbers use special gear to help them get a good grip on the rock. Their tight-fitting shoes have sticky soles. All climbers use ropes, too. These keep climbers safe if they lose their grip on the rocks.

MIDAIR   31

For the past hour, Koushek and Stacy had stared at nothing but steep gray rock. Now, as they hung suspended in midair, they could see miles of river and fields spread out below them.

"That view is amazing." Stacy remarked.

A moment later they heard something above them. Stacy's eyes widened in horror, and she screamed, "Koushek, watch out!"

Looking up, Koushek saw a huge rock tumbling toward him. He braced himself, hoping he could hang on. The next thing he knew, the rock veered sharply to the left, making dust in its path and splintering rock on its way down the cliff.

Compare Fiction and Nonfiction

" *Rockin' Rock Climbing* gives factual information about the sport, including a section about staying safe. "

" *Midair* is about two made-up rock climbers. The author invents what they say and what happens to them. "

Comparison, continued

Compare Characters

Often what makes a story great are the characters. One character may be clever but have dark secrets; another might be kind but easily deceived. Seeing what happens to these different types of people keeps you turning the pages.

Why Compare Characters?

- Comparing characters helps you focus on their traits, or qualities, such as courage or greed. Once you understand what makes them tick, you can better understand their actions.

- Seeing how characters are alike and different may give you new ways to look at yourself, and your family and friends. For example, you may read about two characters who don't seem to have much in common but end up being best friends. Maybe that's happened to you. Or, maybe it will happen some day.

- Comparing two characters who had to face similar situations can shed light on how people make important choices. For example, two different characters may have to choose between their personal beliefs and what others believe. Their different decisions show you the different sides of human nature.

Huck's Reaction in *Huckleberry Finn*	Ralph's Reaction in *Lord of the Flies*
Huck helps Jim run away even though he has been told that slaves are property.	When the boys do their hunting dance, Ralph gets caught up in the excitement and helps them beat Simon.

Which character followed the crowd? Who followed his own beliefs?

In this passage two teens are about to go on stage and dance in front of a large audience. Compare how the two characters react to the situation. What does each character say and do, and why?

Short Story

LAST CALL | Evelyn Stone · 13

"Last call! Five minutes! Ready on stage in five minutes!"

The stage manager's call created panic in the dressing room. Twenty girls all tried to squeeze in one last look in the mirror.

"How do I look?" asked Sari, flashing a dazzling smile at her own reflection.

"Same as always," I answered.

"Is that good?" she asked, deadly serious. Her smile had faded, and for a moment she seemed to let her armor down.

"I'd say so, since you always look perfectly beautiful," I muttered. Sari heaved a sigh of relief and began applying a third coat of lipstick—which she didn't need.

I glanced into the mirror thinking, "And you are perfect, too—perfectly pitiful. But, since you dance in the third row, no one will be looking at you anyway. . . .unless you trip." In my mind I quickly reviewed a tricky cross-step move and hoped against hope that I would pull it off.

Sari, of course, danced in the first row, not because of her looks, but because of her talent. She was a really great dancer—a fact that every one, even she, knew.

"Oh, I'm nervous," Sari exclaimed, checking her costume from every angle. "Are you nervous? You don't look nervous."

Before I could answer, she started heading toward the door. She had spent so long in front of the mirror that she had to step on toes to get to the front of the line. She shoved her way through, oblivious to the other girls' cries and complaints.

"Break a leg!" I called after her, but I don't think she heard me.

How to Compare Characters

- Collect **details about Sari.**

- Collect **details about the narrator.**

- Decide how the two characters are alike or different.

Conclusions

You ring the doorbell at your friend's house. The house is dark and no one comes to the door. You put two and two together and say, "No one is home." You've drawn a conclusion. When you read, you **draw conclusions**, or take information in the text together with what you already know to decide what to believe.

What Are Some Examples?

You draw conclusions as you read fiction and nonfiction texts.

- When you read an interview or biography, you draw conclusions about the person the author is describing. For example, if the author tells you that the person has invented several high-tech gadgets, it may lead you to believe that she studied engineering in college.

- When you read a news report or historical writing, you put together the facts with what you already know and decide what may have caused an event.

- In fictional stories, you put together details from the story with what you know to determine why characters act in certain ways.

Words Related to Conclusions

Conclude and *conclusion* are part of the same word family. Study the chart to learn more about these words.

Academic Vocabulary

Word History	Word and Definition	Example
From the Latin *claudere*, meaning "to shut" or "to close off"	**conclude** (kən-klūd′) *v.*, to come to believe something based on facts	The footprints in the snow led us to **conclude** that a deer had come close by.
	conclusion (kən-klū′-zhən) *n.*, a belief based on facts	When I saw her smiling in class, I reached the **conclusion** that she did well on the test.

Conclusions in Nonfiction

As you're reading, add up the facts and draw on what you know to decide what to believe. When you read about events that really happened, you can check other sources to see if your conclusions are correct.

Magazine Article

ONE GIANT LEAP

Michel Fournier is prepared to break a few world records. He has tried it twice in recent years. But this time, he hopes, he will make history when he jumps from a basket-like gondola carried by a hot air balloon. That balloon will be hovering 25 miles above the ground, making this the highest balloon flight ever. Fournier's jump will be the longest in history, too, and also the fastest—faster than the speed of sound.

This time, Fournier and his team have been extra careful about his equipment. They have ordered a new balloon. As far as the weather is concerned, they have waited for a time when weather conditions should be right. All they can really do now is hope.

How to Draw a Conclusion

1. Collect **facts.**

2. Add them up and think about what you know.

3. Decide what to believe.

Adding Up the Facts

FACT 1: Fournier has tried the jump twice in recent years.

+

FACT 2: He and his team have been extra careful about his equipment.

+

FACT 3: They have waited for a time when all conditions should be right.

➡

CONCLUSION: Fournier has had problems with equipment and weather.

Conclusions, continued

Conclusions in Fiction

Pay attention to the information a writer gives you to draw conclusions about a story's characters, the problems they face, and the story events.

1 **Gather the Details**

Take note of the settings—where events take place—what characters do and say, and key events.

> I put the phone down on the desk and started to weep. How could I tell my mother the news she didn't want to hear? I searched my brain for a way to tell her. I could picture my brother Raymond on his motorcycle the day he left. The image haunted me.

Here are the details one student gathered from this passage:

The narrator started to cry. **+** The mother will be upset by the news. **+** The narrator pictures her brother on his motorcycle.

2 **Put Information Together to Draw a Conclusion**

Think about the details you've gathered. What do they add up to? Make sure that any conclusion you draw is based on the text and makes sense with what you know.

Sample Conclusion

" The narrator has just heard that her brother was in a motorcycle accident. "

3 **Read on to Check your Conclusion**

See whether the author provides any additional information that tells you if your conclusion is accurate.

As you read "One Long Night," add up the details and then draw conclusions to answer these questions:

- Where is Yolanda?

- What is happening in this part of the story?

- Why does she want to go upstairs?

Fiction

ONE LONG NIGHT ❖ 37

There was a low rumbling sound, like a distant train. Then the floor and walls started to shake. Several pictures fell off the wall and crashed on the floor. Yolanda quickly got up from the couch, but wasn't sure what to do.

She looked out the living room window, and saw several large trees swaying under the streetlight. Things inside the house were still falling. A small vase fell off a bookshelf and onto the carpet. The lights blinked once, but stayed on.

Running into the kitchen, Yolanda grabbed the emergency flashlight. She saw a pile of broken dishes on the floor. Then she headed for the stairs. Her brother Rudolfo was upstairs in his crib taking a nap. Before she could set one foot on the stairs, the lights went out. She turned on the flashlight and rushed upstairs.

Details in Fiction

When writers tell stories, they use lots of details, or small bits of information. These details get you to react with feelings and help you picture settings, characters, and events.

Details About the Setting

Details about a setting—or where a story takes place—help create a **mood**, or the feeling the reader gets from a story or poem. The details in this passage produce a particular mood.

> The house creaked in the winter winds, its roof coming off one shingle at a time. Every window had been shattered. A layer of dirt and green mold formed a crust on the white siding. Its only visitors were six large crows.

The writer's description of the setting gives a fearful feeling.

Details About the Characters

Details also help readers imagine what characters are like—how they look, speak, and act. Read the passage to find out what Devon's grandmother is like.

> Devon could smell his grandmother's perfume hanging in the air. It filled the hallway announcing that she had arrived. He heard her laughter coming from the kitchen. Hardy, belly laughs. He went inside to say hello. She was wearing a turban and a flower print dress. Her nails were painted deep red to match her slightly smudged lipstick.

The details help you paint a picture of this unrestrained character.

The details that make characters come alive may help you relate the characters to people you know. Does Devon's grandmother remind you of anyone you know?

As you read the passage below, focus on the details the writer gives about the setting and characters. What feelings, or mood, do they create? How do you picture the two characters in the story?

Mystery

OCTOBER DAWN   17

    Jones and Garibaldi reached the top of the hill and paused to catch their breath. They could hear a dog on a nearby farm. Its howling seemed to float over the hemlock trees, breaking up in the frozen branches. At the bottom of the hill, the silent graveyard waited. Its gray headstones sat under the moonlight.

    Jones—a tall, balding gentleman—shivered in the cold. He wrapped his well-worn, thin coat around him tightly and approached the graveyard fence. Garibaldi was a short, stout and generally nervous type. He was forever blowing his nose or wiping the hairs of his trimmed brown mustache. After stuffing a rumpled silk handkerchief into a back pocket, he put on a pair of thick black gloves. Then he turned on his flashlight.

    Gathering their shovels, the two looked at each other with a heavy silence and began to trudge down the hill. They had no idea what to expect. They only knew that the time had come.

Look for details about the setting that create a mood of gloom and suspense.

Look for details that help you imagine the characters.

Details About the Plot

What keeps you reading a story and guessing what will happen next? Often, it's the **suspense** that the writer builds into the plot of the story. Writers include details that make you wonder how things will turn out. In this way, they keep you interested and keep you reading.

How Writers Build Suspense

Writers use different methods to build suspense. They may:

- raise questions in your mind

- slow down or speed up the action of the story

- hint that you can't trust what the narrator or a character says

- put characters in dangerous situations

- give clues about good or bad things that may happen later in the story

Read the first two stanzas of "The Raven." How did Edgar Allan Poe create suspense in the poem?

THE RAVEN

—EDGAR ALLEN POE

Once upon a midnight dreary, while I pondered, weak and weary,
Over many an old and curious book filled with forgotten lore—
While I sat there, nearly napping, suddenly there came a tapping,
As of someone gently rapping, rapping at my bedroom door.
"It is some visitor," I muttered, "tapping at my bedroom door—
        Only this, and nothing more."

Ah, clearly I remember it was in cold and dark December,
And each separate dying ember formed a ghost upon the floor.
Eagerly I wished for tomorrow—I had tried but failed to borrow
Help from books to cease my sorrow—sorrow for the lost Lenore—
For the rare and beautiful maiden whom the angels name Lenore—
        Nameless here for evermore.

The narrator is startled by a sudden sound.

Here, he uses words like *dying* and *ghost* to add to a mood of fear and uncertainty.

Read the scene from a mystery set on the Caribbean island of St. John. Pay attention to how Forrest reacts when Mr. Landon asks him some questions. How do the writers build suspense?

Mystery

ESCAPE FROM FEAR | Skurzynski & Ferguson 17

"Where are your cousins?"

"They're around here, somewhere," Forrest said, shaking his shoulder free. He crossed his arms as if daring Steven to ask him more questions.

"I'd like to meet them."

"No! I mean, thank you for your concern." Jack noticed a bead of perspiration roll down the end of Forrest's face. He must be wilting in the moist evening heat. Or maybe he was more nervous than he was letting on. "Look, Mr. Landon, I don't want to be rude, but what I do really isn't any of your business."

"I'm afraid it is," Steven answered quietly. "I was just talking to Jack about that. You're only 13 years old, you're thousands of miles from home, and you're here all alone. That makes it my business."

Details that Build Suspense

- The way Forrest acts shows that he may have something to hide.
- Other details suggest that something bad may happen.

Fact and Opinion

A hummingbird's heart can beat 1260 times a minute. That's a **fact**—a statement that can be proven to be true or false. *Hummingbirds are amazing animals.* That's an **opinion**—what someone considers to be true. Knowing the difference keeps you from believing just anything you read.

What Are Some Examples?

You can find facts and opinions in all sorts of texts.

- Reference books, such as encyclopedias or almanacs, give facts about a topic. These sources may also quote famous people's opinions about the events of their time.

- Editorials are opinion pieces. The writer states an opinion such as *Teens should have curfews.* Then the writer presents facts to support the opinion, for example, *Many cities that imposed curfews have helped keep kids safe from crime.*

- Advertisements usually contain favorable opinions about a product. Sometimes ads include facts such as the number of cars sold or the ingredients in a food.

Words Related to Fact and Opinion

Are you *opinionated*—that is, do you have a lot of strong opinions? You better have some *accurate* facts to back them up. Study the chart to learn more words related to fact and opinion.

Academic Vocabulary

Word History	Word and Definition	Example
From the Latin *accurare,* meaning "to take care of"	**accurate** (aʹ-kyər-ət) *n.,* exactly true or correct	To check the **accuracy** of my report, I used two reference books.
From the Latin *auctoritat* meaning "decision, power"	**authority** (ə-thôrʹ-ə-tē) *n.,* someone who is an expert on a subject	My aunt is an **authority** on genetic diseases.
From the Latin *valēre,* meaning "strong"	**valid** (vaʹ-ləd) *adj.,* exactly true or correct	Evidence showed that his claim of innocence was **valid**.

Fact and Opinion in Persuasive Writing

When you read editorials, essays, and advertisements, look for words that signal an opinion such as *think, believe, must,* and *should.*

Newspaper Editorial

EDITORIAL

The Question of Soda

This week the parents of students at Franklin High School received a letter. It explained a plan to remove soda from the vending machines at school. As a student at the high school, I am writing to address this issue.

The school should not take away students' ability to choose what they would like to drink. It would not be wise to follow the suggested plan. Instead, the school should provide students with information to help them make good decisions.

In 2005, four states passed laws that required companies to print nutritional information on foods sold in schools. Better labeling means better choices. The best solution is to add bottled water to the vending machines. Then students would have a healthier alternative to soda.

—Bill Martínez, 10th Grade, Jefferson High

How to Identify Facts and Opinions

- Words like *should, think, believe* are clues to an **opinion.**
- Statements of **fact** can be proven true or false.

In an advertisement trying to get you to buy a product, you are likely to find both facts and opinions.

Advertisement

THE SOFT DRINK WITH THE BIG TASTE

One sip, and you'll never go back to those other soft drinks. We've added real orange juice, and some surprises, too. Together, these flavors produce a taste that is sparkling smooth. The flavor is so big, we could hardly fit it into a glass!

Fact and Opinion, continued

Fact and Opinion in a News Article

Usually, news reporters stick to the facts, telling *who, what, where, when, why,* and *how.* But often, reporters include people's opinions of an event or topic. And sometimes, they put in their own opinions, too. If you can tell facts from opinions, you'll get the real story!

What Should I Know?

Here are some things to do as you read a newspaper article.

- After each statement, ask yourself: *Can this be proven to be true or false?*

- If you're not sure whether a statement is a fact, look it up. Encyclopedias, periodicals, and other references are good sources to use. You can ask an expert, or authority, too.

- Look for adjectives that give away a writer's feelings. For example, if a writer describes someone as *attractive,* you can tell how the writer feels about the person.

Fact or Opinion?

The following statements might be found in a newspaper article. See what makes each statement a fact or an opinion.

Facts	Opinions
Last week, three new convenience stores opened in the North Side neighborhood.	It is not necessary to have three convenience stores in one neighborhood.
Funding was cut for the music program at King High School.	By cutting the music program, students at King High School are being cheated.

You can prove that this information is true.

The phrase *not necessary* is a clue that this is an opinion.

The adjective *cheated* reveals how the writer feels about the topic.

As you read this news article, ask yourself whether the statements are facts or opinions.

Newspaper Article

Just One Spoonful of Sugar

Tomás Rivas,
Lake County science reporter

Americans are in love with sugar. The amount of added sugar that Americans consume rose 30 percent in the last two decades. Studies show that each individual ate an average of 64 pounds of sugar per year.

Does the body really need sugar to keep it going? The answer to this question is "yes," but the type of sugar that is good for your body is in the form of starches. Foods like whole grains, cereal, and fruit contain sugars. But besides sugar, they are also full of vitamins and minerals. Starchy foods taste really good, too!

Most people do not take in enough healthy sugars. Instead, a lot of the foods and drinks that people consume are full of added sugar. This added sugar contains empty calories. So, these foods do not have the vitamins and minerals that the body needs to be healthy.

How to Identify Facts and Opinions

Ask yourself if the writer's statements can be proven. If so, they're **facts.** If not, they are **opinions.**

You can use a chart like this to identify facts and opinions.

Fact and Opinion Chart

Statement	Fact or Opinion?	Why?
Studies show that each individual ate an average of 64 pounds of sugar per year.	Fact	I can look this up on the Internet to check if it is true.
Starchy foods taste really good, too!	Opinion	This statement tells what the author thinks about starchy foods. Not all people agree.

Inferences

Writers do not always come right out and say what they want you to know. You have to make an **inference**, or logical guess.

What Are Some Examples?

To make an inference, you combine clues in the text with your own knowledge and common sense.

- When you read magazine and newspaper articles, you may make inferences about how the writer feels about the subject.

WRITER'S WORDS	READER'S INFERENCE
There should be a law that requires all motorcycle riders in the U.S. to wear helmets.	The writer must think that riding motorcycles is dangerous. She may even know someone who was hurt riding a motorcycle.

- You make inferences when you read history texts, too. Suppose you read that in the 1960s, police were called in to remove students who were demonstrating. You may know that during the Vietnam War there were a lot of student protests, so you guess that the demonstrators were protesting the war.

- In fictional stories, you make inferences about characters' feelings, actions, and personalities. If a character steps in to defend someone from the school bully, you might infer that he or she is courageous.

▼ Demonstrations protesting the Vietnam War

Inferences in Nonfiction

When you read nonfiction, pay attention to the facts and think about what you already know about the topic.

Magazine Article

TROUBLE IN THE ALEUTIAN ISLANDS

Aleutian children before the forced evacuation

The Aleutian Islands, now part of the United States, lie southwest of Alaska. According to the 2000 census report, about 8,000 people call the islands home. They are the Aleuts, and like their ancestors, they are fishermen.

During World War II, the Aleuts experienced true hardship. They were forced to leave their homes. After Japan attacked the islands, the U.S. military moved in. The military used the islands as a base. To do this, they removed people from areas that were considered important to security.

The Aleuts were given no time to prepare to leave their homes. They were allowed to take only a few things with them—a small suitcase and a bedroll. The people were moved to internment camps. The camps did not provide enough food for everyone, and medical care was poor. Nearly 10 percent of the Aleuts in the camps died.

How to Make an Inference

1. Look closely at the **information** the writer gives about the events.

2. Add what you know.

3. What can you infer about the military's decision to send the Aleuts to internment camps?

Reader's Inference

What the Writer Says
The military removed Aleuts from areas considered important to security.

+

What I Know
Even Japanese Americans who were U.S. citizens were sent to internment camps.

=

Inference
During World War II the mood in the U.S. must have been very tense.

Inferences in Fiction

Getting to know a character in a story is like getting to know people in real life. You piece together information to create the full picture.

- Readers may make inferences about a characters' **feelings.**

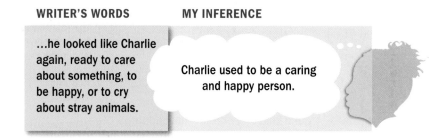

WRITER'S WORDS

Some days he'd just sit on that bed with his hands hanging down between his knees.

MY INFERENCE

He sounds like he doesn't have the energy to move. People who are depressed sometimes act that way.

- Readers may also make logical guesses about a characters' **traits**, or qualities such as honesty, kindness, or greed.

WRITER'S WORDS

...he looked like Charlie again, ready to care about something, to be happy, or to cry about stray animals.

MY INFERENCE

Charlie used to be a caring and happy person.

All parts of the text can give you clues to what a character is like.

- **Read the writer's description.** Look for describing words that help you picture the character.

- **Look for what the character does.** Actions like sitting on a bed with hands hanging down are important clues.

- **Look for dialogue.** If the character is speaking, are there clues in what the character says or how the character says it? If other characters are speaking, look for their attitudes toward the character you are trying to understand.

When you read fiction, try to figure out what makes characters the way they are. Use what the writer tells you, and combine those details with what you know from your own experience.

Novel

Right after he came home from Rahway, I got up in the middle of the night to look at him. He'd been away for more than two years, and the guy sleeping across from me was a stranger. Some days he'd just sit on that bed with his hands hanging down between his knees. Just staring out the window and looking evil. But when he was asleep, his face spread out—all the frowns and scowls just kind of faded and he looked like Charlie again, ready to care about something, to be happy, or to cry about stray animals.

Make Inferences

From these **details**, you can guess that:

- In the past two years Charlie has changed.
- Now he seems depressed and angry.

Use a chart like this one to help you make inferences.

One Reader's Inference

Details from the Story	**What I Know**	**Inference**
Charlie used to be happy and care about things.	People worry when friends or family act depressed.	The narrator must be worried about Charlie.

▼ City row houses like the one where Charlie and his brother lived

Main Idea and Supporting Details

The **main idea** is the central, or most important, point that a writer makes. **Supporting details** are the bits of information that tell more about the main idea.

How to Find the Main Idea

No matter what topic you read about—from the Harlem Renaissance to cloning in the 21st century—focus on what the writer thinks is important for you to know.

- The first step in figuring out the main idea of a nonfiction text is to identify the **topic**, or subject. Then decide what the writer is mostly saying about the topic. For example, if the topic of an article is reality shows, ask yourself: *What is the writer mostly saying about reality shows?*

- Often writers will directly tell you their main idea. They include a **main idea statement** right at the beginning of a passage. Other times writers state the main idea at the end or in the middle of the text.

- You can also use **headings and subheadings** to identify what the writer considers to be important information. For example, in a biography of Gandhi, you might come across the heading *Gandhi's Achievements*. So as you read that section, ask yourself: *What were Gandhi's achievements?*

Words Related to Main Ideas

Whether you're reading or writing, it's important to know what the writer's *thesis*, or contolling idea, is. Study the chart to learn more about words related to main ideas.

Academic Vocabulary		
Word History	**Word and Definition**	**Example**
From the Greek *topos*, meaning "place"	**topic** (top'-ik) *n.*, the subject of a written text	The **topic** of Nate's essay is elephants in captivity.
From the Greek *tithenai*, meaning "to put down"	**thesis** (thē'-sis) *n.*, an idea or opinion for discussion	Nate's **thesis** is that elephants should not perform in the circus or be kept in zoos.

To help you focus in on the main idea, think about the author's purpose, or reason for writing the text. It may be to explain something to you, to entertain you, or to change your mind about something.

Magazine Article

Philanthropists Carry on an Old Tradition

Today, as in the past, the United States has been home to philanthropists. A philanthropist is a person actively involved with bettering the lives of other people. Philanthropists generally donate money and time to help other people in their community.

Benjamin Franklin was one of the nation's first philanthropists. He helped raise money to build hospitals, libraries, and colleges. When Franklin died in 1790, he left a portion of his money to the cities of Philadelphia and Boston.

Andrew Carnegie of Carnegie Steel also used his great wealth to help others. Among other things, he donated money to help build more than 2,500 public libraries. The first of those libraries was built in 1881.

Today, there are still men and women who want to make a difference in the larger community. Three modern-day philanthropists are successful businesspeople Bill Gates, Warren Buffett, and Oprah Winfrey.

How to Find the Main Idea

1. Think about the **author's purpose**, or reason for writing the text.

2. Identify the topic:
   - Read the title.
   - Examine the pictures and captions.
   - Look for repeated, key words.

3. Look for a **main idea statement.**

4. Check to see that the **details** support the main idea.

Use a diagram to trap the main idea and details that support it.

Details

Benjamin Franklin was one of the first philanthropists.

Main Idea

Today, as in the past, the United States has been home to philanthropists.

Andrew Carnegie donated money to build libraries.

Bill Gates, Warren Buffett, and Oprah Winfrey are modern-day philanthropists.

What If the Main Idea Isn't Stated?

Sometimes, authors do not tell you the main idea directly. Then you have to figure it out on your own.

1 **Think About the Author's Purpose**

Ask yourself: *Why is the author writing this?* The author's reason for writing may be to inform, entertain, or persuade you.

2 **Identify the Topic**

Ask yourself: *Who or what is the passage mostly about?* Check the title, pictures and captions, and repeated words.

3 **Focus on Important Details**

The main idea is what the writer mostly says about the topic. You can figure it out by focusing on the most important details. What idea do they add up to?

In 1996, Lance Armstrong discovered he had cancer.

He left cycling for a few years while he got treatment.

Since 1997, he has been raising money to fight cancer.

4 **Combine the Details with What You Know**

Since the main idea isn't stated, different readers may sum up the writer's main idea in different ways. Draw on your experience and the details provided to come up with a main idea that makes sense. Make sure there's evidence in the text for your main idea statement.

As you read the article on the next page, focus on the most important details. See two possible main idea statements on page 449. What other main idea could the details add up to?

Lance Armstrong
Rides into History

LANCE ARMSTRONG accomplished something no other athlete has. Between 1999 and 2005, he won seven consecutive Tour de France bicycling races. Born in 1971, Armstrong grew up in the hill country of Texas. In 1996, he was at the peak of his career, ranked first among all the cyclists in the world.

But on October 2, 1996, he learned that cancer was beginning to weaken his body. During the next few years, Lance took time off from professional cycling. He was treated and began to recover from the disease. In 1997 he started a charity foundation to raise money for cancer research and treatment. In 2004, the foundation began giving out yellow rubber wristbands. The wrist bands have brought tens of millions of dollars to the fight against cancer. Today, more than 7,200 volunteers help Lance raise money for a cure.

What do these **important details** add up to?

Lance Armstrong won seven consecutive Tour de France races.

Sample Main Idea Statements

" Getting cancer changed Lance Armstrong's life. "

" Lance Armstrong has spent years raising money to fight cancer. "

Plot

When you tell your friends you're reading a book about a 16-year-old orphan who *travels back in time from 2025 to 2005 to stop a worldwide flu epidemic,* you are describing the book's **plot**. The **plot** is the action of a story—the series of events that connect the beginning to the ending.

What Are Some Examples?

Short stories, novels, and plays all revolve around a plot.

- In most plots, the main character has a **goal** or faces a **conflict**—a problem or struggle that he or she has to deal with. The goal or the conflict triggers the action.

- All plots have a beginning, middle, and ending. For example, you may meet the characters, find out about the conflict, see how it gets worse and worse until the characters solve their problem by the end of the story.

Words Related to Plot

Some words such as *conflict* and *resolution* have everyday meanings and also special meanings related to the plot of a story. Study the chart below to learn more.

Academic Vocabulary

Word History	Word and Definition	Example
From the Latin *calumniari*, meaning "to accuse falsely"	**challenge** (cha'-lən) *n.*, a difficult and sometimes exciting situation or problem	In this story, the main character has the **challenge** of living with his stepmother.
From the Latin *conflictus*, meaning "a contest, or dispute"	**conflict** (kon'-flikt) *n.*, a problem that characters in a story face	The **conflict** is that two brothers want to date the same girl.
From the Latin *resolvere*, meaning "to loosen"	**resolution** (re-zə-lū'-shen) *n.*, in fiction, the part where the reader discovers if the characters' problems are solved	I thought the **resolution** was realistic, but if I tell you what it is, I'll give away how the story ends.

When you read fiction, ask yourself: *What goal does the main character have?* Or, *What problem does the main character try to solve?* As is true with real people, sometimes a character has more than one problem.

Short Story

It was spring break, and Will and Vladimir were shooting hoops at school.

"Hey, Vlad, what are we going to do next summer? I'm going to finally have a car," Will said as he dribbled the ball down the court and took a shot.

Vladimir sighed in frustration. "I want to go to the Erie County Fair, but I don't have the money for tickets or for gas. Besides, my mom doesn't like me to go out of the city."

Will said, "I think I'll be able to save some money doing odd jobs. I have a few lined up already."

Vladimir thought for a minute then said, "I hadn't really thought about working, but if I earn some money I might be able to change my mom's mind."

"You can find tons of jobs around here," Will said. "I'm painting Mrs. Greene's kitchen tomorrow. Then her sister wants me to take a bunch of cans and bottles to the recycling place. And mow her lawn, too."

Vladimir's eyes lit up. "Man, you're right. My neighbors need someone to take care of their dog, and I'm sure other people in my building could use my help, too."

What **conflict,** or problem, does the main character have?

This shows how the main character **tries to solve the problem.**

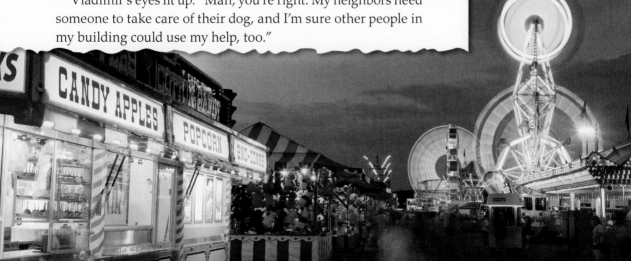

▼ The Erie County Fair, in Hamburg, New York.

Plot, continued

How Do Writers Develop the Plot?

Sometimes plots seem confusing and hard to follow. But behind all that confusion there is a structure, or parts that work together in a certain way. The parts of plot are: the exposition, the conflict, complications, climax, and resolution.

Track the Plot with a Diagram

The diagram below shows the parts of a plot. It gives you a picture of how the action builds to a high point (rising action) and then winds down to a resolution (falling action).

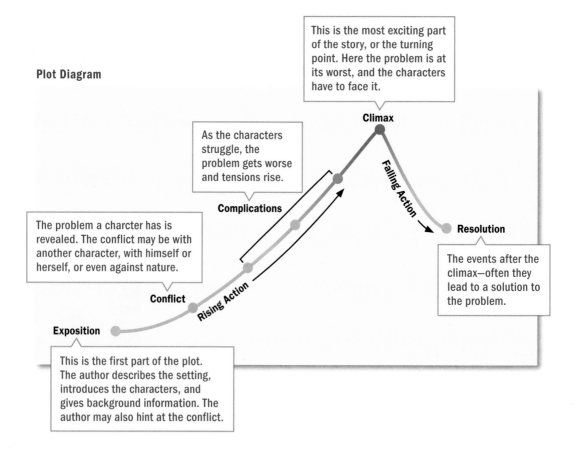

Plot Diagram

This is the most exciting part of the story, or the turning point. Here the problem is at its worst, and the characters have to face it.

Climax

As the characters struggle, the problem gets worse and tensions rise.

Complications

Falling Action

The problem a charcter has is revealed. The conflict may be with another character, with himself or herself, or even against nature.

Resolution

The events after the climax—often they lead to a solution to the problem.

Conflict

Rising Action

Exposition

This is the first part of the plot. The author describes the setting, introduces the characters, and gives background information. The author may also hint at the conflict.

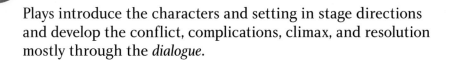

Plays introduce the characters and setting in stage directions and develop the conflict, complications, climax, and resolution mostly through the *dialogue*.

LOSING OUR LUCK   85

ACT TWO
Scene One

RAY *and* JAMAL *are talking in the locker room before a big basketball game. Both boys look excited as they await the arrival of the rest of the team. Suddenly,* DANILO *bursts in the door with a panicked look on his face.*

Stage directions describe where the action takes place and introduce the characters.

DANILO: You guys (*panting*) will never guess what happened. (*He struggles to catch his breath.*)

JAMAL: Calm down, dude. What are you talking about?

DANILO (*sadly*): Our lucky team ball is missing. You know, the one we've used in every game. The one that's helped us get our 10–0 record.

RAY (*laughs hesitantly*): What? You've got to be joking.

JAMAL: Can't you tell he's serious? We have to find that ball. Let's go look and see if we can find it. (*The three boys exit the locker room and go off in search of the ball. Minutes later the boys meet back in the locker room.*)

The play's **conflict** is revealed through lines of dialogue, or the words the characters speak.

RAY: Please tell me you had better luck than I did. (JAMAL *and* DANILO *shake their heads.*)

RAY: Well, that does it. We're going to lose for the first time tonight.

JAMAL (*with intensity*): We can't let a small setback stop us. We've been practicing for months. We can win without that ball.

(RAY *and* DANILO *nod their heads.*)

DANILO: I hope you're right, Jamal. Let's go show the Cougars what we got! (*The three boys high-five each other and head out to find the rest of the team.*)

Look for **clues** to how the characters will deal with their problem.

Sequence

The **sequence of events** is the order in which events happen. Writers often organize their work by describing events in time order sequence, one after the other. They tell what happened first, then what happened next, then the next event, and so on.

What Are Some Examples?

You can find time order sequence in nonfiction and fiction texts.

- In a biography, the writer often follows the course of someone's life—a character is born, grows up, goes to school, gets a job, and discovers the Theory of Relativity.

- Most history texts also are written in sequence, beginning with the earliest event and ending with the latest. This helps you see how things changed as events unfolded over time.

- Many pieces of fiction are organized in time order sequence. For example, short stories tell what happens to the main character first, next, then, and last.

Words Related to Sequence

Chronology is another way to say "sequence of events." It comes from the Greek word *khronos*, which means "time." Study the chart to learn more words related to sequence.

Academic Vocabulary

Word History	Word and Definition	Example
From the Latin *sequi*, meaning "to follow"	**consequence** (kon'-sə-kwens) *n.*, something that naturally follows; effect **sequential** (si-kwen'-shəl) *adj.*, following a natural order	Success often is a **consequence** of hard work. The plot is **sequential**, starting with the earliest event and ending with the last.
From the Greek *khronos*, meaning "time"	**chronic** (kro'-nək) *adj.*, lasting a long time **chronological** (kro'-nə-lo-ji-kəl) *adj.*, following time order	Hunger has been a **chronic** problem in Africa. The photographs in her album are in **chronological** order.

Sequence in Nonfiction

When you read nonfiction, look for clues to the sequence of events. These clues include times, dates, and signal words such as *first*, *next*, and *later*.

News Article

NEWS ACROSS THE NATION

Celebrating Chávez

Linda Hiu, staff writer

On March 17, 1966, César Chávez changed our country forever. He led a march out of Delano, California. Along with 70 farmworkers he headed to Sacramento, the state capital. They were protesting low pay and poor working conditions on the farms where they picked grapes.

Twenty-five days later, 10,000 supporters greeted Chávez in Sacramento. There, he announced that one large grape-growing company had agreed to raise workers' pay. The company agreed to improve working conditions, too.

In the late 1960s, César Chávez led peaceful protests to help farmworkers.

Chávez fought tirelessly for farmworkers and all workers until his death in 1993. Now in March 2006, we celebrate the 40th anniversary of his victory in Sacramento.

How to Identify Sequence

- Look for **dates.**
- Pay attention to **words that signal time order.**
- Photographs and captions may clarify when events took place.

Time Line

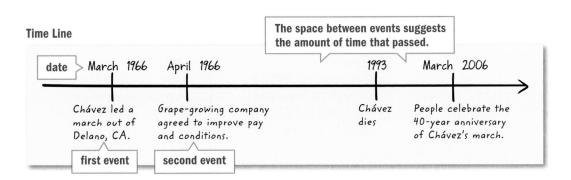

The space between events suggests the amount of time that passed.

| date | March 1966 | April 1966 | | 1993 | March 2006 |

Chávez led a march out of Delano, CA. | Grape-growing company agreed to improve pay and conditions. | Chávez dies | People celebrate the 40-year anniversary of Chávez's march.

first event **second event**

Sequence in Fiction

Writers of fiction usually describe events in time order. However, sometimes they present events out of sequence. One technique is called **flashback**.

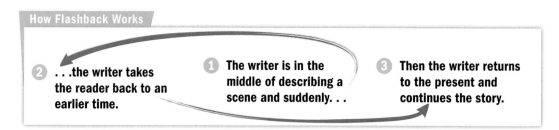

How Flashback Works

② . . .the writer takes the reader back to an earlier time.

① The writer is in the middle of describing a scene and suddenly. . .

③ Then the writer returns to the present and continues the story.

You probably have seen movies that use flashbacks as a way to fill in important details about a character's background. These details help you see what shaped his or her personality and motivation.

Foreshadowing is another technique that fiction writers use. It adds an element of suspense and gets the reader interested in finding out how the plot will unfold.

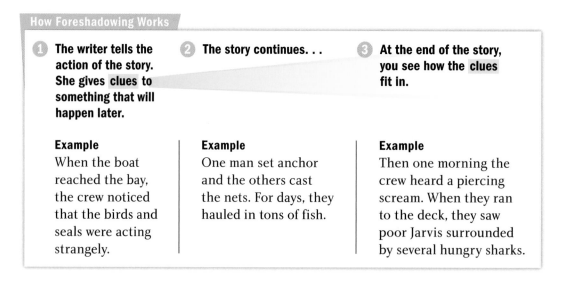

How Foreshadowing Works

① The writer tells the action of the story. She gives clues to something that will happen later.

② The story continues. . .

③ At the end of the story, you see how the clues fit in.

Example
When the boat reached the bay, the crew noticed that the birds and seals were acting strangely.

Example
One man set anchor and the others cast the nets. For days, they hauled in tons of fish.

Example
Then one morning the crew heard a piercing scream. When they ran to the deck, they saw poor Jarvis surrounded by several hungry sharks.

When you read fiction, look for time order words, flashback, and foreshadowing.

Science Fiction

THE PORTAL   37

The August heat was stifling as Arlo walked through the backyard. He checked the pockets of his jacket. Yes, the gloves and hat were there. Slowly he opened the door to the basement, and made his way through the dark, damp room. He looked behind him for his sister Ruby. She followed him inside, already wearing her hat and gloves. Had anyone seen them?

The trunk was exactly where they had left it. The cracked leather reflected years of wear. On the lock, instead of a keyhole, was a red hourglass shape. Arlo remembered when he had stumbled across it last year. The hourglass was the first thing he noticed. He was frightened then, but also intrigued.

Now, Arlo placed his hand on the familiar hourglass. The lid popped open. All they had to do was slip through the portal to go back or forward in time. On this sticky summer day, they planned to travel to the Ice Age. Little did they know what would await them in that strange frozen world.

How to Identify Sequence

Look for a **flashback** to an earlier event. The phrases *remembered when* and *last year* are clues.

Look for **foreshadowing.** Words like *would* and *could* suggest possible future events.

When fiction includes flashback, you can map the story to help you keep track of the events. Use a sequence chain to locate the action in time.

Sequence Chain

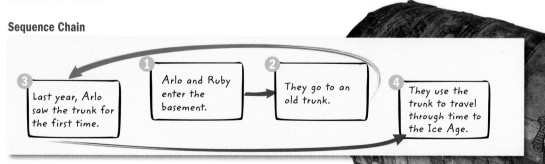

3 Last year, Arlo saw the trunk for the first time.

1 Arlo and Ruby enter the basement.

2 They go to an old trunk.

4 They use the trunk to travel through time to the Ice Age.

Setting

On that brisk December night in Montana, the full moon rose over the snowy peaks. This sentence describes a **setting**—when and where a story takes place.

What Are Some Examples?

The setting is an important part of fiction and drama. It often affects the characters and the events.

- Some stories are set in a very specific time and place. Steinbeck, for example, wrote about Monterey, California, in the 1930s and 1940s. Other writers use a more general setting like an unnamed city in modern times.

- The setting helps to create the **mood**, or feeling you get about a story. For example, a story that takes place at night on a dark, deserted street might create a feeling of tension and suspense.

- Characters are influenced by the setting. For example, a character who suddenly finds himself on that dark, deserted street might panic and not think clearly.

Words Related to Setting

The words *local*, *locale* and *location* are all part of the same word family. Study the chart to learn more about these words.

Academic Vocabulary

Word History	Word and Definition	Example
From the Latin *locus*, meaning "a place"	**local** (lō'-kəl) *adj.*, having to do with a particular place **locale** (lō-kal') *n.*, the place where a story happens; scene **location** (lō-kā'-shən) *n.*, a place or area	The **local** politicians were not happy when the family decided to raise goats. Monument Valley was the perfect **locale** for a story about cowboys. As a child, she had lived in a quiet **location**, far from busy highways and tall skyscrapers.

Short Story

FAMILY DIARY ❧ 87

Felix could feel the ocean even before he got out of the car. His family was moving in slow motion after driving all night, but he suddenly felt refreshed. He bounded out of the car, heading straight for the water. He ran to the railing and looked down at the waves crashing below. A flock of seagulls circled above his head, screeching noisily.

To Felix's surprise, the beach was covered with jagged rocks and boulders. The tide was coming in, bathing the rocks in foam. Sunlight broke through the clouds and the water changed from shades of pale blue to dark green. Felix turned to see his father walking toward him. He was smiling.

How to Identify Setting and Mood

Look for clues to the setting, including descriptions of how it looks, smells, and feels.

As you read, pay attention to the mood, or feeling, the setting creates.

Setting and Characters

Just like people in real life, fictional characters are affected by the time and place in which they live. Suppose you are reading a story and the main character is about to turn eighteen. If the story were set in Dallas in 2000, he would have a number of choices about his future—whether to go on to college, or find a job, or both.

Now suppose that the story is set in France in the late 1800s and the character is female. What choices would she have? How would she be affected by the time and place in which she lived?

Short Story

The Necklace
—Guy de Maupassant

She was one of those beautiful, charming women who are born as if by accident, into a lower-class family. Because of this, she did not have even a chance of meeting and marrying a rich, important man. Instead, she married a lowly clerk from the Ministry of Education.

She had to dress plainly because she could not afford fine clothes or jewelry. This made her feel like someone of little worth. She thought that if she could dress well, other people might consider her more important.

In France in the 1800s, women had few options for improving their social status.

To impress people, she feels her only choice is to wear fancy clothes.

Setting and Plot

Sometimes the setting is so important to the plot that it becomes one of the main characters. In the story, "Deadly Waters," three teens come across two very hungry alligators. The setting makes this encounter possible. Read to find out how the different characters react.

DEADLY WATERS | Skurzynski & Ferguson   21

Upstream, two round alligator eyes blinked just above water. The gator was middle-size: about five feet from its tail tip to its blunt nose. As it skimmed forward, it left behind a rippled wake that barely disturbed the canal's surface. While Jack Landon fumbled for his camera, his sister, Ashley, pointed following the path of the dark shape in the water. The gator was closing in fast.

"Look, Bridger, he's after that duck, or whatever it is," Ashley murmured to the boy standing beside her. "Should I yell to warn it?"

"Gator's got to eat, too," was all Bridger answered. A tall, lean, tow-headed 14-year-old wearing a Stetson hat, jeans, and cowboy boots, Bridger Conley had already proved himself to be a boy of few words. And strong opinions.

The three of them—Jack, Ashley, and Bridger—stood beside a canal in the Florida Everglades, watching the large bird that kept swimming underwater, with its whole body submerged. Every minute or so, the bird's small head and long, skinny neck would snake upward, breaking through the sun's reflection on the water. Then back down it would go, gliding beneath the surface like a seal. It didn't seem to notice the danger it was in.

"Hold it...hold it," Jack muttered, twisting his lens to focus. Catching both animals in one picture would make a magnificent shot.

What mood do these **details** create?

How do the two characters **react?**

▼ Alligators in the Everglades

Index of Skills and Strategies

Spanish-English cognates 78, 79, 80–81, 83, 86–87

Speech 235

Sports terms 100, 104, 158–159

Story elements *See* **Literary elements and devices**

Structural analysis 78, 79, 82, 84, 106, 106–107, 108–109, 110–111, 112–113, 114–115, 116–117, 118, 119, 120–121, 146, 154, 155, 163, 164, 172, 248, 250

Suffixes 78, 84, 106–107, 112–113, 114–115, 118, 163, 248, 250

Summarize 208, 217, 262–263, 264–271, 278

Synonym scale 161

Synonyms 88–89, 91, 149, 152, 153, 161, 163, 170, 177–199, 410

Synthesize
  form generalizations 205, 217, 260, 320, 322–324, 325–326, 328–329, 331, 332–333, 338–340, 358, 361, 368, 372, 374–375, 376–377, 378–383, 384–390, 392–394, 395, 396–398, 399, 400–401, 406, 430, 431, 443, 445, 448

  draw conclusions from one text 214, 374–375, 376–377, 384–385, 400–401, 430, 431, 432–433

  draw conclusions from multiple texts 374–375, 376–377, 386–391, 392–394, 395, 396–398, 399, 400–401

compare and contrast ideas 229, 297–299, 331, 374–375, 376–377, 392–395, 423

take a position 217, 374–375, 376–377, 378, 380, 382, 384–385, 386, 392–394, 395, 396–399, 400–401, 431

T

Test 69

Text features
  acronyms 42, 45

  art 43, 47, 52, 60, 66, 71, 219, 222–223, 225, 258, 304, 308

  captions 48, 51, 71, 219, 220, 222–223, 225, 258–259, 264–265, 274, 447, 448, 455

  charts, graphs, and tables 58, 68, 71, 222, 228, 352, 353, 355

  dated entries 38, 455

  diagrams 48, 71, 222, 307

  electronic links 38, 75

  fine print 66, 72

  footnotes 65, 71

  maps and legends 52–53, 71, 222–223, 226

  numbered steps 48, 233, 353

  photographs 34, 40, 50–51, 66, 71, 219, 220–221, 222, 258–259, 264–265, 266, 274, 305, 352, 353, 447, 448, 455

  quotations 355

  repeated words 211, 213, 258, 260, 265, 266, 274, 323, 357, 370–371, 447, 448

  stage directions 356, 420–421, 453

  stanzas 222–223, 340, 355, 357

  title, headings, and subheadings 219, 220–221, 222–223, 224–225, 227, 228, 255, 258–259, 264–265, 266–267, 270, 274, 275, 282–283, 286, 323, 352, 370, 410, 411, 423, 446, 447, 448

  verses 356, 357, 370

  words in bold type 220, 222–223, 265, 266

Text structures
  cause and effect 229, 237, 414–417

  chronological 229, 232, 233, 308, 342, 350, 353, 454–457

  compare and contrast 229, 234, 297–299, 392–395, 422–429

  goal and outcome 229, 231

  logical order 229, 236, 271, 353

  narrative 222–223, 229, 230, 270–271, 344–346, 348, 426, 432–433, 434, 436–437, 450–453, 460–461

  problem and solution 229, 271, 293, 450–453

  strength of arguments 229, 235

Textbook 70–71, 217, 225–226, 227, 229, 236, 243, 267, 302, 306, 307, 343, 352, 379–380, 387–388, 410, 411, 414, 422, 438, 442, 454

Thesaurus 140, 148–149, 152–153, 251

Topic 222, 225, 256–257, 258–259, 260–261, 262, 264, 266–267, 272, 274, 278, 320, 322, 323, 326, 328, 332, 392, 395, 411, 423, 424, 425, 446–448

Index of Skills and Strategies, continued

Word consciousness, continued

multiple-meaning words 94–95, 96–99, 142–143, 154–155

synonyms 88–89, 91, 149, 152, 153, 161, 163, 170, 177–199, 410

word families 78, 79, 80–81, 82, 84–85, 146, 163, 170, 176, 177–199, 410, 430

word origins 82, 86, 114–115, 117, 120–121, 128, 129, 130, 131, 149, 154, 155, 157, 163, 170, 171–172, 174

Word diagram 176

Word families 78, 79, 80–81, 82, 84–85, 146, 163, 170, 176, 177–199, 219, 238–239, 248–251, 252–253, 410, 430

Word history 128, 129, 130, 131, 149, 154, 155, 163, 170, 171–172, 173, 174, 410, 414, 418, 422, 430, 438, 446, 450, 454, 458

Word map 146, 159, 160, 170, 176

Word origins 82, 86, 114–115, 117, 120–121, 128, 129, 130, 131, 149, 154, 155, 157, 163, 170, 171–172, 174

Word parts

base words 85, 106–107, 110, 112, 116, 146, 154, 163, 176

compound words 84, 106, 108–109, 119, 414

Greek and Latin roots 82, 86, 106, 110, 112, 114–115, 117, 120–121, 152, 155, 163, 164, 172, 174, 176, 414, 418, 422, 430, 438, 446, 450, 454, 458

prefixes 78, 79, 106–107, 110–111, 112–113, 114–115, 116–117, 163, 248

suffixes 78, 84, 106–107, 112–113, 114–115, 118, 163, 248, 250

Word-learning strategies *See* **Vocabulary strategies**

Wyland 20–25

Z

Zephaniah, Benjamin 4–5, 253

Acknowledgments and Credits

Grateful acknowledgment is given to the authors, artists, photographers, museums, publishers, and agents for permission to reprint copyrighted material. Every effort has been made to secure the appropriate permission, but if any omissions have been made, please contact the Publisher.

Agencia Literaria Carmen Balcells: Pablo Neruda, "La Poesía" from MEMORIAL DE ISLA NEGRA © Fundación Pablo Neruda, 2007. Reprinted by permission.

Liz Sohappy Bahe: "Printed Words" by Liz Sohappy Bahe.

BOA Editions, Ltd.: Naomi Shihab Nye, "Ducks" from FUEL. Copyright © 1998 by Naomi Shihab Nye. Used with the permission of BOA Editions, Ltd.

Christian Burial Music: "Cherry Tree" by Natalie Merchant. Copyright © 1996 Christian Burial Music. All Rights Reserved. Used by permission.

City Lights Books: Photo of open book is THE ESSENTIAL NERUDA: SELECTED POEMS by Pablo Neruda, edited by Mark Eisner, Copyright © 2004. Used by permission of City Lights Books.

Maurice E. Duhon, Jr.: "There's a Harlem Renaissance in My Head" by Maurice E. Duhon, Jr.

Farrar, Straus & Giroux: Excerpt from "Poetry" from ISLA NEGRA by Pablo Neruda, translated by Alastair Reid. Translation copyright © 1981 by Alastair Reid. Reprinted by permission of Farrar, Straus and Giroux, LLC.

Patrick Jones: "Wrestling with Reading" by Patrick Jones from GUYS WRITE FOR GUYS READ edited by Jon Scieszka. Copyright © Patrick Jones. Reprinted by permission.

King Features Syndicate: "Parents Think Movie Making Kid Is Wasting His Time" from HELP ME HARLAN by Harlan Cohen © KING FEATURES SYNDICATE. Reprinted by permission.

Little, Brown and Company (Inc.): "Who Am I?" from THE CODE by Mawi Asgedom. Copyright © 2003 by Mawi Asgedom. By permission of Little, Brown and Co.

National Geographic Society: Reprinted with permission of the National Geographic Society from the book DEADLY WATERS by Gloria Skurzynski and Alane Ferguson. Text copyright © 1999 Gloria Skurzynski and Alane Ferguson. Reprinted with permission of the National Geographic Society from the book ESCAPE FROM FEAR by Gloria Skurzynski and Alane Ferguson. Text copyright © 2002 Gloria Skurzynski and Alane Ferguson. "Murdering the Impossible" by Caroline Alexander originally appeared in NATIONAL GEOGRAPHIC, November 2006. Copyright © 2006 National Geographic Society. Graph copyright © 2004.

Penguin Group (UK): Photo of open book (pp.20-1) of THE COMPLETE POEMS by Christina Rossetti, translated by R W Crump, notes and introduction by Betty Flowers (Penguin Books 2001). Texts copyright © Louisiana University Press, 1979, 1986, 1999. Editorial Matter copyright © Betty S Flowers, 2001. Reproduced by permission of Penguin Books Ltd.

Penguin Group (USA) Inc.: From MIRACLE'S BOYS by Jacqueline Woodson. Copyright © Jacqueline Woodson, 2000. From THE PEARL by John Steinbeck, copyright 1945 by John Steinbeck, © renewed 1973 by Elaine Steinbeck, Thom Steinbeck and John Steinbeck IV. Used by permission of Viking Penguin, a division of Penguin Group (USA).

Perseus Books LLC: From WHEN I WAS PUERTO RICAN by Esmeralda Santiago. Copyright © 1993 by Esmeralda Santiago. Reprinted by permission of DA CAPO PRESS, a member of Perseus Books Group.

The Peters Fraser and Dunlop Group Ltd. (PFD): "I Love Shelley" by Benjamin Zephaniah (Copyright © Benjamin Zephaniah) is reproduced by permission of PFD (www.pfd.co.uk) on behalf of Benjamin Zephaniah.

Press); p317 (marathon © Associated Press); p341 (Rivers © Associated Press); p350 (Sojourner © Associated Press); p381 (protest © Saurabh Das/Associated Press).

Art Resource: p125 (pectoral © Reunion des Musees Nationaux/Art Resource, NY); p223 (map © Bildarchiv Preussischer Kulturbesitz/Art Resource, NY).

Artville: p75 (headlight); p167 (vibraphone); p167 (saxophone); p167 (piano); p167 (guitar); p175 (telephone); p246 (eye).

Barry Lawrence Ruderman Antique Maps: p52 antique map; Courtesy of Barry Lawrence Ruderman Antique Maps (www.raremaps.com).

Big Stock Photo: p242 (gamepad © Big Stock Photo).

Bridgeman Art Library: p171 (reconstruction of lyre © Museo della Civilta, Romona, Rome, Italy, Roger-Viollet, Paris) The Bridgeman Art Library International.

Chandra X-ray Center: p51 infrared nebula © 2MASS/ UMass/IPAC-Caltech/NASA/ NSF); p51 (radio nebula © NRAO/AUI/NSF).

Chuck Close: p256 ("Lyle, 2003" © Chuck Close) Courtesy of Chuck Close, published by Pace Editions, Inc.

Corbis: p2-p3 (wall with old posters © Paul C. Pet/zefa); p11 (duck feathers © Niall Benvie); p14 (Malcolm X with Ilyasha © Bettmann); p16 (Malcolm X in a crowd ©

Bettmann); p24-p25 Cannery Row whale mural © Richard Cummins); p25 (whale mural in Hawaii © Morton Beebe); p53 (mosque © Robert Harding World Imagery); p71 (Copernicus © Paul Almsy); p71 (Medieval map © CORBIS); p71 (Amerigo Vespucci © Bettmann); p89 (braille page © CORBIS); p113 (diving © Peter Guttman); p114-115 (Anza-Borrego Desert © Pat O'Hara); p117 (warning sign © Lawrence Manning); p117c (Danger Drop sign © Stock disc); p123 (umbrella © Leonard de Selva); p134 (Amelia Earhart posing with airplane © Bettmann); p135 (Amelia Earhart in cockpit © Bettmann); p139 (fishing boats © Annie Griffths Belt); p143 (background of brushed metal © W. Cody); p149 (summit © CORBIS); p159 (net © Randy Faris); p205 (background of brushed metal © W. Cody); p207 (Chasma Boreale – Mars © NASA); p225 (William H. Seward © CORBIS); p225 (political cartoon by Frank Bellew © Bettmann); p226 (map © MAPS.com); p227 (NASCAR race © George Tiedemann/NewSport); p259 (avalanche © Galen Rowell); p261 (firefighter © Raymond Gehman); p269 (creek © Craig Tuttle); p277 (Andes plane crash survivors © Group of Survivors); p277(The Andes © Lary Dale Gordon/zefa); p282 (shoot basketball © Zack Gold); p308 (Chuck Yaeger beside Bell X-1 © Bettmann); p309 (Bell X-1 Glamorous Glinnis in flight

© Smithsonian Institution); p315 (fire eaters © Matthias Schrader/dpa); p325 (Amerigo Vespucci © Bettmann); p363 (Hayao Miyazaki © Haruyoshi Yamaguchi); p372 (subway sign © William Manning); p379 (coal mine © CORBIS); p380 (harvest tea © Jeremy Horner); p382 (sacks of coffee beans © D. Amon/photocuisine); p401 (fingers in ears © Duncan Smith); p405 (groovy van © Marvy!); p415 (listening to music © Zave Smith); p419 (flames © Charles O'Rear); p426 (front page of New York Times reporting loss of Titanic ©Bettmann); p427 (rock climbing © CORBIS); 433 (using a flashlight in a dark room © image100); p435 (cemetery © Brian Cenclar); p442 (demonstation at Kent State University © Reuters); p442 (Anti-Vietnam war protesters © Leif Skoogfors); p447 (hands around globe © Images.com); p455 (Cesar Chavez © Ted Streshinsky).

Craig Lovell: p51, p65, p70, p71.

Dana Berry: p51 (technical drawing © Chandra X-Ray Center).

Dark Horse: p47 "Shock Rockets" (tm) © 2006 Kurt Busiek and Stuart Immonen, pages 4-5.

Digital Stock: p173 (penguin); p289 (planet); p294 (planet).

Fotosearch.com: p73 (Laundromat © age Fotostock); p166 (marimba); p203 (teenage boy, top © Design Pics); p249 (hands reach © age footstock); p285 (spider web © Stock Connection); p292-p293 (female robot © Blend Images).

Gary Friedman: p33, p40 (flying © Gary Freidman, FriedmanArchives.com); p40 (hand-stand © Gary Friedman, FriedmanArchives.com).

Getty Images: p5 (Benjamin Zephaniah © Getty Images); p11 (reeds © Greg Kuchik); p15 (Malcolm X with daughters © Time & Life Pictures); p16 (Malcolm X and daughters © Robert L. Haggins/Time & Life Pictures); p17 (Malcolm X at podium © Time Life Pictures); p21 (Wyland © Getty Images); p21 (Jacques Cousteau © AFP) p22 (turtle © Getty Images); p22-23 (humpback whale mural – Miami © AFP); p32 (windsurfer © Digital Stock); p33 (girl in jacket © Photo Disc); p34, p241 (hallway © Stone); p36 (coffee shop © Scott Van Dyke/ Beateworks); p38 (fountain pen © Stockbyte); p40 (girl on skateboard © Stan Liu); p53 (Darulaman Palace © Lonely Planet Images); p71 (midnight sun © Arnulf Husmo/Stone); p82 (Mt. Everest © National Geographic); p86 (pizza © Butch Martin/Photographer's Choice); p88 (empty cheese grater © Robertson, Lew/ Stockfood); p89 (flat screen monitor © Ryan McVay); p91 (sunglasses © CSA Plastock); p94 (bus driver strike © AFP); p95 (fingerprint card © Robert Clare); p100 (executive at desk ©Stephen Swintek); p106 (microphone with cord © Benoit Jeanneton); p109 (girl with mobile

phone © Getty Images) p117 (Proceed with Caution sign © George Diebold Photography/Iconica); p117 (thin Ice sign © Don Ferrall); p117 (Trip Hazard sign © C Squared Studios); p132-133 (Stonehenge © Panoramic Images); p133 (Stonehenge, UK © Peter Adams); p137 (Mary Celeste © Keystone); p137 (sextant © Stockdisc); p139 (eyes © Chad Baker); p141 (smiling © Gala Narezo); p145 (car © David McNew); p149 (mountain climber © Melissa McManus); p150-151 (rainforest © Panoramic Images); p158 (hockey goalkeeper © Terie Kakke); p158 (soccer goalie © Mike Powell/Allsport Concepts); p163 (band © Holly Harris); p177 (graduate © Getty Images) p206 (monarch butterflies in tree © Ken Lucas); p206 (monarch butterfly ©PhotoDisc); p215 (duck © PhotoDisc); p219 (boy standing in bus doorway © Lisa Peardon); p220 (winding road © Laurance B Aiuppy); p238 (remote control © Raul Touzon/ National Geographic); p240 (girl in jacket © Photo Disc); p243 (construction worker © SW Productions); p251 (monitor © Ryan McVay); p253 (Benjamin Zephaniah © Getty Images); p255 (teenage boy holding book/pen © Jack Hollingsworth); p255 (teenage girl at desk © Digital Vision); p259 (avalanche © Aurora); p271 (flower © Getty Images); p273 (Aurora Borealis © Johnny Johnson); p275 (ocean floor © Stephen Frink); p281 (first female

student © Flying Colours Ltd); p281 (second teenage female © David & Les Jacobs); p288 (girls shopping © Blasius Erlinger); p289 (monitor © Ryan McVay); p290-291 (cityscape © Getty Images); p303 (girl in wheelchair © David Buffington); p303 (girl in front of lockers © Andersen Ross); p303 (boy on bus © Matt Henry Gunther); p305 (migrant workers © Michael Rogier/Time Life Pictures); p307 (water & sky © Jeff Divine); p309 (B29 & XS-1 © Keystone); p319 (girl, top © Vicky Kasaly); p319 (teenage boy, second © Getty Images); p319 (teenage girl, bottom © Jack Hollingsworth); p321 (Mexican tiles © Spike Mafford); p323 (young man © Pando Hall); p333 (mortarboards © Frank Whitney); p336 (neon sign © Getty Images); p342 (Silver Star © Time & Life Pictures); p346-347 (paper money © Photodisc); p361 (teenage boy © Bruce Ayres); p377 (monitor © Ryan McVay); p377 (brick wall © Getty Images); p398 (shaking hands © White Packert); p413 (Crab Nebula © NASA-JPL/digital version by Science Faction); p420 (theatre stage © Robert Daly); p423 (monster truck © David Zaitz/Photonica); p427 (El Capitan, background © Paul Nicklen/National Geographic); p437 (palm tree © Kza Mori); p442 (anti-war demonstrators protest in Bryant Park © Getty Images); p445 (row housing © Lambert); p449 (Lance Armstrong © Getty Images); p451 (amusement

Author Photos, continued

Patrick Jones: p7 Courtesy of Patrick Jones.

Naomi Shihab Nye: p11 Courtesy Naomi Shihab Nye.

Jacqueline Woodson: p60 Courtesy of Jacqueline Woodson.

Ilyasha Shabazz: p15 (© Associated Press).

Wyland: p21 (© Getty Images).

Benjamin Zephaniah: p5, p253 (© Getty Images).

Book Covers

'Bunmi Adebayo: p157 By permission. "Dictionary of African Names, Vol 1" ©'Bunmi Adebayo.

Arte Publico Press: p63 "Zoot Suit and Other Plays", Luis Valdez © 1992, Arte Publico Press.

DA CAPO PRESS: p351 Cover of "When I was Puerto Rican". Reprinted by permission of DA CAPO PRESS, a member of Perseus Books Group. Copyright © 1993 by Esmeralda Santiago.

HarperCollins Publishers Ltd.: p156, p251 Reproduced from "Collins Cobuild Student's Dictionary Plus Grammar" with the permission of HarperCollins Publishers Ltd. © HarperCollins Publishers Ltd 1997, 2002, 2005. Updated from the Bank of English. Based on the Cobuild series, developed in collaboration with the University of Birmingham. Collins ®, Cobuild ® and Bank of English ® are registered trademarks of HarperCollins Publishers Ltd.

HarperCollins Publishers: p61 MONSTER by Walter Dean Myers. Text copyright © 1999 by Walter Dean Myers. Used by permission of HarperCollins Publishers.

Merriam-Webster, Inc.: p154 By permission. From Merriam-Webster's School Dictionary ©2004 by Merriam-Webster, Incorporated (www.Merriam-Webster.com); p156 By Permission. From Merriam-Webster's Geographical Dictionary, Third Edition © 2001 by Merriam-Webster, Incorporated (www.Merriam-Webster.com).

National Geographic Society: p20 THE SILENT WORLD cover image originally appeared in "Fish Men Explore a New World Undersea" in NATIONAL GEOGRAPHIC, October 1952. Copyright © 1952 National Geographic Society; p50 Cover and TOC National Geographic Magazine, December 2003 – Vol 204. No. 6. Copyright National Geographic Society; p51 "X-Ray Vision" National Geographic Magazine, Dec 2002, page 46-47. Copyright © National Geographic Society; p71 "Defining the Laws of Motion", pages 8-9, Copyright © 2003 National Geographic Society.

Oxford University Press, Inc: p251 Jacket cover from "Oxford American Writer's Thesaurus" edited by Lindberg, Christene (2004).

By permission of Oxford University Press, Inc.

Penguin Group (UK): p295 Front cover of THE TIME MACHINE by H. G. Wells (Penguin Books, 2005). Copyright © H. G. Wells, 2005.

Penguin Group (USA) Inc.: p61 Front and back covers of MIRACLE'S BOYS by Jacqueline Woodson. Copyright © Jacqueline Woodson, 2000. Cover illustration copyright © Trevor Brown, 2000. Cover design by Linda McCarthy.

Random House, Inc.: p63 From A RAISIN IN THE SUN - BOOK COVER by Lorraine Hansberry, copyright © 1958, 1959, 1966, 1984, 1986, 1987. Used by permission of Random House, Inc.; p157 Cover from THE NEW BIOGRAPHOCAL DICTIONARY OF FILM by David Thomson, copyright © 1975, 1980, 1994, 2002 by David Thomson. Used by permission of Alfred A. Knopf, a division of Random House, Inc.

Simon & Schuster, Inc.: p20 Cover design THE SILENT WORLD courtesy of Pocket Books, a Division of Simon & Schuster, Inc. Used by permission.

Thomson Learning: p63 "Hamlet", Edited by Harold Jenkins, The Arden Shakespeare, 1982. Courtesy of Thomson Learning.

Illustrations

Norm Bendell: p30, p80, p142, p244, p412.

Harvey Chan: p12-13.

Paula Cohen-Martin: p102, p103, p104, p105.

Dave Cutler: p0-1, p30, p76, p78, p140, p200, p202, p218, p254, p280, p302, p318, p360, p374, p408.

Lane du Pont: p4-5.

Barry Gott: p262.

Charles Glaubitz: p371.

Michael Krider: p127.

Aaron Leighton: p128, p129, p130, p131.

John Mantha: p147.

Chris MacNeil: p152 (walking), p152 (pacing), p152 (strutting), p161.

Lisa Papp: p239.

Edward Tamez: p439 (fizz ad).

Greg Stoermer: p75, p101 (antique car), p75, p101 (old style car); p75, p101 (future car).

Benjamin Wachenje: p111.

Wendy Wax: p204.

Kris Wiltse: p28-29.

The Good Reader's Guide Development Team

Hampton-Brown/National Geographic School Publishing extends special thanks to those who contributed so much to the creation of *The Good Reader's Guide*.

Editorial: Shirleyann Costigan, Kristin Cozort, Leslie Hall, Ramona Jafar, Phillip Kennedy, Sheron Long, Jacalyn Mahler, Debbi Neel, Diane Silver, BrainWorx Studio, and Words and Numbers

Design and Production: Marcia Bateman-Walker, George Bounelis, Christy Caldwell, Jen Coppens, Wendy Crockett, Denise Davidson, Alicia DiPiero, Michael Farmer, Jeri Gibson, Annie Hopkins, Karen Hunting, Ernie Lee, Eva Morris, Mary McMurtry, Katherine Minerva, Russ Nemec, Marian O'Neal, Ruthy Porter, Deborah Reed, Scott Russell, Sumer Tatum-Clem, Alex Von Dallwitz, and Liz Garza Williams Photography

Publishing Operations: Jennifer Alexander, Dawn Liseth, and Debbie Saxton

Permissions: Katrina Saville